This We
Believe

**An overview of the teachings of
Seventh-day Adventists**

Erwin Gane &
Leo Van Dolson

Pacific Press Publishing Association
Boise, Idaho
Oshawa, Ontario, Canada

Edited by B. Russell Holt
Designed by Tim Larson
Cover art by Lorenzo Ghiglieri/Theater of the Universe©
Typeset in 10/12 Century Schoolbook

Library of Congress Cataloging-in-Publication Data:
Gane, Erwin R.
    This we believe : an overview of the teachings of Seventh-
  day Adventists / Erwin R. Gane and Leo R. Van Dolson.
       p.   cm.
     ISBN 0-8163-1138-2
     1. Seventh-day Adventists—Doctrines. I. Van Dolson, Leo R.
  II. Title.
  BX6154.G36   1993
  230'.6732—dc20
                                              92-39733
                                              CIP

93 94 95 96 97 ● 5 4 3 2 1

Contents

Chapter 1

Words
to Grow By

When the *Lyon*, on which John Eliot was a passenger, sailed into Boston Harbor, the young Englishman leaned over the railing, feasting his eyes on the green shoreline. Watching, Eliot saw something that he never had seen in England. A canoe manned by Algonquin Indians was skimming across the water toward the *Lyon*. John was fascinated by their bright feathers and clothing made of skins.

When the *Lyon* docked, Governor Winthrop greeted John warmly, assuring him that a church and congregation were awaiting his services. John served the people faithfully as their pastor, but he could not forget the Algonquins. He invited a young brave, Job Nesutan, to live with him, and from the Indian he learned the difficult Algonquin language. In October 1646, John preached his first sermon to the Indians. From then on, he met with them each week.

Because the Algonquins had no written language, John Eliot spent years developing one and teaching them to read it. About twenty years after first preaching to the Indians, John completed translating the Bible into the Algonquin language. This was the first Bible printed in the Western Hemisphere. It is said that before Eliot died at age eighty-six, he could repeat the entire Bible from memory.

Today, most of the world's people have the Bible, or portions of it, in their own language. But possessing a Bible and actually studying it are two different things. A Gallup poll indicates that 85 percent of Americans have a Bible, but few read it regularly.

The conclusion is that the people of the United States are becoming Bible-loving biblical illiterates. The best way to assure that you spend time with the Word of God is to dust off your Bible and study it every day.

"Our daily bread"

What a privilege it is to hold the Word of God in our hands! But even more, what a privilege it is to read it, to study it carefully, and to discover the truths it contains!

We know that we have to continue to eat nourishing food on a daily basis if we are to stay alive and healthy physically. In the same way we cannot expect our Christian experience to be meaningful and growing unless we eat the food of God's Word. But once we learn to partake daily of the Bread of Life, we develop a taste for it and find ourselves malnourished without it.

One of the major excuses for neglecting the Bible is that it takes too much time to study it in the way it should be studied. Is this true? Stop and consider how much time it takes to prepare and eat your daily food. In figuring, be sure you count the hours spent in the supermarket. Somehow we seem to be able to find time to satisfy our physical hunger. Perhaps finding time for Bible study depends on how hungry we are for the Word of God. It also is a question of priorities.

It has been said that "life stripped to its essentials is freedom." Perhaps that is one reason Jesus said, "The truth shall make you free" (John 8:32). When we set aside a specific amount of time each day for Bible study, we find that we truly are free—free from self and free from many of the problems that we learn to leave with God.

In *The Pilgrim's Progress* John Bunyan describes the experience of the man with the muck rake. This fellow was so busy removing the dirt around him that he never looked up to see an angel above him holding a crown of gold. The angel was patiently waiting to give the crown to the muck raker, but he was never ready to receive it. Why not? Because he was so preoccupied with what he was doing that he never turned, or lifted up his eyes. We need to take time each day to turn our eyes of thought heavenward.

Where the Bible came from

Because He loves us far more than we realize, the God of the Bible has done all He can to reveal Himself to us. After sin came into this world, God did not leave us alone in our lost state, alienated from Him. Through the Bible and the work of the Holy Spirit, He comes to us, showing us His character, revealing His will, and urging us to accept the salvation He has provided in His Son, Jesus Christ.

In giving us the Bible, God did not use human secretaries to take word-for-word dictation. Instead, He inspired the Bible writers with His thoughts. The prophets then wrote these revelations in their own words. Thus, while God used many people to produce the Bible, it has just one Author.

Even those who wrote the Bible understood that they did not originate the messages that they transmitted. The apostle Paul recognized the writings of the prophets before him to be the "holy scriptures" (Romans 1:2) and the "oracles of God" (Romans 3:2).

For that reason, the Bible claims to be inspired. "All scripture is given by inspiration of God" (2 Timothy 3:16, KJV). The New International Version of this verse says, "All Scripture is God-breathed."

Bible comes from the Greek word *biblos*, which means "book." Actually the Bible is a collection of sixty-six books—thirty-nine in the Old Testament and twenty-seven in the New Testament in most Bibles. The Old Testament, originally written for the most part in Hebrew, contains the five books of the law, followed by (in order) the historical books; the "writings," or poetic books; the major prophets, and the minor prophets. These do not necessarily follow a chronological sequence. The New Testament, written in Greek by Christians of the first century A.D., can be divided into four categories: (1) the history of the church of the first century, including the four Gospels and the book of Acts, (2) Paul's epistles (letters), (3) the general epistles, the rest of the books through Jude, and (4) the book of Revelation.

Although other books are sometimes included in published Bibles, those mentioned above have been accepted generally as the canon, the collection of the sacred books that are considered as inspired and sacred and as possessing divine authority.

Why Bible study is essential

The chief reason for reading the Bible is to become better acquainted with its Author. The ultimate purpose of Bible study is to lead us into a personal relationship with the God who loves us and to an acceptance of the salvation provided through Christ's sacrifice. Studying the Bible makes a difference in our lives. If we will let it, the Bible will become the instrument the Holy Spirit can use most effectively to enable us to become all that God makes possible.

God's Word is valuable to us. Scripture is given for:

1. doctrine.
2. reproof.
3. correction.
4. instruction in righteousness (see 2 Timothy 3:16).

Its ultimate objective is "that the man of God may be complete, equipped for every good work" (2 Timothy 3:17, RSV).

The main reason people do not enjoy studying the Bible is because they find things there that cut across their desired way of living. But after all, that's the purpose of the Bible, isn't it? God's Word wouldn't be much good to us if reading it didn't make us better people. The one thing we have to grasp is that *better isn't bitter*! God wants us to have the very best life possible in a sin-drenched world.

The realization that all God's commandments are promises that will enable us by His grace to get the most out of life should change our attitude toward the Bible. Instead of ignoring God's requirements and hoping that they'll go away or somehow won't apply in our case, we'll long to search them out, take delight in them, and put them into daily practice.

Power in the Word

There is tremendous power in the Word of God—creative power. Psalm 33:9 tells us, "He spake, and it was done; he commanded, and it stood fast."

Two missionary couples were dining out in a hotel restaurant in Tokyo. One of the men, a fun-loving individual, was intrigued by some of the magic-stunt gadgets for sale in Japan and had just purchased a little receptacle attached to a spool of string that would wind up quickly. This would cause an item placed in the receptacle to apparently disappear. He had this gadget mounted under his coat. While the group waited to be served, the fun-lover called the waitresses to come over and watch. He stuffed his napkin in the little receptacle, then threw his hands into the air to distract their gaze while the napkin disappeared. However, the stunt backfired. Somehow the string caught on one of the buttons of his coat, and the giggling waitresses pointed to the napkin—still in plain sight.

We cannot picture the Creator in that kind of situation. We cannot imagine Him saying, "Now, all right everyone. Gather around and watch this." Then He cries out, "Let there be light!" but nothing happens. If such a scene could take place, we might imagine the Creator getting a little frustrated as someone begins to giggle—"I said, let there be light! Come on, light, what are you waiting for?"

There is absolutely no way that could happen, is there? Yes, it *can* happen. How? Where? The rebellious human heart alone can stymie the all-powerful Word of God. That Word pronounces that He wants to bring light and life into the darkness of every heart. But the waste and void of sinful human nature is the only thing in all the universe that can resist the all-powerful Creator's command.

However, if we are willing to lay aside our Creator-proof armor, then when He speaks, it *will be done*. He commands, and the sinful dust of our human nature is surely shaped anew in the image of God. Then His Spirit breathes into the old dead bones of our carnal nature, and suddenly, through His all-powerful word, the new creation comes to life.

God speaks through His written Word, and it is done. Just as His word upholds and sustains our physical lives, His written Word upholds and sustains our spiritual lives. The power of the Bible to change human hearts and to sustain spiritual development is one of the great evidences that it is what it claims to be—the Word of God.

Another evidence of its inspiration is that God's Word endures forever (see Isaiah 40:8). It is "settled in heaven" (Psalm 119:89), and so will we be if we allow Christ to take over our lives. God's Word heals, and we are whole again. Think of what can happen, both now and in the future, if we let the Holy Spirit fill us with the power of God's Word!

Finding hidden treasure

Under the sponsorship of wealthy Lord Carnarvon, Howard Carter engaged in off-and-on archaeological explorations in the area of ancient Thebes beginning in 1908. The two men had been responsible for several interesting discoveries, but World War I nearly stopped their exploration. From 1919 to 1921 Carter worked over the entire section of the Valley of the Kings between the tombs of Merneptah, Ramses III, and Ramses IV. Still no important discovery was made, and the concession to dig there had only a few more weeks to run.

Carter had just about given up hope of making any major discovery in that area, when on the morning of November 4, 1922, he found a rough-hewn step below the entry to the tomb of Ramses IV. Following this lead, he uncovered the entrance to another royal tomb—one that was to prove more fabulous in the richness of its contents than any other Egyptian royal sepulcher uncovered in modern times. As he came to the last barrier across the passageway, Carter was able to read the hieroglyphic inscription, which indicated that the occupant of the tomb was the long-sought Tutankhamen.

Excitedly, Carter summoned Lord Carnarvon from England. The wealthy patron and his daughter arrived in Alexandria on November 20, and on November 25 the first stone was removed from the tomb wall, allowing Carter, Lord Carnarvon, and Carnarvon's daughter, Lady Evelyn Herbert, to catch the first breathtaking glimpse of the strange golden animals, statues, and furniture that are now world famous. The treasure they discovered that memorable day is said to be one of the greatest single discoveries ever of concentrated wealth.

But there is an even more valuable concentration of treasure waiting for our discovery in the Bible treasure chest. In the Palestine of Christ's day, it was not uncommon to find treasure hidden in a field. Because there were no bank vaults in those days, persons with valuables to preserve frequently buried them either in the earthen floors of their houses or somewhere in their fields. If the owners were killed in an invasion or carried away into exile, the place of concealment might soon be forgotten. Later, someone plowing such a field might uncover the buried treasure.

Imagine the joy that would follow such a discovery! Jesus told a story about a man who came across buried treasure in a field he was plowing. But he did not own the field! To buy the field and make the treasure his, he had to sell everything he possessed. But, because the treasure was worth far more than all he had, he did not hesitate to do so.

Jesus did not tell this story to teach us how to take advantage of our neighbors. His point was that when we find the treasure of the kingdom of heaven we should be more than happy to give all that we have, and are, for it. The parable also illustrates the tremendous joy that comes from discovering the hidden treasures of the Word of God. The reward we receive as we study is worth far more than the effort it takes to discover the truths that are placed there for us to find. And the effort itself becomes joyful, just as it was with the man in the parable who gladly sold all that he had in order to obtain the treasure.

Words to grow by

Knowing the Word and will of the Lord is not enough. We must be willing to follow it completely. In this we have the example of Jesus:

The Son of God was surrendered to the Father's will, and dependent upon His power. So utterly was Christ emptied of self that He made no plans for Himself. He accepted God's plans for Him, and day by day the Father unfolded His plans. So should we depend upon God, that our lives may be the simple outworking of His will (Ellen G. White, *The Desire of Ages*, p. 208).

What it takes to respond this way is a total commitment to God's will and such a love for Him that everything we do, say, or even think may be the simple outworking of His will for us.

If our spiritual diet is impoverished, if we try to feed our souls on the husks of the commonplace and uninspired, our minds and souls will become dwarfed and cheapened. Peter counsels, "As newborn babes, desire the sincere milk of the word, that ye may grow thereby" (1 Peter 2:2). Jesus informed the devil, "Man shall not live by bread alone, but by every word that proceedeth out of the mouth of God" (Matthew 4:4).

One of the laws of nutrition is that we are what we eat. This law is true in the spiritual sense too. In order to grow spiritually, we must have daily spiritual nourishment. Through a return to careful, daily Bible study, we can find a heaven in our hearts now and actually partake, even before we go to heaven, of the healing leaves of the tree of life (see Revelation 22:2).

Chapter 2

What Is God Like?

Four-year-old Karen lived with her grandmother, an old woman who did not expect to live very long because she had heart trouble. Karen did not often have a chance to go anywhere; she was usually confined to home. Her father was a criminal who was in trouble with the law, and her mother was a lady of the night who did not come home very often. The little girl was bright, intelligent, and very pretty, with long black hair, beautiful big brown eyes, and a lovely smile.

One day some friends decided to take Karen and Grandma for a drive. Because the car was so full of people, there was nowhere for Karen to sit except on the knee of the family's teenage son. But Karen did not mind that at all. She chatted with him, and he pointed out interesting sights, explaining things they saw as they drove along.

Karen was enjoying herself so much that she threw her arms around the neck of the young man and kissed him. He was very embarrassed. The car was full of people, and he hardly knew how to react to little girls who were so affectionate. He gently pulled her arms from around his neck and pushed her away. Karen was terribly hurt. She did not know what she had done to warrant the boy's reaction. Her lip dropped, and tears welled up in her big brown eyes. In a voice breaking with emotion she said, "Nobody doesn't love me!"

That was too much for the young man. He spent the rest of the day trying to convince her that, indeed, he did love her and that she was a very important little girl.

"Nobody loves me." That is the universal heart cry of humanity—nobody cares, nobody understands. The world is a very lonely place for those who feel that they are not loved or accepted—and millions of individuals feel that way. Even when surrounded by crowds of people, they feel alone and miserable.

How can such lonely ones find love and a sense of self-worth? There is only one sure way, and that is to come to know God as the tender, caring heavenly Father He really is. For centuries, the devil has convinced multitudes that God is a cruel, legalistic, exacting judge who is waiting for people to do wrong so that He can punish them. But that is a very inaccurate depiction of our heavenly Father. He is infinitely merciful and wonderfully patient and forgiving. Because He loves you as if there were no other to love, He works for you and shepherds you through life, even when you feel rejected and unwanted. There is no love like the love of God; it is real, immeasurable, and for you!

How do we know there is a God?

Millions of people are afraid to trust God's love, because they are not even sure He exists. Being sure of God's existence and knowing Him are not the same as being able to *prove* His existence. Can the existence of God be proved? It depends upon what you mean by proof. If you are looking for scientific proof from experiments that can be conducted under controlled conditions and from which undoubted conclusions can be drawn, you cannot "prove" the existence of God. The Deity cannot be put in a test tube.

Scientific proof is possible only in a limited area of life. Mathematical, chemical, or physical proofs are limited to narrow segments of thought and discovery. Logical proofs have validity only if the premises (or first statements) are undeniably true. Many logical proofs may be overturned by seriously challenging their premises.

Most of life is outside the realm of mathematical, laboratory, or logical proof. For example, how would you prove scientifically the superiority of honor, justice, loyalty, or love? How would a man prove scientifically that his wife loves him? He may have very strong evidence one way or another, but is that "proof"? The fact is that most of life depends on enormous probabilities.

Sometimes people are convicted of murder, not on the basis of absolutely certain fact, but on the basis of probability. People have been executed or condemned to life in prison on the testimony of honest citizens who were mistaken in their identifications or incorrect in their perception of what happened. Yet the "proof" of guilt was accepted, and the accused was condemned.

People who reject the existence of God often think that faith is a matter of putting on blinders. They fail to realize that faith is by no means confined to religion. Faith is necessary in every area of life. We exercise faith when we go into a restaurant to eat, when we put our money in the bank, when we get on a bus or an airplane. We exercise faith when we send our children to school. A teacher or another student may poison their minds. We display a great deal of faith when we get married. Think of the staggering divorce rate! All life is lived by faith. Why should we be surprised when we are confronted by the need of faith in religion?

It is not possible to provide scientific proof for the existence of God. But it is possible to be aware of such impressive evidence that we are willing to pray to God and trust Him. Looking at the evidence, we can have a personal certainty that allows us to say, "I know God."

What is that evidence? First, there is the evidence of intuition. Intuition is the immediate knowing or learning of something without the conscious use of reasoning. It is instantaneous awareness. People everywhere believe in a god or gods because of an intuitive response to the things they see and hear.

In his little book, *Give God a Chance*, William E. Sangster explains:

> There are some things we know without being told. . . .
> We always knew . . . that love was better than hate and kindness than cruelty. . . .
> We always knew that beauty pulled us. People vary in the way they respond to beauty, but all feel it—in a flower, in a landscape, in a sunset, in a symphony . . . it needed no justification. Its "proof" was in itself.
> We always knew that truth was better than a lie—however convenient lying might be on occasion! . . .

We always knew that goodness was better than bad-
ness. . . .

Beauty, truth, goodness . . . how real and high they are!
Even when we spurn them, we know in ourselves that we
are spurning the best. How *do* we know? *We just do!* They
are inside us. Animals don't feel like this. We have sight
and *insight*.

If we follow these insights, they lead us to a Being to
whom beauty, truth, goodness are supremely precious
([London: Epworth Press, 1959], p. 22).

The Bible teaches that our intuitive knowledge of God comes
directly from Him (see Romans 1:18-20). People are without
excuse, not because they have scientific proof, but because God
Himself impresses their minds as they view the things He has
created. "God has shown it to them" (verse 19, NRSV). That is
why the Bible so confidently calls the atheist a fool; not because
he is dumb or ignorant, but because he denies the impressions
implanted in his mind by God Himself. Intuitive knowledge of
God is convincing evidence of His existence.

Through the ages, Christian philosophers have used their
reasoning faculties to arrive at five arguments for the existence
of God. Even though none is a proof, each has some value as
supporting evidence.

1. The argument from cause (the cosmological argument) tells
   us that all existing things have a cause—God.
2. The argument from design (the teleological argument)
   emphasizes that our world reveals order, intelligence, harmony, and purpose—provided by God.
3. The argument from being (the ontological argument) says
   that man has in his mind the idea of an absolutely perfect
   being. Therefore, that absolutely perfect being must exist—
   God.
4. The moral argument (the anthropological argument) is
   that humankind's moral sense of right and wrong comes
   from God.
5. The historical argument (the ethnological argument) is
   that every nation and culture in history has had a basic

sense of the divine and a need for worship. This sense comes from God.

The Bible teaches that reason alone cannot discover God (see Job 11:7; 37:23; Ecclesiastes 8:17; Isaiah 40:28). God chooses to reveal Himself as our Saviour from sin and as our Guide through life, but He hides from us the infinite mysteries of His person. The arguments from reason provide strong *probability* of God's existence, but not *proof*.

Bible writers offer evidence that the Scriptures are inspired by God (see 2 Timothy 3:16; 2 Peter 1:19-21). Because only God can predict the future, Bible prophecy comes from Him (see Isaiah 46:9, 10; Daniel 2:28; Acts 3:18). Fulfilled prophecies are evidence that God exists and knows the end from the beginning.

The Bible also offers the evidence of personal experience. Those who have a personal friendship with God know that this is the only kind of knowledge of Him that is of lasting value. To *know about* Him is one thing; to *know Him* by entering into a spiritual relationship with Him is quite another. As you seek Him in His Word and in prayer, the Lord comes to you (see John 14:18, 23) and reveals His love and truth to your heart. Your fellowship with Him is the source of peace, joy, and happiness in service for Him and for others.

What is God like?

The Bible teaches that there is only one God. The Bible writers were monotheists, and so are Bible-believing Christians today. Moses expressed Israel's confidence in one God: " 'The Lord our God is one Lord' " (Deuteronomy 6:4, RSV). " 'To you it was shown, that you might know that the Lord is God; there is no other besides him' " (Deuteronomy 4:35, RSV). The prophet Malachi underlined the point: " 'Have we not all one father? Has not one God created us?' " (Malachi 2:10, RSV).

Jesus emphasized the truth of Moses' teaching. The "first of all" the commandments, Jesus said, is, " 'Hear, O Israel: The Lord our God, the Lord is one' " (Mark 12:29, RSV). The apostle Paul added his testimony: "As to the eating of food offered to idols, we know that 'an idol has no real existence,' and that 'there is no God but one' " (1 Corinthians 8:4, RSV). Paul wrote of "one Lord, one faith, one baptism, one God and Father of us all, who is above all and through all and in all" (Ephesians 4:5, 6, RSV). James agreed: "You believe that God is one; you do well. Even the demons believe—and shudder" (James 2:19, RSV).

The Bible teaches that Jesus Christ and the Holy Spirit are Deity, equal with the Father in authority and power and mysteriously one with Him. Jesus is not another God, or an inferior God, but Deity in the fullest sense. And so is the Holy Spirit. Here is a divine mystery that human minds cannot completely grasp. The Father, the Son, and the Holy Spirit are three separate personalities, but so bound together in nature, attributes, and character that they are one God. When you pray to One, you are praying to all Three. When one member of the Deity suffers, so do the other two. God is one, manifested in three "personalities," but mysteriously bound so closely together in nature that the three are one Deity. This we call the doctrine of the Trinity.

Jesus declared that He was equal with the Father. "This was why the Jews sought all the more to kill him, because he not only broke the sabbath but also called God his own Father, making himself equal with God" (John 5:18, RSV). In dialogue with His enemies Jesus claimed to be "I am" (John 8:58), Yahweh, or Jehovah, of the Old Testament. This is the name for Himself that God gave Moses. "God said to Moses, 'I AM WHO I AM.' And he said, 'Say this to the people of Israel, I AM has sent me to you' " (Exodus 3:14, RSV). Jesus explained: "I and the Father are one" (John 10:30, RSV). This was too much for His enemies; they took up stones with the intention of stoning Him to death. They asserted: " 'It is not for a good work that we are going to stone you, but for blasphemy, because you, though only a human being, are making yourself God' " (John 10:33, NRSV).

When the apostle Paul taught the Gentiles that, in the Person of Jesus Christ, God "was manifested in the flesh" (1 Timothy 3:16, RSV), they reacted negatively. Greek philosophy taught that the supreme Deity could have no contact with earthly matter. Paul contradicted that philosophy. He taught that in Christ, "the whole fulness of deity dwells bodily" (Colossians 2:9, RSV). By this he meant that the full and complete nature of the Deity dwells in Christ. The word *fulness* (Greek: *pleroma*) means "the sum total." Mysteriously, the Babe that was born in Bethlehem was the sum total of the Deity. The Man who served others so unselfishly and laid down His life for the sins of the world was none other than the King of the universe.

The Holy Spirit is a Person and Deity. He is not merely God's influence; He has the marks of personality: intellect (see John 14:26), will (see 1 Corinthians 12:11), and emotion (see Ephesians 4:30). Peter identified the Holy Spirit as God. He declared that Ananias had lied to the Holy Spirit, to God (see Acts 5:3, 4).

The Holy Spirit is identified with Yahweh of the Old Testament. The "Spirit of the Lord" is "the God of Israel" (2 Samuel 23:2, 3). The "Lord God" is the "Spirit" (Ezekiel 8:1, 3, RSV). God the Holy Spirit inspired the prophets to write the Scriptures (see 2 Timothy 3:16; 2 Peter 1:21). The presence of the Holy Spirit in the believer's heart is the presence of Christ and the Father (see John 14:18, 23).

The one God who created us (see Malachi 2:10) is the Father (see Genesis 1:1), Jesus Christ the Son (see John 1:1-3, 14; Colossians 1:16), and the Holy Spirit (see Genesis 1:2; Psalm 104:30). They each possess the same powers and characteristics. They are each all-powerful (see Job 42:1, 2; Matthew 28:18; Romans 15:19). They are each all-knowing (see Psalm 147:5; John 16:30; 1 Corinthians 2:10-12). And they are each omnipresent, capable of being everywhere at once (see Psalm 139:7, 8; Matthew 28:20).

God is love. The entire Bible speaks to our hearts of God's love. Even the ugly stories of Satan's perversity and man's sin remind us that such things would not have happened if only God had been trusted, loved, and served. God revealed His infinite love to Moses in a personal way (see Exodus 34:6, 7). God's love involves forgiveness for those who seek Him, patience, and willingness to guide and protect.

God's unfathomable love is justice too. He is so free from sin and so opposed to it that He can never accept it as normal or right (see Exodus 20:5, 6). This is why He sometimes allows hard experiences to come upon us because we are so naturally sinful, and He wants us to turn to Him for deliverance (see Hebrews 12:6; Revelation 3:19).

Christ's life exemplified God's love. Jesus made it clear that such a close union exists between Him and His Father that to know the one is to know the other (see John 1:18; 14:8-11). The disciples of Jesus know God because they know Jesus. When we find Jesus in the Gospels, we find our heavenly Father, for Jesus is the perfect exemplification of God's infinite character. His work was to heal and to save (see Luke 4:18). These two aspects of His ministry went hand in hand; He forgave sin and healed the sick as an illustration of His ability to transform the sinner. Bodies and minds touched by Jesus of Nazareth were restored to perfect health. He delivered struggling souls from the dominion of sin and evil powers. Thus He revealed, as no one else could, what God is like.

The death of Jesus Christ on the cross of Calvary for the sins of the entire world was the greatest evidence of God's love that could possibly have been given to humans (see 1 John 2:2). No sacrifice could equal this, no suffering compare with it; no other atonement could ever be sufficient to pay the penalty for our sins and reconcile us to God (see Isaiah 53:5, 6; 2 Corinthians 5:21; 1 Peter 2:24). Because Jesus bore our guilt in His body on the cross, He became separated from the Father and the Holy Spirit (see Matthew 27:46). The members of the Deity chose to endure this severing of the mysterious, infinite unity that exists between them. And the suffering they endured was infinite! This is the supreme evidence of God's love.

Without God's love in our hearts, we become selfish and earthly. The sensitive appreciation of things beautiful and pure, as well as the capacity to feel genuine concern for other human beings, are attitudes created by God's love reigning in our lives. A person without God's love becomes selfish, proud, and thoughtless of others. Christ is the One who makes us the loving people God intends us to be (see 1 John 3:1-3; 4:7, 12, 13).

If you allow Jesus to come into your heart by the Holy Spirit, you will become a new creature in Christ (see 2 Corinthians 5:17). Your old ways will be replaced by His ways. You will have peace in place of passion, trust in place of fear, and love in place of hate. God's love will elevate you to the status of a true child of God.

Chapter 3

"How Much
He Cares"

God the Eternal Father is the Creator, Source, Sustainer, and Sovereign of all creation. He is just and holy, merciful and gracious, slow to anger and abounding in steadfast love and faithfulness. As the apostle John summarized it, "God is love" (1 John 4:8).

Jesus came to reveal the Father to us (see John 1:1, 14; 14:9). If Jesus were to talk to us personally, what do you suppose He would say? Because His favorite theme when He talked with His followers while here on earth was the paternal character and abundant love of God, Jesus probably would speak to us about how much our Father in heaven loves us.

What would He be likely to choose for His text? Perhaps it would be Hosea 11, a chapter in which God comes right out and says, "I love you." In the eleventh chapter of Hosea, we find the gospel in the Old Testament.

This little book that begins the minor prophets is not appreciated as it should be. Some people feel a bit embarrassed at the story. They find it hard to believe that God would tell a prophet to marry a woman such as Gomer. Then, after the profligate wife was no longer wanted by anyone, God told Hosea to do another strange thing.

Gomer was on the auction block as a slave, but she was so worn out and unattractive that she was for sale at half price. God sent Hosea down to buy her back, which he did. But he didn't take her home to be a slave, although he had every right to do just that. Instead, he reinstated her as his wife, the mother of their three children, the queen of his household. This is a tender illustration of what God is willing to do for us.

In its power and majesty, Hosea 11 surely is one of the most beautiful chapters in the Bible. Again and again throughout the Bible, in the midst of messages warning of the consequences of unfaithfulness, we find tender, loving pleas from God. Hosea 11 is one of the most heartwarming. The first two verses read this way in the Revised Standard Version: "When Israel was a child, I loved him, and out of Egypt I called my son. The more I called them, the more they went from me; they kept sacrificing to the Baals, and burning incense to idols."

The fourth verse is God's answer to our carelessness and backsliding. Jesus bends down, it says, to minister to our needs—to feed us, as it were. He bends down in compassion and interest. But we, His people, are bent in another direction.

In spite of it all, God lovingly pleads in verse 8, "How can I give you up, O Ephraim! How can I hand you over, O Israel!" (RSV). Unrepentant Israel deserves total annihilation, but God is loathe to visit His judgments on His apostate people.

"How can I give you up! . . . My heart recoils within me, my compassion grows warm and tender. I will not execute my fierce anger, I will not again destroy Ephraim; for I am God and not man, the Holy One in your midst, and I will not come to destroy" (verses 8, 9). God's compelling love reaches out and binds us when we try to escape from Him. His boundless love will not let us go, yet He cannot force us to receive that love.

What does it mean to be the recipients of God's love, to be accepted into the heavenly family? Would you be willing to adopt a deformed infant? Would you take it into your home and into your heart? That's what God has done for us because of His great love for us.

We have been marred and deformed by six thousand years of sin, but God still wants us! And His greatest desire is to make us whole again in the truest sense.

The Bible tells us that in the beginning, God made humanity and the earth perfect. When Adam and Eve sinned, an all-pervasive, full-blown, "4-D" evil resulted—disease, despair, decay, and death. However, we still can find evidences of how much God loves us. Even the decaying leaves in their magnificent fall colors make us pause and wonder at our Creator's thoughtfulness.

God invites us as His earthly children to trust Him with a trust deeper and stronger than that which children have for their parents. The love of God for us is larger, broader, and deeper than human love. It is immeasurable.

What evidences have you seen in your life of God's care, love, and concern for you?

My first glimpse of God's sustaining care came when my twin brother was hit by a car on the busy San Francisco street where we lived. When the doctors told my parents that it seemed impossible that six-year-old Freddie could live, my mother called the elders of the Adventist church to pray for his recovery. In an amazingly short time the child's badly fractured skull began to heal. This miracle was most important to our family. In it we saw God's love and mercy firsthand.

How we can know God

In Job 11:7, Zophar asks the patriarch, "Canst thou by searching find out God?" Certainly we cannot. The greatest scientists cannot produce evidence of God's existence that will bring their colleagues to give up deep-seated doubts. How, then, can we know God? Only through His self-revelation. But God wants us to know as much about Him as human beings can possibly grasp.

Edwin Abbott turned to fantasy in an attempt to demonstrate how difficult it is for us to accept and understand what is outside our sphere of existence. In his fascinating little book *Flatland*, he describes a two-dimensional world peopled by creatures that remain blissfully unaware of a third dimension. The story is narrated by a square. His configuration makes him a fairly substantial citizen in a society in which circles make up the highest caste. Straight lines not only are the lowest caste, but also can be quite dangerous. Because the inhabitants are limited to a flat plane of vision, they find it nearly impossible to recognize straight lines coming directly at them. All they can see of these citizens of low caste is a minuscule dot.

The square relates that, after a discussion with a sphere that was trying to explain the concept of a third dimension, the sphere snatched him away from the comfortable plane in which he existed and carried him to the three-dimensional world known as Spaceland. As the amazed square looked back at Flatland, he could see for the first time what squares, straight lines, triangles, and pentagons looked like from above. In Spaceland he discovered such unbelievable creatures as cubes, cones, pyramids, and other solid figures. At the end of his experience, he was sent back to Flatland to proclaim the existence of a third dimension.

Of course, the square's revolutionary gospel was met with scoffing and jeering. Shouting turned to anger as he persisted in trying to explain what he had seen. He ended up in lifelong imprisonment because of his "heresy."

We have as much difficulty accepting and understanding the dimension in which God exists as the mythical inhabitants of Flatland had in understanding our familiar third dimension. Many consider belief in God unscientific nonsense, taking the attitude that they cannot believe that which is beyond the plane of their own existence. Our only means of understanding God is to accept by faith what He communicates to us about Himself and His kind of existence.

Learning to know God

How does God go about revealing Himself in ways we can understand? The Bible suggests at least five methods:

1. Earthly parents: father (see Psalm 103:13), mother (see Isaiah 66:13).
2. Jesus (see John 14:7-9).
3. Nature (see Psalm 19:1-4).
4. The Bible—under the guidance of the Holy Spirit (see 1 Corinthians 2:10-14).
5. The image of God as reflected in born-again people (see Isaiah 43:10-12).

When we turn to these divinely appointed means of revelation, we soon find that the skeptics, as well as the insurance companies, have given God a "bad press." Unfortunately, even many Christians have a badly distorted picture of our heavenly Father. From childhood they have been told, "If you don't do what is right, God won't love you!"

How wrong that is!

The Creator, who still loves fallen Lucifer, certainly loves little children who barely know right from wrong.

One prevailing myth is that God is waiting to slap us down as soon as He catches us doing something wrong. He is pictured as a stern judge with whom Jesus must plead and beg in order to persuade Him, rather reluctantly, to forgive us.

But Jesus' intercessory ministry will be viewed in a very different light if we study carefully Ellen White's description:

God's appointments and grants in our behalf are without limit. The throne of grace is itself the highest attraction because occupied by One who permits us to call Him Father. But God did not deem the principle of salvation complete while invested only with His own love. By His appointment He has placed at His altar an Advocate clothed with our nature. As our Intercessor, His office work is to introduce us to God as His sons and daughters. Christ intercedes in behalf of those who have received Him. To them He gives power, by virtue of His own merits, to become members of the royal family, children of the heavenly King. And the Father demonstrates His infinite love for Christ, who paid our ransom with His blood, by receiving and welcoming Christ's friends as His friends. He is satisfied with the atonement made. He is glorified by the incarnation, the life, death, and mediation of His Son.

No sooner does the child of God approach the mercy seat than he becomes the client of the great Advocate. At his first utterance of penitence and appeal for pardon Christ espouses his case and makes it His own, presenting the supplication before the Father as His own request.

As Christ intercedes in our behalf, the Father lays open all the treasures of His grace for our appropriation, to be enjoyed and to be communicated to others. "Ask in My name," Christ says; "I do not say that I will pray the Father for you; for the Father Himself loveth you, because you have loved Me. Make use of My name. This will give your prayers efficiency, and the Father will give you the riches of His grace; wherefore, 'ask, and ye shall receive, that your joy may be full.' " John 16:24 (*Testimonies for the Church*, vol. 6, pp. 363, 364).

How much God wants to give us

Jesus touched a large number of people with healing, but Matthew 9:20-22 introduces us to a desperate woman who reached out to touch Jesus. Her faith was much stronger than her body. For twelve years she had been suffering from a disease that the doctors were unable to cure. Some believe that she had been a woman of wealth, but all that she possessed was spent on trying to find a cure. Now nothing was left but a crippled body and a spark of hope—her faith in Jesus.

This sufferer had to see Jesus. Painfully she made her way to the seaside. The little fishing boat, just then being dragged up on the shore, was returning from the Decapolis area. But because a large crowd was pushing around it, there was no way she could get through to Jesus.

The woman could hear the Master's gentle, lovely voice speaking with the authority of heaven. Then the crowd began to move toward Capernaum. When Jesus entered Matthew's house, people filled the doorway and the narrow street outside. Suddenly there was a stir in the waiting crowd as they made way for Jairus, a ruler of the synagogue, who had come to plead for Jesus' help.

People still pressed around Jesus as He slowly began to make His way on a mission of mercy to the home where a little girl was dying. The sick woman was desperate. "I must reach Him, I must!" she thought to herself. "Perhaps I can manage to touch the hem of His garment. If I do, I know I will be healed." But she could not push through the crowd in her weakened condition. Just then, Jesus began to make His way toward her. Would He pass her by? Dignity forgotten, the woman dropped down into the dust. She did not care what people thought. Crawling through a forest of legs, she reached out in desperation, just managing to touch the border of Jesus' robe.

An electrifying thrill came from that touch as she was instantly healed. In that touch the faith of her life was concentrated. Instantly her pain and feebleness were replaced by the vim and vigor of perfect health.

More than satisfied with the change that took place, the woman shrank back into the crowd, hoping to go unobserved. But Someone had noticed. Jesus felt the touch of faith and the power that had been drawn from Him.

When He asked, "Who touched Me?" Peter, as we might expect, answered boldly, "What do You mean, 'Who touched Me'? The whole crowd is pressing around You. Everybody is trying to touch You." But Jesus "could distinguish the touch of faith from the casual contact of the careless throng" (*The Desire of Ages*, p. 344). He was on the way to raise a little girl from the sleep of death, but the touch of faith stopped Him in His tracks.

There was a great crowd pressing about Christ. None of them realized any accession of vital power. But when the sick woman reached out to touch Him, believing that she would be healed, she felt that healing power. We might apply that to spiritual things. It does us no good merely to talk of religion in a casual way or to pray without soul hunger and living faith. A faith that accepts Christ merely as Saviour of the world will not bring healing to the soul. The only faith that will benefit us is that which embraces our Lord as a personal Saviour.

Although the woman's strong faith led her to reach out and touch the hem of Christ's garment, she then tried to fade away in the crowd. But Christ had much more for her—hers was to be the blessing of personal testimony and witness that reaches down to us today. How wonderful it is to touch the hem of His garment! But we are living in a time when we cannot be satisfied with only this.

It is natural that when we get a little money we want more. We taste a bit of delicious food, and we want more. It is human nature to desire more of what is pleasant. But we receive a mere taste of heaven's infinite blessing and steal away satisfied, as though God has no more to give. Oh, that we could understand how much God wants to give His people today. How His heart of divine love must hurt when He sees us turn away with so little when He has so much to give!

Even God's prohibitions, which many people use as an excuse to turn away from the gospel today, are evidence of His care. His great love is revealed in the fact that He is interested in every aspect of our lives, even what we eat and wear. What God wants more than anything is to give us the more abundant life (see John 10:10).

"How much He cares"

A young singer bore a cross that seemed so heavy she was tempted to give up her trust in God. She had a measure of faith. She knew that God had power to do all things. But she could not believe that He cared enough about her to give individual attention to her needs. Because she didn't believe, she couldn't pray. In her distress she picked up the phone. The moment her friend answered, the young woman blurted out, "Something terrible has happened. I'm not a Christian anymore. I've given up everything!"

Then she hung up. But as she did so, she saw on the wall before her a copy of the famous painting of Christ in Gethsemane. The heart she thought so cold began to weep. Through her tears she began singing once again these words:

> Because His love for me led through Gethsemane,
>   I know He cares, He cares for me;
> Because His plan for me led to the cross of Calvary,
>   I know He cares, I know He cares for me.

These words gave the lie to all she had been thinking and saying. She could not sing them and still doubt. Casting herself at the Master's feet, she wept out a prayer from a heart that knew He cared.

Don't ever think that God does not care. He cares so much that He was willing to give His only begotten Son to be one with us, not just for a little while, but for all eternity.

The question we must face as we realize how much God cares is not, "Does He really care for me?" but rather, "How much do I love Him in return? Am I willing to give my all in complete surrender and full confidence to Him?"

Chapter 4

God
Came to Us

It is the spring of the year A.D. 31. A visitor has come to Jerusalem to celebrate the Passover at the temple. On Friday morning he is walking through the streets of the ancient city when he hears the clamor of a great mob coming from the direction of Pilate's judgment hall. He hurries through the streets and sees a huge crowd of people swaying this way and that, clamoring for the life of a prisoner. The visitor presses through the crowd so that he can have a closer look. On the balcony before him he sees the condemned Man. He is wearing a long purple robe; in His hand is a ruler's staff, and on His head a crown of thorns. The thorns have been pushed down upon His brow, and the blood trickles down His cheeks.

At that moment Pilate, the Roman governor, appears and shouts to the mob, "Shall I crucify your King?" And, with a yell that seems to come from hell, the people cry out, "Crucify Him, crucify Him. We have no king but Caesar."

Jostled this way and that by the angry crowd, the visitor watches with amazement as Pilate hands the prisoner over to the Roman soldiers. They drag Him down the stairs and push back the surging crowd as they lay a great heavy cross on His shoulders. They push two other prisoners in behind Him and command Him to walk—and He starts walking. But He looks ill and in pain, and every labored step seems to cause Him agony. He collapses beneath the weight of the cross, and the Roman soldiers drag a man from the crowd and command him to carry the cross.

All along the road leading out of the city the crowd is jeering, abusing Him with cruel, profane words and bitter accusations. If it were not for the Roman soldiers, the crowd would have torn Him to pieces.

When the mob arrives at a place called Calvary, outside the city walls, the Roman soldiers lay the huge cross on the ground and stretch the condemned Man out on it. They take a hammer and pound nails through His hands and feet, fastening Him to the cross. They pick up the cross and force it down into a hole in the ground while the priests and people shout in satisfaction that at last the "impostor" is brought to justice. The soldiers fasten the two other prisoners to crosses and place them on either side of Him.

The tortured One who is the focus of the angry crowd's accusations shows no hatred or anger. In a voice full of sorrow and pain He prays, "Father, forgive them; for they know not what they do" (Luke 23:34). He sees a young man supporting His weeping mother and says to her, "Woman, behold thy son!" And to the young man He says, "Behold thy mother!" (John 19:26, 27). And the visitor thinks to himself, "How could a dying criminal be so kind? Is He really the liar and impostor they say He is?"

The hours pass by, and intense darkness shrouds the cross, the soldiers, and the angry crowd. But the visitor stands with his eyes pinned to the spot where hangs the kindest face he has ever seen. Then, about three o'clock in the afternoon, the darkness lifts, and the face of the condemned One lights up with glory as He exclaims, "It is finished." "Father, into thy hands I commend my spirit" (John 19:30; Luke 23:46). Then He bows His head and dies.

At that moment the earth rumbles and heaves, as lightning flashes and thunder explodes around the surrounding hills. The jeering crowd takes fright and rushes for shelter. The visitor to Jerusalem, ignoring the confusion around him, walks slowly, sorrowfully, and pensively back to the city, unable to control his surging emotions. Who was this saintly Man? Where did He come from? Why did they want to kill Him? How could He show such gentleness and love in the face of such abuse?

Who was Jesus of Nazareth?

This is the question that many visitors to Jerusalem were asking that terrible Passover weekend. And it is the question that millions have asked since that time. His followers said that He was the Son of God, the promised Messiah, who came to our world to suffer the punishment for all human sin. They pointed to the predictions of the Old Testament Scriptures and explained that His birth, life, death, and resurrection fulfilled all that the ancient prophets had foretold.

For example, the disciples of Jesus explained that He was the "Seed" of the woman spoken of in Genesis 3:15 (see Galatians 3:16, 19). Although He was temporarily wounded by Satan, ultimately His death and resurrection will result in Satan's destruction.

Jesus' followers pointed inquirers to the prediction made hundreds of years before that the Messiah would be born in Bethlehem (see Micah 5:2). They explained that Jesus *was* born in Bethlehem (see Matthew 2:1). They declared that Jesus was born of a virgin, as Isaiah had predicted. The Messiah would be called Immanuel, meaning "God with us." Jesus was that Messiah (compare Isaiah 7:14 with Matthew 1:23).

The disciples of Jesus taught that even the star followed by the wise men was foretold by an Old Testament prophet (compare Numbers 24:17 with Matthew 2:1, 2, 7, 9-11). They joyfully pointed out that the Spirit-filled life of Jesus was a fulfillment of an ancient prophecy (compare Isaiah 61:1, 2 with Luke 4:16-19). The manner of His death was outlined centuries before (compare Psalm 22 and Isaiah 53 with Matthew 27 and John 19).

Jesus' followers taught enthusiastically that He had not remained in the grave, but had risen from the dead on the Sunday morning after He was crucified. On the day of Pentecost, seven weeks after the death of Jesus, the apostle Peter applied the prophecy of Psalm 16:8-11 to Jesus' resurrection:

God raised him up, having loosed the pangs of death, because it was not possible for him to be held by it.
For David says concerning him,
"I saw the Lord always before me,

> for he is at my right hand that I may not be shaken. . . .
> For thou wilt not abandon my soul to Hades [the grave],
> nor let thy Holy One see corruption" (Acts 2:24-27, RSV).

Peter declared that David "foresaw and spoke of the resurrection of the Christ. . . . This Jesus God raised up, and of that we all are witnesses" (Acts 2:31, 32, RSV).

The writings of Jesus' disciples establish conclusively that Daniel's predictions regarding the Messiah were fulfilled by Jesus. Daniel wrote that the Messiah, the anointed One, would come sixty-nine weeks of years (483 years) after "the going forth of the commandment to restore and to build Jerusalem" (Daniel 9:25). Jesus became the anointed One when He was baptized by water and by the Holy Spirit "in the fifteenth year of the reign of Tiberius Caesar" (Luke 3:1, 21, 22; compare Acts 10:38). That was the year A.D. 27, 483 years after the enactment in 457 B.C. of Artaxerxes' command to restore Jerusalem (see Ezra 6:14). Daniel had predicted that Jesus would be killed halfway through the seventieth week of years (see Daniel 9:27). Three and a half years after His baptism in the autumn of A.D. 27 Jesus was crucified—in the spring of A.D. 31.

Four Passovers occurred during Jesus' ministry: (1) John 2:13, the Passover of A.D. 28; (2) John 5:1, the Passover of A.D. 29; (3) John 6:4, the Passover of A.D. 30; (4) John 13:1, the Passover of A.D. 31, when Jesus was crucified. Therefore, Jesus was crucified three and a half years after His baptism, as Daniel had predicted.

The Bible does not offer scientific proof that Jesus of Nazareth was the Son of God. Acceptance of Jesus as the Christ is an act of faith inspired by the conviction of the Holy Spirit. But the evidence is convincing and overwhelming. The Messiah of the ancient prophecies is the One who allowed Himself to be cruelly slain by His unbelieving countrymen.

Jesus—fully God

Jesus claimed to be the Son of God. He accepted Peter's statement: " 'You are the Christ, the Son of the living God' " (Matthew 16:16, RSV). Jesus responded: " 'Blessed are you,

Simon Bar-Jona! For flesh and blood has not revealed this to you, but my Father who is in heaven' " (verse 17, RSV).

Jesus did not mean to imply that He is inferior to the Father as earthly sons are inferior to their fathers. In fact, a number of times He claimed equality with the Father. When Jesus announced to His hearers, " 'My Father is working still, and I am working' " (John 5:17, RSV), they correctly interpreted Him to mean that God was His Father, "making himself equal with God" (verse 18, RSV). Because they thought He was blaspheming, they wanted to kill Him.

Jesus took the name for God given to Moses centuries before and claimed that, like the Father, He had eternal preexistence. There never was a time when He did not exist in the closest union and fellowship with the Father. Jesus taught: " 'Before Abraham was, I am' " (John 8:58, RSV). God had identified Himself to Moses as I AM (see Exodus 3:13, 14). That means that the LORD (Yahweh or I AM) of the Old Testament is the LORD of the New Testament (compare Deuteronomy 6:4-6 with 1 Corinthians 12:3).

Jesus' apostles repeated over and over again that He is Lord, Deity in the fullest sense of the term. The apostle Paul taught: "If you confess with your lips that Jesus is Lord and believe in your heart that God raised him from the dead, you will be saved" (Romans 10:9, RSV). A few sentences later, Paul wrote of Jesus: "The same Lord is Lord of all and bestows his riches upon all who call upon him" (verse 12, RSV).

To those of Greek culture, Paul explained that in Jesus Christ the supreme Deity had come in human flesh. "For in him the whole fulness of deity dwells bodily" (Colossians 2:9, RSV). Writing to Titus, Paul referred to Jesus Christ as "our great God and Savior" (Titus 2:13, RSV).

The apostles were convinced that the God of the universe who created our world was Jesus Christ (see John 1:1-3, 14; Colossians 1:16, 17). When Paul referred to Jesus as "the *first-born* of all creation" (Colossians 1:15, RSV, emphasis supplied), he used the Greek word *prōtŏtŏkŏs*, which means "the preeminent one." Jesus was not the first in time to be created; as the Creator, He is preeminent over creation.

For those who doubt that Jesus is Deity, we would point out that there are only three alternatives as to who He is: God, bad, or mad. Jesus claimed that He is God in the fullest sense. Either He was telling the truth, or He was a bad man, an imposter who lied about His identity. Or He was insane, deluded into imagining that He was God. But there is absolutely no evidence in all the literature about Him that Jesus ever lied or that He was in any way mentally deranged. Quite the contrary, even His opponents have seen in Him supreme purity and emotional and psychological balance. Then, when He claimed to be God, He must have been telling the truth—because good men in their right minds do not tell lies.

Jesus—fully human

Jesus' favorite name for Himself was "Son of man" (see Matthew 8:20; 9:6; Mark 10:33). The angel told the virgin Mary: " 'The Holy Spirit will come upon you, and the power of the Most High will overshadow you; therefore the child to be born will be called holy, the Son of God' " (Luke 1:35, RSV). Because His mother was human, Jesus was human in every respect, except that He was not sinful. Paul emphasized that Jesus "was descended from David according to the flesh" (Romans 1:3, RSV). He was "born in the likeness of men" (Philippians 2:7, RSV).

Notice, the angel explained that at birth He would be "holy" (see Luke 1:35). The rest of humanity has been "brought forth in iniquity." With David we can all say: "In sin did my mother conceive me" (Psalm 51:5, RSV). "The wicked go astray from the womb, they err from their birth, speaking lies" (Psalm 58:3, RSV).

Although Jesus was holy at birth, He took upon His perfect nature our fallen, sinful nature and was tempted while bearing it. That is why the Bible teaches that as Jesus overcame sin completely, so may we—by relying upon Him for power as He relied upon His Father for power.

Peter wrote that Jesus left us "an example, that you should follow in his steps. He committed no sin; no guile was found on his lips" (1 Peter 2:21, 22, RSV). Speaking through the apostle John, Jesus said: "He who conquers, I will grant him to sit with

me on my throne, as I myself conquered and sat down with my
Father on his throne" (Revelation 3:21, RSV).

Jesus—sin bearer for all

The most wonderful truth in the Bible is that Jesus Christ
suffered on the cross for the sins of all humanity. Isaiah wrote:
"He was wounded for our transgressions, he was bruised for
our iniquities; upon him was the chastisement that made us
whole, and with his stripes we are healed. All we like sheep
have gone astray; we have turned every one to his own way;
and the Lord has laid on him the iniquity of us all" (Isaiah 53:5,
6, RSV).

Paul repeated the same truth in his second letter to the
Corinthians: "For our sake he [the Father] made him [Jesus] to
be sin who knew no sin, so that in him we might become the
righteousness of God" (2 Corinthians 5:21, RSV). Jesus took our
guilt upon Himself, identifying with every sinner who has ever
lived and ever will live. "He himself bore our sins in his body on
the tree, that we might die to sin and live to righteousness"
(1 Peter 2:24, RSV).

No one can ever claim that he or she had no opportunity of
salvation. Jesus died for the sins of all (see 1 John 2:2). His Holy
Spirit convicts all human beings of sin and of their need of the
Saviour (see John 12:32; 16:8-11). Our part is humbly to accept
Jesus as Saviour and Lord, allowing Him to reign in our hearts
by the Holy Spirit (see Romans 5:17; 8:9, 10).

Because He rose from the dead, Jesus is able to save completely all who surrender their hearts to Him (see 1 Corinthians
15:17-23). All faithful believers before and after the cross are
forgiven their sins and given eternal life because Jesus died for
their sins and rose again. "He who believes in the Son has eternal
life" (John 3:36, RSV).

Jesus—mediator, judge, and king

After He rose from the dead, Jesus ascended to heaven, where
He shares the throne with the Father in the heavenly sanctuary.
"We have such a high priest, one who is seated at the right hand
of the throne of the Majesty in heaven, a minister in the sanctu-

ary and the true tent [tabernacle] which is set up not by man but by the Lord" (Hebrews 8:1, 2, RSV).

As our High Priest in the heavenly sanctuary, Jesus forgives our sins when we confess them to Him (see 1 John 1:9). He purifies us from all spiritual uncleanness. He purifies the "conscience from dead works to serve the living God" (Hebrews 9:14, RSV). That means He gives us victory over the sins that we could not overcome in our own strength. No temptation is too powerful for Him to overcome for us if we put our complete trust in Him (see 1 Corinthians 10:13).

The Bible teaches that a short time before His second coming, Jesus, along with the Father, conducts a judgment in heaven to see whose names can be retained in the heavenly book of life (see Daniel 7:9-14; 12:1; Matthew 22:11-14). If you believe in Him, your name is in the book of life now (see Luke 10:20). The purpose of the pre-advent judgment is to determine who have retained the born-again experience so that their names can be kept in the book of life and they can be taken to heaven when Jesus comes. "He who conquers shall be clad thus in white garments, and I will not blot his name out of the book of life; I will confess his name before my Father and before his angels" (Revelation 3:5, RSV).

At the end of the pre-advent judgment in heaven, Jesus ceases His work of mediation in the sanctuary (see Revelation 8:5; 22:11). Probation closes for all humanity—the saved are saved for eternity, and the lost are lost for eternity. Shortly after that, Jesus comes with the holy angels (see Matthew 24:30, 31). As "King of kings and Lord of lords" (Revelation 19:16), He destroys the wicked, raises the righteous dead, and, with them, takes the righteous living to the heavenly kingdom (see 1 Thessalonians 4:16-18).

Jesus promised, "I will come again and will take you to myself, that where I am you may be also" (John 14:3, RSV). What a day of relief and rejoicing that will be! Jesus Christ Himself, the One who died for our sins on Calvary's cross, is coming again soon to give His faithful people immortality (see 1 Corinthians 15:51-54) and to give them an eternal home with Him.

Have you accepted Jesus as Saviour and Lord? Are you allowing Him to reign in your heart every day? Do you pray and study the Bible regularly, allowing the Lord to speak to you by His Holy Spirit? Have you let go all the sins that you like so much? Do you depend on Jesus constantly for victory in your life, just as He depended on His Father? There is an eternity of joy ahead for you if you will enter into this experience.

Chapter 5

"When He Comes"

God the eternal Holy Spirit was active with the Father and the Son in creation, incarnation, and redemption. He inspired the writers of Scripture and filled Christ's life with power. He draws and convicts human beings and renews and transforms those who respond into the image of God.

Long ago in London a famous preacher was forced to deliver his sermons on the streets because the churches would not allow him to speak inside. Although crowds flocked to hear him, he was not successful in reaching what he considered to be the upper classes.

One day, while preaching, he saw his opportunity when a stylish carriage approached. Interrupting his sermon, the speaker inquired as to who owned this splendid coach. He learned that it belonged to Lady Ann Erskine, a social butterfly noted for squandering her husband's wealth. As Lady Ann's carriage approached, the minister prayed that the Holy Spirit would lead him to say something that would reach her heart. When she drew within earshot, he announced loudly that he was about to hold an auction for Lady Ann's soul.

Quickly he recognized a bidder. "It's Satan. Satan, what do you bid for the soul of Lady Ann Erskine?"

Then he replied for Satan, "All the wealth of the world, fine clothes, fine company, and pleasures of all sorts."

"All right, Satan, but what about after this life has ended? What do you offer then?" The answer was nothing but a long silence.

"Oh!" exclaimed the preacher, "here's another bidder. It's Jesus. Jesus, what do You offer for Lady Ann's soul?"

"I offer a life of service for others—a cross of self-denial for her to carry in this life—but it will bring her true happiness if she is willing to bear it. And after that, I offer eternal life in the kingdom I'm preparing for those who love and serve Me."

The preacher's daring message strongly moved Lady Ann. She ordered the carriage stopped, stepped out, and walked over to the platform from which her soul had been put up for auction. Tearfully she told the crowd that she realized the hopeless condition of her self-seeking and gladly accepted Christ's bid.

Lady Ann held true to her decision, becoming known as the angel of the slums of London. She also wrote many inspiring Christian hymns. Her conversion demonstrates the first part of the commission given to the Holy Spirit (the Comforter) when He came in a special way to represent Christ on earth after the ascension. "When he comes," Jesus promised, "he will convict the world of guilt in regard to sin" (John 16:8, NIV).

Because of His omnipresence, the Holy Spirit is able to convict and convert human beings wherever they may be. A professional diver, working in salvage off the Florida coast, was making his way toward a sunken ship when he noticed something white in the mouth of a shellfish. The diver had to move carefully in order to preserve his balance, but was able to retrieve the white object that had attracted his attention. Holding it close to the window in his helmet, he recognized it as a gospel tract. Later, intrigued at finding a message from God at the bottom of the sea, he read it carefully. As he continued thinking about the Spirit of God following him to the depths of the ocean, he gave his heart to the One who was that interested in saving his soul.

From where did the Comforter come?

In John 16, Jesus said that the Comforter was yet to come. However, He had previously stated: "I will pray the Father, and he shall give you another Comforter, that he may abide with you for ever; even the Spirit of truth; whom the world cannot receive, because it seeth him not, neither knoweth him: but ye know him; for he dwelleth with you, and shall be in you. I will not leave you comfortless: I will come to you" (John 14:16-18).

This leaves us with an enigma. How could the Comforter "come" if He already was "dwelling with" them? Also, why did Jesus tell His disciples a little later, "It is expedient for you that I go away: for if I go not away, the Comforter will not come unto you; but if I depart, I will send him unto you" (John 16:7)?

When Jesus was with the disciples, they had their "Comforter." But He was about to return to heaven to take up His intercessory ministry. Thus, they needed "another Comforter" (John 14:16). That leaves us with the question, Why was it best for them that Jesus go away? Part of the answer is that if He stayed on earth, He would be limited to one geographical locale at a time, whereas the Holy Spirit, because of His omnipresence as God, could be everywhere at once—He could be winning souls on the streets of London at the same time that He might also influence a diver to accept the Word of God at the bottom of the sea.

The Holy Spirit had been working in and for this world from the very beginning. It was He who "moved upon the face of the waters" (Genesis 1:2) as the divine Agent of Creation. It was He who inspired the prophets (see 2 Peter 1:21). But now He was to "come" in a new way, accepting a new office—that of the Comforter, the Representative of Christ on earth.

Because Christ took our humanity, forever to retain it, He could not be in every place personally at once. Therefore, it was for His followers' interest that He should return to the Father and send the Spirit to be His representative on earth. No one would then have any advantage because of his location or his personal contact with Christ. By the Spirit the Saviour would be available to all.

The Greek word translated "Comforter" is *paraklētŏs*, a compound word made up of *para*, "alongside," and *klētŏs*, "one called." He is the One called to stand by our side and help us with every need.

R. A. Torrey found himself walking along a narrow path near a lake one night after speaking at a Bible conference in New York State. Under most circumstances, it would have been a pleasant walk, but a storm had come up, darkening the sky. The unfamiliar path followed the edge of a bluff. The storm had gullied out deep ditches along the path, which made the journey even more dangerous. Occasionally a flash of lightning would reveal the hazards ahead, but then it would be darker than ever. Torrey reports,

> Just then the thought came to me, "What was it you told the people there at the Conference about the Holy Spirit being a Person always by our side? Does He not walk by your side now?". . . Then I at once realized that the Holy Spirit walked between me and the edge of the bluff, and that four miles through the dark was four miles without fear, a gladsome instead of a fearsome walk (*The Holy Spirit* [Westwood, N. J.: Fleming H. Revell Co., 1927], p. 31).

The office work of the Holy Spirit

Because the Holy Spirit came as the representative of Christ, His office work is to make effective in our lives the redemption that Jesus wrought for us on the cross. In doing so, the Spirit makes Christ's presence real to us by dwelling in our hearts and leading us step by step to live the same kind of life that He enabled Jesus to live. Not only does He convict us of sin, but also "of righteousness" (John 16:8).

In His Sermon on the Mount, Jesus promised, "Blessed are they which do hunger and thirst after righteousness: for they shall be filled" (Matthew 5:6). In a special sense, filling us with righteousness is the work of the Holy Spirit.

Our sense of unworthiness and need leads us to hunger and thirst after righteousness. As we do, we can claim the promise that all who long to bear the likeness of God's character will be satisfied. The Holy Spirit leads us to fix our eyes on Christ and works within us, enabling us to be conformed to Christ's image.

The Beatitudes demonstrate the kind of righteousness Jesus was talking about in the Sermon on the Mount—conformity to the image of Christ.

Think what the reaction of Christ's listeners must have been as He made His presentation. They seem to have been amazed at His teaching, which was so at variance with what the Pharisees taught. Those religious leaders had led the people to think that happiness consisted in the possession of material bounties and that fame and honor were to be coveted.

But Jesus pointed out the duty of His followers to help others understand what is involved in righteousness and eternal life. Jesus assured His disciples then, as well as those who would become His disciples through the ages, that "blessed are they which are persecuted for righteousness' sake: for their's [sic] is the kingdom of heaven" (Matthew 5:10). Obviously, the "righteousness" that the believers would be persecuted for was not a mere transaction in the books of heaven but involved instead a moral righteousness that would be demonstrated in their lives.

Imagine the reaction of the Pharisees and Jewish leaders who were present on that occasion. As Jesus presented the principles of righteousness, the Pharisees must have whispered to those around them that what He was teaching was contradictory to the Ten Commandments. Of course, as Jesus explained, that was not at all what He intended. While many were thinking that He had come to do away with the law, Jesus clearly revealed His attitude toward the Decalogue. "Think not that I am come to destroy the law, or the prophets," He stated in no uncertain terms in Matthew 5:17. He declared that it was not His purpose to set aside the precepts of the law. He understood that the order and harmony of the natural world and the well-being of the universe depend on God's laws.

The key to Christ's use of the term *righteousness* is found in Matthew 5:20: "Except your righteousness shall exceed the righteousness of the scribes and Pharisees, ye shall in no case enter into the kingdom of heaven." The people considered the Pharisees, who had added many legal requirements of their own to the laws of God, to be the best possible people. That day, in the Sermon on the Mount, Christ pointed out that the Pharisees were good but just *not good enough*.

In His famous sermon, Jesus proceeded to show His hearers that God makes possible, through the righteousness Christ imparts, a reproduction in themselves of His character. In six specific illustrations, Jesus contrasted the kind of righteousness the Pharisees were promoting with His kind of righteousness.

When He finished, the hearers were clearly aware that Christ's standard of righteousness was far stricter than was the legalistic criteria of the Pharisees. In fact, it was so strict that it was impossible for people to achieve such righteousness by their own unaided works.

The people Jesus spoke to had been attempting to reach perfection by their own efforts. Naturally, they had failed. After Jesus pointed out that their kind of righteousness never could enter the kingdom of heaven, He made it plain what kind of righteousness all who enter heaven must possess. In the words "Be perfect as God is perfect," He showed that the law is a transcript of the character of God and that only the children of God can be partakers of His nature, and thus be like Him. In Matthew 5, Jesus contrasted the righteousness-by-works philosophy of the Pharisees with His own concept of righteousness that can be achieved only by allowing the Holy Spirit to lead us step by step into Christ's likeness.

Other aspects of the Holy Spirit's work

The book *Seventh-day Adventists Believe* . . . lists additional items that we might consider to be the "office work" of the Holy Spirit (see pages 64-66).

1. He brings the truth of Christ. As the "Spirit of truth," He is to guide us "into all truth" (John 16:13), the truth as it is in Jesus.

2. He brings the presence of Christ. Jesus gave the assurance that the Spirit was to dwell " 'with you and will be in you.' " He promised, " 'I will not leave you orphans; I will come to you' " (John 14:17, 18, NKJV). Christ's promises—" 'I will never leave you nor forsake you' " (Hebrews 13:5, NKJV) and " 'I am with you always, even to the end of the age' " (Matthew 28:20, NKJV)—are realized through the Spirit.

3. He guides the operation of the church. The book of Acts describes how He does this (see Acts 13:1-4, 9; 16:6, 7; 15:28; 20:28). The church does not have to depend on human organization, leaders, or wisdom.

4. He equips the church with special gifts (see chapter 16 of *Seventh-day Adventists Believe* . . .). Through these gifts,

the Holy Spirit provides all that is necessary to carry on the work of God in the church and in the world.

5. He fills the heart of believers (see Ephesians 5:18). In this way He continues the work of transformation in our lives that was begun at the new birth.

The work of the Holy Spirit is vital in our lives as Christians. What a marvelous "comfort" and blessing Christ bestowed on us when He prayed the Father to send us the Holy Spirit as Christ's special representative on earth! How much we miss when we do not allow Him to accomplish in us all that Jesus explained in John 14-16 He would be able to do for us.

One Christian writer summarizes it this way:

It is the Spirit that makes effectual what has been wrought out by the world's Redeemer. It is by the Spirit that the heart is made pure. Through the Spirit the believer becomes a partaker of the divine nature. Christ has given His Spirit as a divine power to overcome all hereditary and cultivated tendencies to evil, and to impress His own character upon His church (Ellen G. White, *The Desire of Ages*, p. 671).

Chapter 6

Where Were You?

As Creator of all things, God has given us in Scripture the only authentic account of His creative activity. He made the heaven and the earth and all living things in six days, and established the Sabbath on the seventh day as the memorial of His completed work. The first human beings were made in the image of God as the crowning work of Creation. When He finished the work of Creation, God declared that it was "very good."

To those who question His Creatorship, God challenges, " 'Where were you when I laid the earth's foundations?' " (Job 38:4, NIV). That's a fair question. None of us were there, of course. No human observer witnessed either the creation of the universe or the creation of this world. Impressions to the contrary notwithstanding, modern scientists such as Carl Sagan were not witnesses. Isn't it strange, then, that Sagan and the majority of scientists who share his convictions and who are removed by about 6,000 years from the event, are so quick to discount what the Creator tells us about how He put the world together? Instead, they draw inferences from the sin-scarred shell of the perfect world God created, then claim that their assumptions are more scientific than the Creation record. No wonder God questions, " 'Who is this that darkens my counsel with words without knowledge?' " (Job 38:2, NIV).

Science is at its best when it deals with events that are happening right now, or at least can be made to happen now. But, when we get into the area of the origin of matter and life, we go beyond the limits of the scientific method.

4—T.W.B.

Some scientists act as if the discussion that has raged for more than one hundred years between those who accept the hypothesis of evolution and those who accept the Bible record of special creation was settled long ago in favor of evolution. But that is not so. There is not adequate evidence on either side to prove one position or the other scientifically and conclusively. The Bible teaching of specific creation is outside the province and scope of science, but it is not internally unscientific. The evolutionary hypothesis, on the other hand, contradicts such scientific laws as the second law of thermodynamics (the general natural tendency to go from order to disorder) and the law of probability (the chance of life evolving on earth in five billion years is one out of one followed by 40,000 zeroes).

In the long run, which theory of origins we accept boils down to the question of basic assumptions. Here, creationists have the advantage. The Bible record of the creation of life comes from the Creator Himself. He *was* there. He made it happen.

Complicating the picture for investigators today is the biblical fact that the surface of the earth as we now know it consists almost entirely of the flotsam and jetsam of a planet drowned in a great flood. Bible writers and Bible testimony consistently present a literal universal flood that covered the highest mountaintops, destroyed all living creatures except those preserved in Noah's ark, and changed the entire surface of the earth (see Matthew 24:37-39; 2 Peter 2:5; 3:6). Therefore, scientists today do not study the earth as it came from the hand of the Creator. Instead, their conclusions on origins are based on their study of fossils and geological strata that were deposited by a universal flood.

We hear what we want to hear

Naturally, those biased by the assumptions that they have been taught find it difficult to listen to what God has to say about how He made the world.

We hear what we most want to hear. This fact is illustrated by the reported experience of the naturalist Charles Kellogg. One day, when he and a friend were walking down a street in New York City, Kellogg stopped, listened a moment, and said to his friend, "Do you hear that?"

"Hear what, Charlie?"

"That cricket singing."

"What cricket? How can you hear a cricket in the midst of all the noises here in the city?"

"Come," the naturalist replied. "Let me show you." He led his friend to a crack in a nearby wall. Sure enough, a cricket was there.

"Charlie, I still don't understand how you could hear a cricket in the midst of all the noise here in the city."

Kellogg took a dime out of his pocket and dropped it on the street. Several passersby turned to look.

"You see," the naturalist said, "in the midst of all this noise, those people could hear a dime drop. It depends on what you have your ears attuned to. I'm listening for the sounds of nature."

The woodpecker is one of the Creator's most marvelous productions in the natural world. Some of its special features are: a beak that can drive through hard wood that would bend a nail; neck muscles strong enough to deliver jackhammer blows; a skull so thick that it thrives on continuous shocks that would kill some other birds; and stiff tail feathers with sharp spines to brace the bird for hammering.

One of the woodpecker's most amazing features is its tongue. It can be extended four or five times its normal length, enabling the bird to extract insects from hollow trees. This unusual organ is rooted in, of all places, the right nostril! Leaving the nostril, the tongue splits into two segments, wraps around the skull under the skin, passing on each side of the neck bones, then joins together and comes up through the lower jaw. This strange arrangement has puzzled evolutionists for years. How many millions of years would it have taken a bird such as a robin to develop this unique tongue?

We need to have our ears so attuned to the voice of the God who created the cricket and the woodpecker that we are willing to listen when He tells us through such spokespersons as the prophet Isaiah, "The Lord thy maker ... hath stretched forth the heavens, and laid the foundations of the earth" (Isaiah 51:13), and the prophet Jeremiah, who adds: "He hath made the earth by his power, he hath established the world by his wisdom, and hath stretched out the heavens by his discretion" (Jeremiah 10:12).

When we accept the Bible as our guide to understanding the natural world, we find nature pointing to its Creator. In His teachings Christ often spoke of the things that His own hands had made. Even though the earth has been marred by sin, much that is beautiful remains. Today we can follow Christ's example in referring to God's object lessons. When we look at it through eyes that wear Bible spectacles, we can see that nature still reveals its Creator.

Scripture and science

After stating that the Creator can be "clearly seen, being understood by the things that are made" (Romans 1:20), the apostle Paul suggests that "professing themselves to be wise," so many have become "fools" instead because they "changed the glory of the incorruptible God into an image made like to corruptible man, and to birds, and fourfooted beasts, and creeping things" (verses 22, 23).

The apostle's words can be applied not only to the custom of idolatry current in his day but also to a philosophy that even then was being given credence in some circles—the concept that life evolved from simple forms into the many complex forms that now exist. Paul suggests that it is absurd to degrade God to the image of created beings. Why? Perhaps we can supply at least a partial answer. Human beings are not always dependable. We are changeable and often capricious, just as were the ancient gods symbolized by the idols about which Paul was concerned.

When we make our Father in heaven that kind of god, we are forced, in turn, to adopt the concept that there can be no absolute law, order, or harmony in the universe. However, science itself is based on the one essential presupposition that dependable laws govern life as we know it.

Suppose that a being from outer space who had never seen a Boeing 747 visited our planet. In the course of learning about how we work and live, he is shown a jumbo jet. After learning about its purpose, he naturally wants to know how it is made. If we were to tell him that jet airliners come into existence all by themselves through millions of years of evolutionary development, he would find it impossible to believe. How, then, could we expect him to believe that the entire natural world, which is far more complex than an airliner, came into existence through long periods of evolutionary development? We might explain, for instance, the geneticists' current understanding of the double-helixed DNA molecule. It is now thought that the messages sent by the genetic code are dependent upon the specific sequences of nucleotides in the DNA molecule rather than upon the properties of the nucleotide constituents themselves. Chemist Charles Thaxton states that this "so-called 'information problem' of genetics . . . poses the most serious threat to naturalistic explanations about the origin of life" (Charles Thaxton, "Theoretical Clay Feet," *Eternity*, September 1985, p. 16). To think that amino acids could arrange themselves into such a complex information system by themselves is beyond belief. Such a clever and complicated design must have a Designer.

The highly plausible alternative to the evolutionary hypothesis is the Bible record of special creation. But that, too, takes faith to accept. "Through faith we understand that the worlds were framed by the word of God, so that things which are seen were not made of things which do appear" (Hebrews 11:3). In the creation of the world, God was not dependent on preexisting matter. By divine decree the world was created out of nothing.

The advent of nuclear science has made it possible to understand to a limited degree how the power of God could be transformed into the matter needed to bring our world into existence. The energy released in a nuclear explosion testifies to the tremendous amount of power and energy it took to put the atoms together in the beginning.

The earth itself is but a tiny portion of God's total creation. "For by him were all things created, that are in heaven, and that are in earth, visible and invisible" (Colossians 1:16). "All things were made by him; and without him was not any thing made that was made" (John 1:3).

The first human beings, Adam and Eve, were made in the image of God as the crowning work of creation (see Genesis

1:26). God gave them dominion over the earth and charged them with the responsibility to care for it (see Genesis 1:27-30). When the work of creation was finished, God declared that it was "very good" (Genesis 1:31). God brought order to the earth's surface and created all plant and animal life in six literal twenty-four-hour days. All of this is in direct conflict with the hypothesis of evolution.

The greatest evidence

Julian Huxley, in his book *Man Stands Alone*, pictures the human race as a curious byproduct of a universe utterly indifferent to life. This bleak thought—the natural outgrowth of the evolutionist-humanist teaching—has led to the fear, hopelessness, and despair that characterize many today.

Some young people have grown up without anything to believe in; they are lost in the whirlpool of uncertainty. They have searched along many alluring paths for some certainty or truth, only to find blind alleys. Many turn hopefully down the popular paths of wealth, pleasure, fame, and power, only to grow frustrated and disappointed.

One of the brightest paths of our time has been that marked "Education." Thousands have traveled it with eager, expectant feet, but where has it led? Although their heads are crammed full of knowledge, often their souls are spiritual vacuums.

Beyond this, ever since the nuclear age began at Hiroshima, we have lived in a perpetual crisis atmosphere so terrifying, so universal, and so altogether unprecedented that it has numbed hopes for the future. Even though, at this writing, the Cold War has ended, we still exist under the threat of nuclear terrorism.

This century, which was touted back in the thirties as the "century of progress," has more than met its promise technologically. What, then, has taken the golden sheen from our age of promise, progress, and plenty? Human beings, children of the eternal God, have proclaimed themselves as the sons and daughters of Mother Mud. Evolution and humanism can lead only to fear, frustration, and despair, because humanity cannot lift itself out of the mire of sin by its own bootstraps.

Indeed, the greatest evidence of what is basically wrong

with the theory of evolution is seen in the results of its circulation for more than one hundred years. Mother Mud is linked inevitably with Father Fear. But it does not end there. Many years ago, some perceptive college youths recognized the implications of the theory of evolution and organized an atheists' club on their campus, which took as its slogan: "Sons of apes don't need a Saviour."

A tremendous truth is involved in that slogan. Not only did God create this world, but His love and benevolence have also been demonstrated ever since in the fact that He sustains all creation on a moment-by-moment basis (see Colossians 1:17; Hebrews 1:3). Even beyond that is His desire to carry on His relationship with the human beings He had created after their rebellion broke the harmony and destroyed the perfection that existed before the advent of sin. In spite of the disaster sin brought on the physical world and the changes for the worse in the nature of human beings, there still is enough design, order, and beauty in nature to help us understand the love of God for fallen beings.

However, the greatest evidence of both God's love and creative power are to be found in Christ's sacrifice at Calvary. The New Testament makes a point of the fact that Christ was our Creator (see John 1:1-3, 14; Colossians 1:13-17). Therefore, it was our Maker Himself who gave His life on the cross so that we might have eternal life. Our Creator became our Redeemer. He is able to create new hearts within us and to restore us to the privilege of being sons and daughters of God (see Hebrews 10:16, 17; 1 John 3:1, 2). Life takes on meaning and human existence takes on purpose only in the fact that our Creator became our Saviour. But, if we were sons and daughters of apes or of primordial ooze, there would be no permanent values, and we would not need a Saviour. There is no way of reconciling these two opposite approaches to, or philosophies of, life.

Those who believe the Bible record of special creation see every display of God's creative and re-creative power as evidence of His personal interest and love. Not only is this reassuring, but it bodes well for the future. Where is the era of evolutionary science leading? Many believe it will end in nuclear destruction of the earth or in ecological disaster. Where does belief in a loving God who created us and has our best interest in view lead? To "new heavens and a new earth, wherein dwelleth righteousness" (2 Peter 3:13). People who accept God as Creator and His plan for their lives find a more abundant life now as they cooperate with His plan for the present (see John 10:10). But they also have God's assurance that He will restore this world to its original created perfection, where "there shall be no more death, neither sorrow, nor crying, neither shall there be any more pain: for the former things are passed away" (Revelation 21:4).

When it comes to deciding on concepts of origins, we need to keep the future in mind. When you compare the prospects, there is no contest.

Chapter 7

"How Can I Quit?"

Jim was not a practicing Christian, but he knew there was something drastically wrong with his manner of life. He had no peace because of the intense, nagging conviction that he was a sinner. Attending a religious service, in response to the deep moving of the Holy Spirit, Jim accepted Christ as his Saviour and Lord. He was baptized and joined a church. For a short time he had new peace of mind; his sins were forgiven, he had hope for the future, and his lifestyle had changed. But there was an ingrained habit he could not overcome.

Sincerely believing that prayer was the answer, Jim prayed often for victory over this troublesome, besetting sin that he could not quit. But all his prayers and efforts seemed futile. His will was weak, and it seemed that his prayers were not being answered.

In sheer desperation, Jim decided to talk to a pastor about the problem. He explained to the pastor, "I pray and pray often and still fall into this sin. It seems as though my religion has failed me."

The pastor smiled and said, "Jim, your much praying might be a clue to your problem."

Jim was shocked; he thought he had come to the wrong person. He responded, "But doesn't the Bible say we should pray often, always, constantly?"

"Yes," the pastor answered, "I believe that too. But when you are tempted to commit this sin you are talking about, what do you do?"

Jim said, "I pray, 'Please, Lord, give me the victory.' "

"Right," said the pastor, "and what do you do next?"

"Well," Jim replied, "I pray again and again and again for the victory."

"And then you commit the sin?" the pastor asked.

"Yes," Jim said, "that's exactly what happens."

"You see," the pastor explained, "you are asking God for something He dearly wants to give you, but you are not claiming the victory by faith. After you have admitted your helplessness and asked God to give you the victory, the next thing you must do is to thank Him for it—even before you have it! Praise God for answering your prayer and enabling you to avoid committing that sin. That's faith—'and this is the victory that overcomes the world, our faith' " (1 John 5:4, RSV).

Jim learned the secret of victorious Christian living. Now when he is tempted, he prays three prayers: (1) "Lord, I like this sin; I am helpless." (2) "But, Lord, I know it's wrong; please give me the power not to do it." (3) "Thank You, Lord, thank You; I believe you have answered my prayer; You have given me the victory. Praise Your holy name."

Many who are addicted to habits that destroy health and happiness, or whose temperaments are a threat to meaningful relationships, are willing to admit that, despite all their good intentions and strenuous exertions, they cannot quit. Paul admitted that apart from Christ he was helpless in the battle with temptation. He wrote, "I can will what is right, but I cannot do it" (Romans 7:18, RSV). His heart cry has been echoed myriads of times through the centuries by struggling sinners. "Wretched man that I am! Who will deliver me from this body of death?" (verse 24, RSV). In other words, "How can I quit?"

We know that we need a power beyond ourselves—but why? Where did we come from? Why are we like this? Where can we get the power to change? Can the change be permanent?

Human nature before the Fall

The Bible describes the physical and spiritual condition of the first human beings to inhabit our world. "God said, 'Let us make man in our image, after our likeness; and let them have dominion over the fish of the sea, and over the birds of the air, and over the cattle, and over all the earth, and over every creeping thing that creeps upon the earth.' So God created man in his own image, in the image of God he created him; male and female he created them" (Genesis 1:26, 27, RSV).

Our first parents were made in the image of God! What is God like? We know from the Bible that, although God is a Spirit (see John 4:24), He has a definite form. Moses asked God, " 'Show me your glory, I pray' " (Exodus 33:18, NRSV). God replied, " 'You cannot see my face; for no one shall see me and live. . . . I will put you in a cleft of the rock, and I will cover you with my hand until I have passed by; then I will take away my hand, and you shall see my back; but my face shall not be seen' " (verses 20-23, NRSV). Adam and Eve were given perfect physical form, not identical to God's, but a reflection or image of His form.

What is God like in character? He revealed Himself to Moses as " 'merciful and gracious, slow to anger, and abounding in steadfast love and faithfulness' " (Exodus 34:6, NRSV). God is perfectly righteous (pure and holy); He is completely free from sin. The psalmist exclaimed, "You are righteous, O Lord, and your judgments are right" (Psalm 119:137, NRSV). "The Lord is righteous; he loves righteous deeds; the upright shall behold his face" (Psalm 11:7, NRSV). Whatever God expects people to be and to do is entirely just, because "the ordinances of the Lord are true and righteous altogether" (Psalm 19:9, NRSV).

God made man and woman in His own image. Therefore, as Adam and Eve came forth from the hand of the Creator, they were righteous, free from every taint of sin. Their thoughts were always pure and holy. They had no biases toward evil; no inner urges to commit sin; no tendencies to think, speak, or do anything wrong. Their lives were a perfect reflection or image of the perfect Creator.

Because they were in perfect harmony with God, Adam and Eve could hold face-to-face communion with Him. It was not until they had chosen to disobey His will that they lost that direct contact (see Genesis 3:8-11).

God did not create them as robots who had no choice but to obey Him. They were not programmed so that they did not have freedom of choice. Throughout the Bible we are told that God wants only willing obedience from those who love Him. Forced compliance is Satan's invention, not God's. Jesus expressed the standard of God's government when He said, " 'If you love me, you will keep my commandments' " (John 14:15, NRSV).

As a demonstration of our first parents' freedom of choice, God placed in the Garden of Eden one tree, the fruit of which He forbade them to eat (see Genesis 2:16, 17). If they wished to diverge from their loyalty to Him and place their allegiance elsewhere, all they had to do was eat the fruit of that tree. Then God would withdraw His sustaining presence from them, and the consequences would be theirs. God explained very clearly what those consequences would be: " 'In the day that you eat of it you shall die' " (Genesis 2:17, NRSV). Why anyone would choose death over the perfection of life in the most ideal environment is beyond our power to explain.

The Fall of our first parents

The fact is that both Eve and Adam made that fatal choice. Eve was deceived by Satan speaking through the serpent (see Genesis 3:1-6). "Adam was not deceived, but the woman was deceived and became a transgressor" (1 Timothy 2:14, NRSV). Of course, there was no reason for Eve to be deceived. God had created for her the best possible world and given her the most impressive reasons why she should always serve Him. But when Satan argued convincingly that God had misrepresented the truth, Eve believed him. Adam joined his wife in disobedience, fully aware that God was entirely trustworthy, but he felt unable to face the future without the beautiful wife God had given him.

The results of that terrible mistake were immediate. They lost the perfect covering God had provided them (see Genesis 3:7). For the first time they were afraid of God (see verses 8-11), and for the first time they experienced marital disharmony. Each blamed someone else for their disobedience (see verses 12, 13). The Lord cursed the serpent because it had been a tool of Satan (see verse 14), cursed the woman who allowed herself to distrust Him (see verse 16), cursed the ground from which Adam was to extract their living (see verses 17-19), and assured them that ultimate death was inevitable (see verse 19).

Why didn't Adam and Eve die immediately? The Lord had said, " 'In the day that you eat of it you shall die' " (Genesis 2:17, NRSV). In the midst of His declaration of the terrible consequences of their sin, God gave the most wonderful promise: " 'I will put enmity between you [Satan, the serpent] and the woman, and between your offspring and hers; he will strike your head, and you will strike his heel' " (Genesis 3:15, NRSV). That meant that throughout human history there would be continual conflict between Satan and those who choose to serve God (the seed of the woman). The most important Seed was to be the Messiah, the Son of God, who would pay the penalty for all sin by dying in the place of sinners (see Galatians 3:13, 16). By taking Jesus' life, Satan would inflict only a temporary wound but would bring upon himself eternal destruction (see Romans 16:20; Revelation 20:10). God did not allow Adam and Eve to die immediately, because by faith in the Messiah to come they could have eternal life. The death at the end of life would be a temporary sleep from which, at the end of time, they would be called forth to immortality and eternal existence with Christ (see 1 Corinthians 15:20-23, 51-54).

Human nature since the Fall

As soon as Adam and Eve sinned, they lost the perfect spiritual natures with which they were created. No longer were they in the image of God. Their inherent, intrinsic righteousness was now gone. Instead, they had fallen, sinful natures with tendencies to sin. They had within them urges to do evil that they had never known before. Until they repented of their sin, they were Satan's subjects. And even after repentance, they were obliged to depend constantly on God for power to conquer the propensities of their fallen natures.

"When God created humankind, he made them in the likeness of God." "When Adam had lived one hundred thirty years, he became the father of a son in his likeness, according to his image, and named him Seth" (Genesis 5:1, 3, NRSV). "While Adam was created sinless, in the likeness of God, Seth, like Cain, inherited the fallen nature of his parents. But he received also the knowledge of the Redeemer and instruction in righteousness" (Ellen G. White, *Patriarchs and Prophets*, p. 80).

This is why we were born with fallen, sinful natures having natural tendencies to sin. After the Fall, Adam and Eve could not pass on to their children pure, perfect, righteous natures. They could only transmit the natures they had earned by sinning. David acknowledged this truth when he wrote: "Behold, I was brought forth in iniquity, and in sin did my mother conceive me" (Psalm 51:5, RSV). This does not mean that, at birth, David was guilty of the sins of his forebears. The Bible teaches that children are not found guilty of the sins of their parents (see Ezekiel 18:20). David meant that at conception he was a new soul in need of a Saviour—because a fallen human being cannot have eternal life in God's presence (compare Romans 5:12-19). His natural biases to sin were to be overcome by the power of God so that, in his transformed nature, he could live with the Lord for eternity.

The psalmist added: "The wicked go astray from the womb; they err from their birth, speaking lies" (Psalm 58:3, NRSV). The language is metaphoric; newborn infants have natures that predispose them to sin. Apart from the transforming power of the Messiah, Jesus Christ, they will live and die in sin.

> The result of the eating of the tree of knowledge of good and evil is manifest in every man's experience. There is in his nature a bent to evil, a force which, unaided, he cannot resist. To withstand this force, to attain that ideal which in his inmost soul he accepts as alone worthy, he can find help in but one power. That power is Christ (Ellen G. White, *Education*, p. 29).

Those who reject Christ and choose to give in to their fallen natures live in sin and have no power to overcome it (see Ephesians 2:3, 12). Education, mind training, the exercise of the will, autosuggestion, and other psychological techniques have some value. But they can never make a sinner into a saint. Righteousness is never our achievement; it is Christ's gift to those who believe in Him.

How Christ changes human nature

A young woman was asked by a friend, "What happened to your life when you became a Christian?"

"I was saved from sin," she answered.

Curious and interested, he questioned, "What do you mean, you were saved?"

She explained, "Before I found Christ, I used drugs, lived an immoral life, and almost destroyed my health forever. Christ gave me new hope for the future, new peace of mind, and the power to live a better life."

Her friend asked, "You mean that salvation changed your habits of thinking and even affected your health?"

She exclaimed, "Very definitely! Being a Christian is a practical matter. It changed the way I think, feel, and act. And now I have much more capacity to study and work. My health and happiness are vastly improved."

The friend was impressed. "I can't argue with that kind of faith. If it works like that, it must be good!"

When, by faith, we accept Christ as Saviour and Lord, His righteousness becomes our righteousness. "It [Christ's righteousness] will be reckoned to us who believe in him who raised Jesus our Lord from the dead, who was handed over to death for our trespasses and was raised for our justification" (Romans 4:24, 25, NRSV).

At the same moment, and as part of the same divine transforming act, Christ's righteousness comes into our hearts by the Holy Spirit. "You are not in the flesh [lost, unsaved], you are in the Spirit, if . . . the Spirit of God dwells in you. Any one who does not have the Spirit of Christ does not belong to him. But if Christ is in you, although your bodies are dead because of sin, your spirits are alive because of righteousness" (Romans 8:9, 10, RSV). The righteousness of God, which humankind lost when Adam and Eve sinned, becomes ours when by faith we accept Christ into our hearts. The Holy Spirit's presence is Christ's presence (see John 14:18; Ephesians 3:16, 17). And His presence in our hearts provides all the necessary power to overcome sin.

You ask, How can I quit sinning? Through the power of the indwelling Christ. By a divine mystery Jesus Christ gives us the "new birth" experience. We are born anew of the Holy Spirit (see John 3:3-8). This means that our past sins are forgiven and we have the power of Christ to overcome. "So if anyone is in Christ, there is a new creation: everything old has passed away; see, everything has become new!" (2 Corinthians 5:17, NRSV). "For our sake he made him to be sin who knew no sin, so that in him *we might become the righteousness of God*" (2 Corinthians 5:21, NRSV, emphasis supplied). Christ died on the cross "so that, free from sins, *we might live for righteousness*" (1 Peter 2:24, NRSV, emphasis supplied).

The apostle Paul taught that those who were once slaves of sin willingly "become slaves of righteousness" (Romans 6:18, NRSV) when, by faith, they receive Jesus Christ into their hearts. The immoral become pure; thieves become honest; drunkards become temperate; selfish, bad-tempered individuals become generous, kind, and thoughtful of others. How? "You were washed, you were sanctified [made holy], you were justified [declared and made righteous] in the name of the Lord Jesus Christ and in the Spirit of our God" (1 Corinthians 6:11, NRSV).

Born-again believers are still fallen human beings with tendencies toward sin (see 1 Corinthians 9:27; Galatians 5:16-18). But daily they receive the power of Christ to subdue their fallen propensities, enabling them to live according to God's will. They are spiritually "renewed day by day" (2 Corinthians 4:16, NRSV). Every true believer can say, "It is no longer I who live, but it is Christ who lives in me. And the life I now live in the flesh I live by faith in the Son of God, who loved me and gave himself for me" (Galatians 2:20, NRSV).

Have you found Jesus Christ as your Saviour and Lord? The real solution is to let Him find you. He said, "I, when I am lifted up from the earth, will draw all people to myself" (John 12:32, NRSV). That includes you—whatever your past life and whatever your present struggle. In Christ there is forgiveness and victory.

Chapter 8

Why Do Tigers Bite?

Whether we know it or not and whether we like it or not, all of us are involved in the great conflict between Christ and Satan regarding the character of God, His law, and His sovereignty over the universe. This conflict originated in heaven when a created being misused the power of choice God had given and in self-exaltation became Satan. This being not only led a portion of the angels into rebellion, but also introduced the spirit of rebellion into this world when he led Adam and Eve into sin. This human sin resulted in the distortion of the image of God in humanity and the disordering of the created world.

When a group of Vacation Bible School children were invited to ask questions, one little boy came up with a big one. Turning his innocent little face to the teacher's, he asked, "Why do tigers bite?" This question has been presented in many ways ever since Satan brought sin into our world. Philosophers have offered a variety of answers. Atheists, who hold that the planet and all forms of life exist by chance, declare that good and evil are in a kind of "survival of the fittest" competition; eventually only one will remain. Others have maintained that at least two gods govern the world; one is good, the other evil. But such answers are inadequate. The question of what our world is all about and why it is blighted with evil basically depends on how we view the world.

The true view is found in the Bible. According to the Holy Scriptures, many thousands of years ago, before this earth was created, evil originated mysteriously in the heart of Lucifer, the most exalted of the angels in heaven. The fault was not God's, for Lucifer was created perfect (see Ezekiel 28:15).

Lucifer permitted himself to be controlled by envious thoughts. He should have recognized that, as a created being, he had no right to the respect and worship accorded Deity. But he did not. Instead he harbored jealous thoughts and confided them to his angel companions. He proposed questions that were designed to sow seeds of dissatisfaction. Lucifer's subtle insinuations resulted in one-third of the angels committing themselves to his side. Misled by his beguiling lies, they felt that he could set up a government superior to God's. With infinite patience their Creator attempted to explain His actions—to persuade the rebel and his sympathizers to abandon the disastrous course they were following. He attempted to make clear that heaven's laws, grounded in love, were essential to happiness. But when Lucifer and his fellow rebels refused to accept explanations or to respond to entreaties, God had no recourse but to cast them out of heaven.

Even then, God did not at once destroy Lucifer and his followers. He gave them time and opportunity to see that their charges against His character and law were unjustified.

Heaven provided a Saviour

God warned Adam and Eve in the Garden of Eden that the natural consequence of disobedience would be death. Lucifer, who had become Satan, saw this as an opportunity to entice the first humans to eat the forbidden fruit and join him in rebellion. Tragically, Adam and Eve yielded to Satan's temptation. But even after they sinned, God in His mercy spared their lives in order that the guilty pair still might have opportunity to repent. However, the penalty for breaking God's law had to be met, and the members of the Godhead had made provision for this eventuality. Long before the great rebellion, they had agreed that God the Son, whom we know as Jesus, would come to this earth and die for sin, taking the place of sinners. How easy it is to mention what Jesus did without understanding fully all that it means!

In a graveyard in Missouri, a tall marble monument bears this inscription:

Sacred to the memory of
WILLIE LEE
He took my place in the line
He died for me

The background is this: During the Civil War in the United States, a band of guerrillas, known as Quantrill's band, burned a town in Kansas. Some of the men were soon caught and lined up in front of a long ditch they had been forced to dig. The men stood there awaiting execution by a firing squad. Just before the signal was given, a young man dashed out of the nearby woods crying, "Stop!"

He explained to the commander of the firing squad that he had been a member of the band and was just as guilty as any of the others. But he had escaped. Now he was surrendering of his own free will in order to take the place of a man in the line.

"I'm single," he said, "but he has a wife and several children. Please place me in the line in his stead."

The order was given to do so, and Willie Lee took the place of the man he had singled out. Then the order for execution was given. The man who had been freed claimed the body of Willie Lee and buried it in his home state of Missouri. All that he could afford as a marker at that time was a simple wooden slab with the words "He died for me" inscribed on it. Later he erected the fifteen-foot monument that still marks the grave of the man who had died in his place.

We can show our appreciation for what Christ has done for us by giving our hearts as monuments dedicated to the Lamb of God, who was willing to come to die in our stead.

The harvest of evil

The decision by the counsel of heaven for Jesus to die for us was made before sin entered the universe. After the Fall, the effects of sin became more and more evident—not only in the human race but in all of nature. The principles advocated by Satan, at first but dimly seen as dangerous, bore a harvest of evil fruit. Nineteen centuries ago, when Christ was murdered because of our transgression, the inhabitants of heaven and the other worlds saw clearly the horrible nature of sin. Then they realized how right God was and how wrong Satan was.

In December 1955, an Alabama woman, Rosa Parks, defied the law of segregated seating in a Montgomery bus. As a consequence she was arrested. Dr. Martin Luther King, a successful young black pastor in the city, read a newspaper article about the incident that changed the course of his life. As he read, a great anger burned in his soul. "Why must my people sit in the back of the bus? Why must they stay in segregated hotels?"

A dream was born—a vision of an America where everyone was equal regardless of race, color, or religion. But there was a struggle in King's soul. Why not go on enjoying his secure pastoral role? He was tempted strongly to leave the task to someone else. But as Dr. King prayed about it, the conviction grew that it was his responsibility. He resigned his position and was soon appointed president of the Southern Christian Leadership Conference. He adopted the philosophy "Change through nonviolent resistance."

Martin Luther King faced unbelievable brutality—fire hoses, police dogs, and violence. He suffered discouragement, but he fought on. In 1964 the Civil Rights Act was passed by the United States Congress. But Dr. King paid the price with his life. He was shot by a man he had never seen. However, the nation he left behind was never to be the same again.

Another young man once made a similar decision to face opposition and the violence of the establishment. After a few years of struggle, Jesus set His face steadfastly to go to Jerusalem, suffering, and death. His blood ran down from the cross, but today it unites people of all races, cultures, and statuses in life under one glorious title—Christian. That precious blood also demonstrated to the universe the horrible nature of sin and the true character of Satan's rebellion.

When Jesus died, the citizens of heaven and the unfallen worlds recognized for a certainty that God is love and that His law is just and necessary. But to give the citizens of our world ample opportunity to understand the issues in the great controversy between Christ and Satan and to allow the people perfect freedom to choose whose side they wanted to join, God permitted the sin drama to play itself out.

Today the conflict is nearing its close. With great urgency the Holy Spirit and the angels of heaven are seeking to help people choose God's side—to put loyalty to God, righteousness, and truth above even life itself. To assist His people in this controversy, Christ sends the Holy Spirit and the loyal angels to guide, protect, and sustain them in the way of salvation.

The Bible makes it clear that the ultimate outcome will be complete victory for God and the vindication of His character and law. Until that glorious day, good and evil will continue side by side. Today supernatural forces are continuing the deadly warfare begun long ago in heaven. Planet Earth is the battlefield. But only a short time remains until Christ comes to claim the victory He won on the cross so long ago.

Why did Jesus come?

The basic question answered by the Bible worldview outlined briefly above is: Why did Jesus come to this planet? Seventh-day Adventists believe that the cross of Christ has universal, as well as local-planet, significance. Jesus came to live and die for more than our salvation. Much more was at stake. He came to answer a charge against the justice of God that preceded our human need for salvation. Satan's mysterious rebellion began before this world existed. After Creation, Satan claimed that it was impossible for created human beings to keep God's law. This is one of the reasons why the member of the Godhead we know as Jesus became a human being. Jesus demonstrated that human beings can keep the law of God and gain the victory over sin.

Otto Ball went to prayer meeting one night in the little Baptist church within walking distance of his farm home. He spit out his tobacco before entering the church and sat down prepared to enjoy an ordinary prayer meeting, such as he had enjoyed for years. A visiting minister presided. During the course of his remarks he said, "You all know tobacco is no good. It isn't food, it isn't drink. It isn't good for us. It numbs our brains and chains us to a habit we can't break. Brethren, I use it. I suppose I always will. But when

I read the commandments in Exodus 20, I wonder if I'm not breaking the first two commandments every day of my life."

Mr. Ball went home and pondered this as he worked in the hilly acres of his mountain home. Finally, he decided to break with his old friend tobacco, though the wrench caused him intense suffering for weeks. Finally, the anguish eased somewhat, and he began to read those commandments again. He began to see more things, and for Mr. Ball to see the way meant he would walk in it. A simple, earnest mountain man read his way into living the good life. His strength was made perfect through suffering.

Those who are born again will take deep delight in doing God's will and in following wherever He leads. (Josephine Cunnington Edwards, "The Character of the Victorious," *Review and Herald*, 5 November 1970, p. 8).

In order to demonstrate the possibility of our living sin-free lives and allowing Jesus to gain the victory over sin in us, Christ had to come to this world and live here as a human being—not as a God. Satan had no quarrel with the fact that God could keep His own law. He focused on convincing people that it was impossible for created beings to do so. Jesus lived as a man, emptying Himself of the use of His divine powers while here on earth, yet remaining divine (see Philippians 2:5-7). He was fully God on earth, but He lived as a dependent human being, clinging to His Father. This is why He called Himself the " 'true vine' " (John 15:1). The glorious news of the everlasting gospel is that what Jesus did, by His grace and the Spirit's power, we can do too.

In recent years there has crept into the church an idea that might be termed "impossibility thinking." It's the belief that we cannot live as Jesus called us to live when He invited us to take up the cross of self-denial and *follow* Him. We should not be surprised by this attempt by Satan to discourage us in the last moments of time in order to delay Christ's second coming.

What we need is a new infusion of "possibility thinking"—a realization of all that God promises and makes possible for His people today.

In 1928 students of the carpentry class at the Japan San Iku

Gakuin (Threefold Educational School) were invited to build the new Tokyo Sanitarium and Hospital. It was a big order, and the school's president, Dr. Andrew Nelson, wasn't sure they should attempt it. But because the mission president, Elder Victor Armstrong, was confident the young men could do the job, they went to work with a will. One day, after they had been at work for a couple of weeks, Elder Armstrong came out to see how they were getting along. During their lunch break, several of the boys were singing a song with words that, roughly translated, went, "Maybe we can do it. Maybe we can do it."

When Armstrong heard it, he got the other boys to reply, using the same tune, "Yes, we can! Yes, we can! Yes, we can!" Everyone had a good laugh; then all joined in and sang Armstrong's version. With that attitude, the students went on to finish the building in record time.

Isn't it time for all of us to take up that song, singing it, "By God's grace and power, we can, we *can*"?

We dare not be indifferent

Seventh-day Adventists believe that the created beings from the unfallen populated planets, along with heaven's unfallen angels, watched with intense interest as Jesus came to earth (see *The Great Controversy*, p. 503.) They, too, had a stake in His life and death. In Jesus, as a created human, God would demonstrate to the universe that He is just and that Satan's charge of injustice is false.

Yet so many seem indifferent to these great issues in which the entire universe is caught up. In London there is a statue of Christ bearing His cross. Yet thousands of people pass by each day without even noticing it. An inscription under the statue reads: "Is it nothing to you all ye that pass by?" Jesus gladly took up the cross for each of us. What does that mean to us? Are we willing to bear the cross of self-denial for Him?

Christ's victory at the cross had universal significance. Now it could be seen by all created beings that God was just in removing sin from the universe. A long time ago, Satan used a snake to confuse a perfect woman who lived in a perfect garden. The issue was the nature of sin. Satan still tries to perplex us regarding the basic issues involved in the great controversy that is going on for our souls. Too often he is successful.

Burt Hunter, a reporter-photographer in Long Beach, California, found himself on a strange mission one foggy morning. He was to interview and take pictures of a woman snake charmer.

When Burt rang the doorbell at an impressive mansion, he was surprised at the beautiful woman who answered. She didn't look like a snake charmer. He blurted out, "I don't understand why a wealthy, attractive woman such as yourself is engaged in this kind of business."

"Oh," she replied, "I don't do it because I have to. It's a fascinating hobby. I like the element of danger involved. Someday soon I plan to give it up and spend more time with my flowers. I can quit this anytime I want to."

As Burt set up his equipment, the woman brought in baskets containing the cobras. She confidently lifted out some of the deadly snakes as he snapped pictures of her handling them. Then she cautioned, "Be especially quiet now, and don't make any quick moves. I'm going to take out my newest snake. It isn't completely used to me yet."

Suddenly she stiffened, whispering to the photographer, "Something's wrong. I'm going to have to put him back." She opened the basket slowly and began to lower the snake into it. As Burt watched, fascinated, there was a lightning jab of the cobra's head as it buried its fangs in her wrist.

Forcing the snake down and securing the basket, the woman clutched her arm. She spoke quietly to Burt, "Go quickly to my medicine chest and bring the snake serum. Hurry!"

Trembling, Burt returned with the precious vial. She instructed him to take out the syringe and fit the needle on. Then she told him how to withdraw the serum. Burt struggled with the unfamiliar task, his hands shaking. He braced his arm against the table as he tried desperately to get the needle into the vial. Suddenly he gasped. His clumsy fingers had crushed the tiny bottle. The serum, now useless, dripped through his fingers.

"Tell me," he urged. "Where can I get another?"

In a quiet voice she responded, "That was my last one."

Her agony soon ended, but Burt's lived on to embitter the rest of his life. Often he thought of her statement, "I can quit this anytime I want to" (adapted from Marjorie Grant Burns, "Broken," *Youth's Instructor*, 25 December 1951, pp. 5, 6, 18, 19).

Many today who, following Mother Eve's example, play with the deadly serpent of sin feel that somehow it won't hurt them. But soon the vial that contains the only remedy for sin will not be available. We must be willing to accept the provision that heaven made so long ago to provide us a Saviour from sin now, before it is too late.

Chapter 9

Springtime in Life's Garden

Mary Magdalene's original home was Bethany, where she lived with Martha and Lazarus. In Bethany a Pharisee named Simon led her into the sin of immorality. We are not told much about the circumstances, but the evidence suggests that, because of the disgrace to herself and her family, she left home and went to the town of Magdala, near the western shore of the Sea of Galilee.

Much of Jesus' ministry took place in the vicinity of the Plain of Gennesaret near where Magdala was situated. It is probable that Mary heard Jesus' teaching while she was living there, responded in heart, and accepted Him as her Saviour. Mary then joined other women whom Jesus had delivered from sin. They traveled with Him and His disciples on His second Galilean tour (see Luke 8:1, 2).

Even though she had found Jesus, Mary struggled with temptation. Seven times Jesus rebuked the evil spirits that controlled her mind and delivered her from their power (see Mark 16:9).

Mary had been looked upon as a great sinner, but Christ knew the circumstances that had shaped her life. He might have extinguished every spark of hope in her soul, but He did not. It was He who had lifted her from despair and ruin. Seven times she had heard His rebuke of the demons that controlled her heart and mind. She had heard His strong cries to the Father in her behalf. She knew how offensive is sin to His unsullied purity, and in His strength she had overcome (Ellen G. White, *The Desire of Ages*, p. 568).

After Jesus' second Galilean tour, Mary returned to her home in Bethany with Martha and Lazarus. On Jesus' occasional visits there she sat at His feet, hungrily partaking of the spiritual nourishment He had to offer. She was there when Lazarus died; she saw Jesus raise him from the dead. She was there on Jesus' last visit and attended the feast in His honor in the home of the Pharisee, Simon. On that occasion she knelt at Jesus' feet weeping, anointed Him with perfume, and with her long hair wiped away the tears that had fallen on His feet (see John 12:1-8).

The next Friday, Mary was in the surging crowd before Pilate's judgment hall as Jesus was abused and condemned. She stood with the apostle John and a group of sorrowing women before the cross (see John 19:25). She did not understand what was happening. He was the life-giving Messiah, her Saviour from sin, but He was allowing Himself to be crucified.

Mary was still on Golgotha's hill when the body of Jesus was taken down and gently laid in the garden tomb. She saw the protective stone rolled to the mouth of the tomb. The next Sunday morning, Mary was the first to visit the tomb. To her dismay, she discovered that the great stone had been rolled away and the body of Jesus was gone. She rushed off to tell the disciples, and Peter and John ran to the garden to confirm Mary's report (see John 20:1-17).

As Mary sadly returned to the tomb that Sunday morning, can't you imagine her emotional suffering? Jesus had given her new dignity. He had saved her from the impulses that alone she was powerless to control. He had taught her how to live a Christian life. He had raised her brother from the dead. But now the Life Giver Himself was dead. And Mary was alone in the garden.

She approached the tomb and looked in. There were two angels there. One asked, "Why are you weeping?" But Mary was too overcome to be comforted even by angels.

She replied, "Because they have taken away my Lord, and I do not know where they have laid Him."

As she turned and walked away, through tear-dimmed eyes she noticed someone whom she thought was the gardener. She said to him, "Sir, if you have carried Him away, tell me where you have laid Him, and I will go and take Him away."

He replied with just one word, "Mary!" And immediately she knew—it was Jesus! She fell at His feet and reached out her hands to touch Him. But He said, "Don't touch [detain] me, because I have not yet ascended to My Father."

That is one of the most beautiful statements in the entire gospel story. Later that day Jesus allowed His followers to touch Him. By then He had been to heaven to be received by His Father. The feelings of this erstwhile immoral woman were so important to Jesus that He paused to comfort her even before going into the presence of His Father.

Mary found Jesus alone in the garden. No longer need she fear the taunting threats of the powers of darkness. Her Saviour, who had died for her sin, was living and well able to keep her from falling. It was springtime in her soul! Jesus, her saving, understanding Lord, was alive!

Jesus' perfect life

What does Christ's life, death, and resurrection mean to you? Have you passed through the long winter of separation from Him, and do you now crave to find Him as Mary did? You, too, can enjoy springtime in your soul! You, too, can find Him—alone in life's garden.

What is the significance for us of Jesus' perfect life? He always told the truth; no one could accuse Him of any wrongdoing (see John 8:45, 46). Even though He was tempted as we are, He never sinned (see Hebrews 4:15). Peter likened Him to a "lamb without blemish or spot" (1 Peter 1:19, RSV). The lambs that were offered as sacrifices in the ancient Israelite sanctuary were to be without blemish (see Exodus 12:5) because they pointed forward to Jesus Christ, who, as the spotless Lamb of God, would be sacrificed for our sins (see John 1:29). "He committed no sin; no guile was found on his lips. When he was reviled, he did not revile in return; when he suffered, he did not threaten; but he trusted to him who judges justly" (1 Peter 2:22, 23, RSV).

When Jesus becomes our Friend and Saviour, He imparts to us the power to live as He did—without committing sin. "God has done what the law, weakened by the flesh, could not do: sending his own Son in the likeness of sinful flesh and for sin, he condemned sin in the flesh, in order that the just requirement of the law might be fulfilled in us, who walk not according to the flesh but according to the Spirit" (Romans 8:3, 4, RSV).

The law is the standard of righteousness, but it cannot save us from sin. Only Jesus can do that. Because of His perfect life and willing sacrifice, we can have the power of the Holy Spirit to live according to the "just" (RSV) or "righteous requirements" (Romans 8:4, NIV) of the law of God. The passion, pride, and impurity that once mastered our better judgment can be overcome. By the power of Jesus' Spirit, we can live victorious Christian lives.

"His divine power has given us everything we need for life and godliness through our knowledge of him who called us by his own glory and goodness. Through these he has given us his very great and precious promises, so that through them you may participate in the divine nature and escape the corruption in the world caused by evil desires" (2 Peter 1:3, 4, NIV).

Even if we fall, Jesus is near to do for us what He did for Mary Magdalene. When we ask, He forgives and cleanses us (see 1 John 1:9). He gives us the power to rise above our spiritual failures and live again according to His will. "For whatever is born of God overcomes the world; and this is the victory that overcomes the world, our faith" (1 John 5:4, RSV).

Christ's perfect sacrifice

When the great preacher Charles Spurgeon was dying, he testified to a friend, "My theology now is found in four little words: 'Jesus died for me.' I don't say this is all I would preach if I were to be raised up again, but it is more than enough for me to die upon."

The reason Mary Magdalene could have God's forgiveness, the power to live a pure life, and the gift of eternal life is that Jesus Christ suffered and died for her sins. The same sacrifice was for every one of us. John wrote: "He is the expiation for our sins, and not for ours only but also for the sins of the whole world" (1 John 2:2, RSV). "You know that he appeared to take away sins" (1 John 3:5, RSV). Peter exclaimed: "He himself bore our sins in his body on the tree, that we might die to sin and live to righteousness. By his wounds you have been healed. For you were straying like sheep, but have now returned to the Shepherd and Guardian of your souls" (1 Peter 2:24, 25, RSV).

Some Christians think that every time the Eucharist is celebrated, Christ's sacrifice for sins is repeated. But the Bible teaches that in His *one* sacrifice He bore the punishment for all the sins that will be committed till the end of time. "He has no need, like those high priests, to offer sacrifices daily, first for his own sins and then for those of the people; he did this once for all when he offered up himself" (Hebrews 7:27, RSV).

The priests in the ancient Israelite sanctuary were constantly offering animal sacrifices for their own sins and for those of the people (see Leviticus 4 and 16). Every animal sacrifice represented the death of Jesus. Although the believers who brought the sacrifices to the sanctuary were forgiven their sins when the blood of the animal was sprinkled by the priest on the altar or in the Holy Place, the forgiveness was conditional upon Christ's death for the sins of the world. Christ did not die for only the sins that would be committed after His day. He died for all the sins that were committed in Old Testament times. "A death has occurred which redeems them from the transgressions under the first covenant" (Hebrews 9:15, RSV).

Christ suffered only once for the sins of the world from the time of Adam till probation closes at the end of history. "Christ, having been offered *once* to bear the sins of many, will appear a second time, not to deal with sin but to save those who are eagerly waiting for him" (Hebrews 9:28, RSV, emphasis supplied). "We have been sanctified through the offering of the body of Jesus Christ *once for all*. And every priest stands daily at his service, offering repeatedly the same sacrifices, which can never take away sins. But when Christ had offered *for all time a single sacrifice for sins*, he sat down at the right hand of God" (Hebrews 10:10-12, RSV, emphasis supplied).

How could Jesus Christ have suffered sufficiently on the cross so that His suffering can atone for the guilt of all human sin? No human being would be capable of bearing culpability for all humankind's guilt. As we have seen in a previous chapter, Jesus was not only fully man, He was also fully God. As God, bearing the sins of humanity, Jesus was separated from the Father and the Holy Spirit. But God—Father, Son, and Holy Spirit—is One (see Deuteronomy 6:4-6; Malachi 2:10; Ephesians 4:5). On the cross the unity of the Deity was mysteriously severed. That is why Jesus cried out in agony of spirit, " 'My God, my God, why hast thou forsaken me?' " (Matthew 27:46). Because He had taken the guilt of all sin upon Him, Christ's unity with His Father was severed. That involved infinite suffering for the Deity. Father, Son, and Holy Spirit suffered in a manner that is too terrible for human beings to understand.

> Upon Christ as our substitute and surety was laid the iniquity of us all. He was counted a transgressor, that He might redeem us from the condemnation of the law. The guilt of every descendant of Adam was pressing upon His heart. The wrath of God against sin, the terrible manifestation of His displeasure because of iniquity, filled the soul of His Son with consternation. All His life Christ had been publishing to a fallen world the good news of the Father's mercy and pardoning love. Salvation for the chief of sinners was His theme. But now with the terrible weight of guilt He bears, He cannot see the Father's reconciling face. The withdrawal of the divine countenance from the Saviour in this hour of supreme anguish pierced His heart with a sorrow that can never be fully understood by man. So great was this agony that His physical pain was hardly felt (Ellen G. White, *The Desire of Ages*, p. 753).

How Mary Magdalene must have rejoiced when she came to understand the significance of Jesus' death. As she stood before the cross, it seemed that all her hopes were dashed. In reality, the agony she witnessed was the very means by which her sin could be forgiven and her life transformed by grace. Through the eternal ages, Mary and every other repentant sinner will give praise to the Lamb, as well as to the Father and the Holy Spirit, for Their infinite sacrifice.

Christ's triumphant resurrection and intercession

Jesus Christ rose from the dead because the evil one could not hold Him there. Jesus had suffered for the sins of others, not for any sin He Himself had committed. As the sinless Son of God, He came forth from the tomb to represent in heaven those who come to God by faith in Him.

Paul explained to the Christians in Corinth:

> If Christ has not been raised, then our preaching is in vain and your faith is in vain. . . . For if the dead are not raised, then Christ has not been raised. If Christ has not been raised, your faith is futile and you are still in your sins. Then those also who have fallen asleep in Christ have perished. . . . But in fact Christ has been raised from the dead, the first fruits of those who have fallen asleep. For as by a man came death, by a man has come also the resurrection of the dead (1 Corinthians 15:14-21, RSV).

How could sinners be saved by a dead Saviour? His resurrection is the surety of our resurrection if we should die before His second coming. The sin of Adam introduced sin and death into the world. The death and resurrection of Jesus atoned for all sin and made absolutely certain the resurrection to eternal life, at His coming, of those who died believing and of believers who have never died (see 1 Thessalonians 4:14-16).

Meanwhile we are "saved by his life" (Romans 5:10). How? Jesus ascended to be our High Priest in the heavenly sanctuary (see Hebrews 8:1, 2). This means that when, by faith in Him, we come to God for forgiveness and cleansing, Jesus is our heavenly Mediator or Intercessor. "For there is one God, and there is one mediator between God and men, the man Christ Jesus" (1 Timothy 2:5, RSV). Because He retains perfect human nature, and because He knows exactly our struggles with sin, Jesus Christ is able to represent us in heaven. When we come to God for forgiveness, He is able to plead, "Father, I died for this one. He/she has accepted My sacrifice. Father, We can forgive and deliver this person from the power of the evil one."

"He is able for all time to save those who draw near to God through him, since he always lives to make intercession for them" (Hebrews 7:25, RSV).

The apostle John urges us not to sin at all. Then, for our encouragement, he adds: "But if any one does sin, we have an advocate with the Father, Jesus Christ the righteous" (1 John 2:1, 2, RSV).

What wonderful security He gives us! Because we believe in Him, He bestows eternal life upon us (see John 3:36); because we trust Him, He gives us power not to sin (see Jude 24); because we confess our sins by faith in Him, we have forgiveness and cleansing from all sin (see 1 John 1:9). Mary Magdalene, with believers from all ages, one day soon will exclaim with unrestrained joy: " 'Worthy is the Lamb who was slain, to receive power and wealth and wisdom and might and honor and glory and blessing!' " . . . " 'To him who sits upon the throne and to the Lamb be blessing and honor and glory and might for ever and ever!' " (Revelation 5:12, 13, RSV).

Years ago in Melbourne, Australia, I met Pastor Kata Ragoso, the son of a Solomon Islands chief, who became a Seventh-day Adventist minister. His tribe had been headhunters and cannibals. Ragoso once stated, "Not only were we devil worshipers, but we were dirty. The only time we washed was when it rained."

Pastor Ragoso became a much-loved spiritual leader in the Solomon Islands. During World War II, he and his men saved the lives of more than 200 servicemen, treating their wounds and leading them through enemy lines to safety. The rescued soldiers recognized the remarkable transformation Christianity had made in the lives of the Solomon Islanders. They often commented on the fact that, if it had not been for the conversion of these people to Christianity, the soldiers might have been eaten rather than rescued.

Jesus' power to change hearts and lives in a dramatic way is as surely available for us as it was for Mary Magdalene and for the inhabitants of the Solomon Islands. His perfect life, ministry, death, and resurrection are the basis of our hope. "And hope does not disappoint us, because God's love has been poured into our hearts through the Holy Spirit which has been given to us" (Romans 5:5, RSV).

Chapter 10

How Christ Saves Us

On a hot July day in 1505 Martin Luther, a twenty-one-year-old student of the University of Erfurt in Germany, was returning to the university after a visit with his parents. As he trudged along a country road about a mile north of the city of Stotternheim, suddenly a fierce storm blew up. The clouds hung low over the road along which he was walking. There was a blinding flash of lightning, a deafening peal of thunder, and the young student fell in terror to the road. "He cried out to his father's saint, patroness of miners, 'Saint Anne help me! I will become a monk'" (Roland H. Bainton, *Here I Stand* (New York: Abingdon, 1950), p. 34).

After a farewell party with his friends, on July 17, 1505, Luther presented himself for admission to the "Black Cloister" in Erfurt, the chapter house of the Hermits of St. Augustine. Luther became a monk for the same reason that motivated thousands of others. He wanted to rid his soul of guilt and prepare himself to meet his Maker.

Luther accepted the commonly held error that to save the soul it is necessary to punish the body. He fasted on occasions three days in a row. He stretched himself in penitence on the floor of his cell without blankets and nearly froze to death. Sometimes he confessed to a superior priest for six hours a day, trying to relieve himself of his feelings of guilt. He was trying to make himself righteous, to placate the Deity, to earn favor with God, to work his way to heaven.

In 1511, when Luther was made a professor of theology at the University of Wittenberg, he began studying the Bible. Some few years later, as he was lecturing on the Psalms, he was puzzled by Psalm 71. He could not understand verse 2: "In thy righteousness deliver me and rescue me; incline thy ear to me, and save me!" (RSV). Luther pondered, "I know God is righteous, but how can His righteousness deliver me? I am unrighteous; how can a characteristic of God save me from my sin?"

Romans 1:16, 17, also gave him great concern: "I am not ashamed of the gospel of Christ: for it is the power of God unto salvation to every one that believeth; to the Jew first, and also to the Greek. For therein is *the righteousness of God* revealed from faith to faith: as it is written, The just shall live by faith" (emphasis supplied). Luther thought "the righteousness of God" mentioned in verse 17 refers to God's own personal righteousness and His punishment of the unrighteous sinner. He wrote that he came to hate God because He is righteous and we are unrighteous. As he searched the Scriptures, suddenly the truth dawned on him that God's righteousness, referred to in the text, is not only the righteousness that God Himself possesses but the righteousness that He bestows upon those who believe. In 1545, the year before his death, Luther described his early experience:

At last, by the mercy of God, meditating day and night, I gave heed to the context of the words, namely, "In it the righteousness of God is revealed, as it is written, 'He who through faith is righteous shall live.' " There I began to understand that the righteousness of God is that by which the righteous lives by a gift of God, namely by faith. And this is the meaning: the righteousness of God is revealed by the gospel, namely, the passive righteousness with which merciful God justifies us by faith, as it is written, "He who through faith is righteous shall live." Here I felt that I was altogether born again and had entered paradise itself through open gates. There a totally other face of the entire Scripture showed itself to me. Thereupon I ran through the Scriptures from memory. I also found in other terms an analogy, as, the work of God, that is, what God does in us, the power of God, with which he makes us strong, the wisdom of God, with which he makes us wise, the strength

eousness was reckoned to Abraham (see Galatians 3:6-8), so "the blessing of Abraham might come upon the Gentiles, *that we might receive the promise of the Spirit through faith*" (verse 14, RSV, emphasis supplied). The reception of the Spirit is a vital part of justification.

As the sinner, drawn by the power of Christ, approaches the uplifted cross, and prostrates himself before it, there is a new creation. A new heart is given him. He becomes a new creature in Christ Jesus. Holiness finds that it has nothing more to require. God Himself is "the justifier of him which believeth in Jesus." Rom. 3:26 (Ellen G. White, *Christ's Object Lessons*, p. 163).

Sanctification—the result of justification

Justification is the immediate and long-term cause of sanctification (holiness). In justification, the righteousness of Christ is bestowed upon believers because the Holy Spirit comes to live in their hearts (see Romans 8:9, 10; compare 6:18-22). Righteousness is holiness; it is purity, goodness—the opposite of sin. The Greek word for *holiness* means "sanctification." Hence, when we are justified, we are also sanctified, or made holy.

Sanctification is present holiness in Christ enjoyed by the justified believer. The Corinthians had been sanctified (made holy) when they came to Christ. But by harboring bitterness and contention, they were spoiling the wonderful gift Christ had given them (see 1 Corinthians 1:2; 6:11).

"Sanctification is a state of holiness, without and within, being holy, and without reserve the Lord's, not in form, but in truth" (Ellen G. White, *Our High Calling*, p. 214).

Sanctification also involves growth in holiness. Fallen human beings, with tendencies to sin, must constantly maintain a warfare against temptation (see 1 Corinthians 9:27; Galatians 5:17, 18). So that the Holy Spirit can retain control of their minds, it is necessary for believers to come to the Lord and to study His Word every day. Then they grow in holiness in the sense that Christ's presence by the Holy Spirit is the power by which they progressively overcome sinful tendencies (see

1 Thessalonians 3:12, 13; 4:1-7; 2 Corinthians 3:18; 2 Peter 3:18).

We need constantly a fresh revelation of Christ, a daily experience that harmonizes with His teachings. High and holy attainments are within our reach. Continual progress in knowledge and virtue is God's purpose for us. His law is the echo of His own voice, giving to all the invitation, "Come up higher. Be holy, holier still." Every day we may advance in perfection of Christian character (Ellen G. White, *The Ministry of Healing*, p. 503).

Christ gives victory

The goal of sanctification is total victory over sin through the power of Christ in the heart by the Holy Spirit. Jesus commanded His followers: "You, therefore, must be perfect, as your heavenly Father is perfect" (Matthew 5:48, RSV). This does not mean freedom from all human imperfection. It means freedom from acts of sin. All sin is imperfection, but not all imperfection is sin. The Bible teaches that we will be free from human imperfection only at the second coming of Jesus (see 1 Corinthians 15:51-54), when Jesus will "change our vile body, that it may be fashioned like unto his glorious body" (Philippians 3:21).

But by Christ's power, we can have victory over acts of sin now. God's people are to "keep the commandments of God," not some of the commandments some of the time. But how? "This is the love of God, that we keep his commandments. And his commandments are not burdensome. For whatever is born of God overcomes the world; and this is the victory that overcomes the world, our faith. Who is it that overcomes the world but he who believes that Jesus is the Son of God?" (1 John 5:3-5, RSV).

God's ideal for us is that we reflect the character of Jesus and live as He did without committing sin. We are to be free from "every defilement of body and spirit, and make holiness perfect in the fear of God" (2 Corinthians 7:1, RSV). We are to be holy in all our "conduct" (1 Peter 1:15, RSV). We do this by allowing Jesus to live within us by the Holy Spirit and live out His life through us (see Galatians 2:20). "He who does righteousness is righteous, as he [Christ] is righteous" (1 John 3:7, literal translation). We are not righteous inherently, independently of Jesus. We are righteous only because He lives in our hearts by the Holy Spirit—because we retain our born-again fellowship with Him (see 1 John 2:29). And as long as we allow Him to reign within, we have freedom from acts of sin (see Romans 6:12-14, 16, 17).

When tempted to sin, we should pray three prayers: (1) "Lord, I am helpless; I like this thing." (2) "Lord, it is wrong; please give me the victory." (3) "Thank You, Lord. I believe I have the victory; thank You!" That third prayer is essential. Faith is praise! As you ask for the victory, believe that Jesus will give it to you and praise Him for it. Then you will have it.

Jesus' wonderful prayer is to be fulfilled for every one of us: "The glory which thou hast given me I have given to them, that they may be one even as we are one, I in them and thou in me, that they may become perfectly one, so that the world may know that thou hast sent me and hast loved them even as thou hast loved me" (John 17:22, 23, RSV).

Chapter 11

Why Belong to the Church?

Jesus Christ founded the church as a means to an end. The church is not a social club—even though it does provide social interaction for its members. The church is not a one-day-a-week audience for an eloquent orator—even though the congregation assembles every Sabbath to listen to the pastor preach. The church is not an assembly of introspective religious zealots who meet regularly to sharpen their spiritual perception. One would hope that church members are genuinely religious, intelligently zealous, and spiritually perceptive. But the primary reason they have banded together as a church organization is more basic and profound.

Because Christians have fallen in love with God as represented by His Son Jesus Christ, they seek constant fellowship with Him and with others who, like themselves, have committed their lives to Him. "God is faithful, by whom you were called into the fellowship of his Son, Jesus Christ our Lord" (1 Corinthians 1:9, RSV).

The apostle John gave the best reason for the existence of the church when he wrote: "That which was from the beginning, which we have heard, which we have seen with our eyes, which we have looked upon and touched with our hands, concerning the word of life—the life was made manifest, and we saw it, and testify to it, and proclaim to you the eternal life which was with the Father and was made manifest to us—that which we have seen and heard we proclaim also to you, so that you may have fellowship with us; and our fellowship is with the Father and with his Son Jesus Christ" (1 John 1:1-3, RSV).

John and his fellow apostles associated with Jesus. They became spiritually and emotionally bound to the Deity Himself. In the process they received His gift of eternal life. "This is the testimony, that God gave us eternal life, and this life is in his Son" (1 John 5:11, RSV). But John and his fellow apostles were not satisfied to have fellowship with God and eternal life only for themselves; they wanted the whole world to enjoy these magnificent blessings. Their mission was to introduce as many as would respond to fellowship with the Father and the Son, with themselves, and with other believers.

What is the church? It is the spiritual fellowship of all those who have entered into fellowship with God. It is impossible to have fellowship with God without also having fellowship with other believers. To argue that you can be a Christian without belonging to the church is like saying that you can enter into fellowship with Christ without entering into fellowship with His family. But how can you love Christ genuinely and relate to Him meaningfully without also loving and relating to those He loves?

Question: Can I be a Christian without joining the church?
    Answer: Yes, it is possible. It is something like being:
    A student who will not go to school.
    A soldier who will not join an army.
    A citizen who does not pay taxes or vote.
    A salesman with no customers.
    An explorer with no base camp.
    A seaman on a ship without a crew.
    A businessman on a deserted island.
    An author without readers.
    A tuba player without an orchestra.
    A parent without a family.
    A football player without a team.
    A politician who is a hermit.
    A scientist who does not share his findings.
    A bee without a hive (*Wesleyan Christian Advocate*).

"If we say we have fellowship with him while we walk in

darkness, we lie and do not live according to the truth; but if we walk in the light, as he is in the light, *we have fellowship with one another*, and the blood of Jesus his Son cleanses us from all sin" (1 John 1:6, 7, RSV, emphasis supplied).

How are people drawn into the fellowship of the church?

Jesus answered that question in terms that are thoroughly relevant to us today. When approached by a rabbinical lawyer who asked him the question, " 'Teacher, what shall I do to inherit eternal life?' He said to him, 'What is written in the law? How do you read?' And he [the lawyer] answered, 'You shall love the Lord your God with all your heart, and with all your soul, and with all your strength, and with all your mind; and your neighbor as yourself.' And he [Jesus] said to him, 'You have answered right; do this, and you will live.' But he, desiring to justify himself, said to Jesus, 'And who is my neighbor?' " (Luke 10:25-29, RSV).

The lawyer's first question was basic: "What shall I do to inherit eternal life?" Jesus drew from him the answer to his own question. The lawyer's knowledge of the law of Moses gave him the answer: love for God (see Deuteronomy 6:5) and love for one's neighbor (see Leviticus 19:18). In other words, by having loving fellowship with God and His children, you have the gift of eternal life.

But the lawyer's fellowship with God was marred by national prejudice. "Desiring to justify himself," he asked Jesus, " 'And who is my neighbor?' " (Luke 10:29, RSV). The lawyer was seeking to justify his ethnic isolationism. He was unwilling to have loving fellowship with those of God's children whom he regarded as less favored. His church was highly selective of its membership. The Samaritans, for example, were left out; in fact, they were despised as unfit for eternal life.

Jesus provided a classic answer—the parable of the good Samaritan. On the lonely and dangerous road from Jerusalem to Jericho, a man was mugged by robbers. They left him bruised and bleeding by the roadside. Walking by, a priest, one of the church's respected leaders, saw the half-dead man, but, evidently thinking he was a Samaritan or another of those not favored by God, passed by on the other side of the road. Likewise a Levite, also a religious leader, saw the man's plight but hurried on without offering assistance. But a Samaritan, traveling the same road, saw the bleeding victim, and with great compassion tended his wounds. He placed the sufferer on his donkey, took him to the nearest motel, and all that night did what he could to relieve his pain. The next morning the Samaritan gave the motel manager money, saying, " 'Take care of him; and whatever more you spend, I will repay you when I come back' " (Luke 10:35, RSV).

Jesus' point is that the Samaritan was a true neighbor to the man who had been robbed and beaten. Jesus instructed the lawyer as He instructs every one of us, " 'Go and do likewise' " (Luke 10:37).

Suppose you were the one whose life had been saved by the Samaritan. Wouldn't you want to know more about him? Wouldn't you want to know something about the God he served and the church to which he belonged? Wouldn't you start by finding out where he lived so that you could contact him and express your deep appreciation? And wouldn't that contact be likely to lead to earnest investigation of the religious convictions that motivated such loving service for others? Probably it would not be long before you would enter into fellowship with that Samaritan; his God would become yours too, and his church would be your church. Toward the end of His life Jesus prayed, " 'I in them and thou in me, that they may become perfectly one, *so that the world may know* that thou hast sent me and hast loved them even as thou hast loved me' " (John 17:23, RSV, emphasis supplied).

Upon whom is the church built?

By now it should be perfectly clear that only Christ can be the foundation of the church. Because the church consists of those who have entered into fellowship with Him, He alone is the One upon whom the church depends for its spiritual life. Jesus is the Rock upon whom the church is erected (see Matthew 16:16-18). "For no other foundation can any one lay than that which is laid, which is Jesus Christ" (1 Corinthians 3:11, RSV). He is the cornerstone upon whom believers "like living stones" are "built into a spiritual house, to be a holy priesthood, to offer spiritual sacrifices acceptable to God through Jesus Christ" (1 Peter 2:5, RSV).

Not only is Jesus the foundation of the church; He is also its head. "God placed all things under his feet and appointed him to be head over everything for the church, which is his body, the fullness of him who fills everything in every way" (Ephesians 1:22, 23, NIV).

There is nothing in the Bible that gives authority to bishops and popes to rule God's people, stipulating what they should believe and commanding them to worship according to their will. Jesus instructed His disciples that they were never to assume the role of rulers. " 'You know that those who are supposed to rule over the Gentiles lord it over them, and their great men exercise authority over them. But it shall not be so among you; but whoever would be great among you must be your servant, and whoever would be first among you must be slave of all. For the Son of man also came not to be served but to serve, and to give his life as a ransom for many' " (Mark 10:42-45, RSV).

God's Word instructs the ministers or elders of the church to be gentle, faithful shepherds, showing God's people how to live, teaching them the truth, always following the leadership of the Chief Shepherd (see Acts 20:28-32; 1 Peter 5:1-4). Jesus' teaching should have ruled out for all time the tendency for church leaders to become ecclesiastical monarchs. " 'You are not to be called rabbi, for you have one teacher, and you are all brethren. And call no man your father on earth, for you have one Father, who is in heaven. Neither be called masters, for you have one master, the Christ' " (Matthew 23:8-10, RSV). How differently the history of the Christian church would read if Jesus' counsel had been followed!

Jesus did not give the keys of the kingdom of heaven exclusively to Peter, but to all the disciples (compare Matthew 16:19 with Matthew 18:18). In fact, Jesus retains the keys Himself: " 'Fear not, I am the first and the last, and the living one; I died, and behold I am alive for evermore, and I have the keys of Death and Hades' " (Revelation 1:17, 18, RSV). Jesus shares the keys of the kingdom with every believer who faithfully presents to others the message of His saving grace.

The decisions of the church do not bind God. By His Spirit He imparts His will to His people, and they make decisions that put

His will into action. Matthew 18:18 is correctly translated: "Truly, I say to you, whatever you bind upon the earth *shall have been bound in heaven*, and whatever you loose upon the earth *shall have been loosed in heaven.*" The decisions are first made in heaven, and then they are imparted to the church as the members seek the guidance of the Holy Spirit.

How was the church organized after Jesus' ascension?

Because Jesus' apostles had associated with Him during His earthly ministry, receiving instruction and training directly from Him, they were recognized as the authoritative leaders of the first Christian church. The book of Acts and the New Testament epistles make it clear that the writings of the apostles and their united decisions were treated as inspired by Christ Himself (see Acts 1; 15; 1 John 1:1-4). The apostle Paul had not been a disciple of Jesus during His ministry. But he was chosen by God after Jesus' ascension as an apostle to the Gentiles (see Acts 9:15, 16). Because Paul's messages were given by the special inspiration of the Holy Spirit, his writings are included in the sacred canon of Scripture (see 2 Corinthians 12:1-12).

Whenever the apostles raised up churches, they appointed pastors (called "elders" or "bishops") to care for the spiritual needs of the believers (see Acts 14:23; Titus 1:5-9). A bishop was not a ruler but a pastor of the church.

Because there were practical business matters that the pastors did not have time to care for, deacons were appointed (see Acts 6:1-6). The deacons did not care only for the mundane affairs of the church; they were also spiritual leaders who taught and preached. Philip was a deacon (see Acts 6:5), but he was also a great soul winner, used by the Holy Spirit to win new believers and raise up churches (see Acts 8:5, 6).

What work has Christ given His church?

Jesus gave the great commission to every member of His church. "Go therefore and make disciples of all nations" (Matthew 28:19, RSV). The great work of making disciples is to continue until every inhabitant of earth has had an opportunity to hear and respond to the good news of salvation through Christ.

Jesus promised: "This gospel of the kingdom will be preached throughout the whole world, as a testimony to all nations; and then the end will come" (Matthew 24:14, RSV).

How can we fulfill this great commission? Not only by supporting those who preach the gospel publicly, but also by personally entering into fellowship with Christ and with those who believe in Him and by sharing Christ with others. Church members are called to pray constantly (see Ephesians 6:18), to study the Word of God regularly (see 2 Timothy 3:14-17), and to impart to others the encouraging truth the Holy Spirit has given to them (see Acts 1:8; Romans 14:19; 2 Timothy 2:2). "Be filled with the Spirit; speaking to yourselves in psalms and hymns and spiritual songs, singing and making melody in your heart to the Lord" (Ephesians 5:18, 19). "Preach the Word; be prepared in season and out of season; correct, rebuke and encourage—with great patience and careful instruction" (2 Timothy 4:2, NIV).

Only as church members have warm and meaningful fellowship within the church are they able to witness effectively to those outside the church (see Hebrews 10:24, 25). The dynamic witness of the apostolic church resulted from the Spirit-filled fellowship that bound the believers together. The record is that "all who believed were together and had all things in common; and they sold their possessions and goods and distributed them to all, as any had need. And day by day, attending the temple together and breaking bread in their homes, they partook of food with glad and generous hearts, praising God and having favor with all the people. And the Lord added to their number day by day those who were being saved" (Acts 2:44-47, RSV).

When the world observes the love Christians have for one another and the warmth of fellowship that characterizes their worship services, many are attracted to the church. Witnessing is not only public proclamation; it also involves loving concern for others manifested in kindly deeds of service. In the final analysis, the good Samaritan is the best soul winner.

How can you become a church member?

The first step is to commit your life fully to Jesus Christ by accepting Him as Saviour and Lord. Jesus explained to Nicodemus,

"Except a man be born again, he cannot see the kingdom of God" (John 3:3). When you willingly give Jesus possession of your heart by allowing His Holy Spirit to dwell within, you have the presence of His righteousness in your heart (see Romans 8:9, 10). Then God's Word, the Bible, will be meaningful to you.

The second step is to discover prayerfully from the Bible as much about the teaching of Jesus as you can and to commit yourself to living according to His will. "If any man will do his will, he shall know of the doctrine, whether it be of God, or whether I speak of myself" (John 7:17). The Bible is Jesus' teaching. All of Holy Scripture centers in Him and points to Him (see John 5:39). True believers are willing to worship in the manner and at the times taught in God's Word. They are willing to forsake all those habits that God's Word condemns and to practice those things it recommends (see John 14:15; 15:10).

The third step is to enter the waters of baptism as a sign of your born-again commitment to Jesus Christ and all that He teaches. Jesus taught: " 'Unless a man is born of water and the Spirit, he cannot enter the kingdom of God' " (John 3:5, NIV). Jesus was baptized by John the Baptist "to fulfil all righteousness" (Matthew 3:15). In other words, He was baptized as an example to believing, repenting sinners. When you are publicly baptized into Christ, you proclaim to all the world that you have died to sin and have been resurrected to a new life in Christ (see Romans 6:4).

The fourth step is to enter into fellowship with God's children by joining the church that believes and practices all that Jesus instructs. "If they do not speak according to this word, they have no light of dawn" (Isaiah 8:20, NIV).

What is that church? It is the church that keeps "the commandments of God" and has "the testimony of Jesus Christ" (Revelation 12:17). It is the church that accepts every truth taught in the Bible and lives by it.

We pray that the Lord will lead you to saving fellowship with Christ and loving fellowship with His church.

Chapter 12

"Here They Are!"

Editors often laugh at typographical errors they find in galleys. Here are a few I picked up while working on the *Adventist Review*: "The Brainerd, Minnesota, Red Squirrels Pathfinder Club activities during the past year included singing in nursing homes, sending greeting cards, collecting canned *goos* on Halloween . . ."

"Religious belief, denominational *affliction*, cultural differences . . . join the natural tendency to dislike those who are separated from us."

"On [Jesus'] trip across the lake to the *dessert* place . . ."

"A campus surrounded by a *pinscented* forest . . ."

"The fact that certain passages of the *Bile* are obscure should not discourage us."

"The hardened earth served as a floor in the new chapel which provided room for one hundred worshipers, on backless benches made from *plants*."

In one manuscript that was sent to our reading committee, *believers* was spelled three times as *belivers*. One sarcastic responder wrote, "What about A-livers, C-livers, and D-livers? Are all your livers B-livers?"

Typos sometimes are amusing, but seldom significant. Once in a while, however, they can be meaningful. After hearing about a group of pious Protestant monks in France who had chosen the motto "Do not be afraid to precede the dawn," I thought that would be an appropriate sermon theme for an Adventist audience. I abbreviated the slogan into the title "Dare to Precede the

Dawn." When asked to preach at a California church, I decided to use this sermon. After arriving at church that morning, I was appalled to see the title listed in the bulletin as "*Daze* to Precede the Dawn." My introduction became more interesting than planned as I pointed out that our world, our country, and sometimes even our church seem to be caught up in the daze that will precede the dawn of eternity.

Events are happening so fast that even those who expect the last movements to be rapid ones are left in a daze. As a result of what is going on in our world, many are turning to the cults or New Age proponents in a search for something they can hold on to.

In his book *Gaily the Troubadour*, Arthur Guiterman penned the following words, which are much more relevant today than when he wrote them fifty years ago:

First dentistry was painless;
    Then bicycles were chainless
    And carriages were horseless
    And many laws, enforceless.
Next, cookery was fireless,
    Telegraphy was wireless,
    Cigars were nicotineless,
    And coffee, caffeineless.
Soon oranges were seedless,
    The putting green was weedless,
    The college boy, hatless,
    The proper diet, fatless.
Now motor roads are dustless,
    The latest steel is rustless,
    Our tennis courts are sodless,
    Our new religions, godless.

Times such as these challenge us to heroic efforts. To continue living and working for the Lord in the same halfhearted way simply is not good enough. It's time to dare great things for God— to address ourselves to the challenge of our unfinished work with new vim and vigor.

The remnant

The *remnant*, or *remaining ones*, is a familiar Bible term used to describe a small group who, while passing through some great crisis, remain loyal to God. Most often the term is used in the Old Testament to designate those who would return from Babylonian captivity.

Isaiah 10:21 predicts that "the remnant shall return, even the remnant of Jacob, unto the mighty God."

Jeremiah 23:3 adds: "I will gather the remnant of my flock out of all countries whither I have driven them, and will bring them again to their folds; and they shall be fruitful and increase."

But because Israel never fully submitted to God's plan for the nation, many of the remnant predictions that could not be fulfilled then will be fulfilled in the eschatological Day of the Lord. One of these is Joel's prediction: "It shall come to pass, that whosoever shall call on the name of the Lord shall be delivered: for in mount Zion and in Jerusalem shall be deliverance, as the Lord hath said, and in the remnant whom the Lord shall call" (Joel 2:32).

Zechariah 8:12 adds: "The seed shall be prosperous; the vine shall give her fruit, and the ground shall give her increase, and the heavens shall give their dew; and I will cause the remnant of this people to possess all these things."

In Revelation, however, John uses the term *remnant* to designate those who remain loyal during earth's final crisis: "The dragon was wroth with the woman, and went to make war with the remnant of her seed, which keep the commandments of God, and have the testimony of Jesus Christ" (Revelation 12:17). As we compare this verse with Revelation 14, we see that those who keep God's commandments in the last moments of time are given the responsibility of warning the world that the coming of Christ is soon to take place. They do their best to prepare the world for its final crisis by proclaiming the three angels' messages. But example is more effective than proclamation. This "remnant" keep the commandments of God and keep the faith of Jesus.

The 144,000

Revelation 14:1-5 paints a word picture of the 144,000 in

heaven, but when moving down to verse 12 we find a word portrait of the 144,000 on earth, before they go to heaven. "Here is the patience of the saints: here are they that keep the commandments of God, and the faith of Jesus."

A hasty reading of this verse may miss the excitement of what God is saying. We need to recognize that all heaven is thrilled as God exclaims, "Here it is! Here's what I've been waiting for! Look! See the patience of the saints. What I've been waiting for so long finally is taking place. Look, everyone, *here they are*! Who? The *keepers* of My commandments, the *keepers* of My faith."

God's people no longer will have to hang their heads in shame and disappointment when this announcement is made. By His grace and power, the 144,000 have emerged before the world perfectly reproducing the character of Christ. In spite of the fierce attacks of Satan, they have, through the effective work of the Holy Spirit in their lives, accomplished what seemed impossible. They have been sealed. They are so settled in the truth that they cannot be moved, in spite of the all-out efforts of Satan to cause people to fall.

Satan today is employing even some in the church to echo his witless challenge, "Show me one person who can keep God's commandments. Show me just one." Of course, this charge ignores Enoch, Moses, Joseph, and John the Baptist—among many others.

The Lord soon will silence Satan and those who attempt to keep the remnant from achieving God's promise. God exclaims, "Look! Here they are! Here are 144,000 who have done exactly what you claim could never be done. See their patience. See, they are keeping My commandments and the faith of Jesus."

When are these remarkable people living such lives? Right at the last moments of time, when it seems more impossible than ever. Right when the world is worse off morally, physically, and mentally than it has ever been, even in the days of Noah. How are they able to do it? God has filled them with His patient, enduring, steadfast love. They are reflecting that love and the faith of Jesus to all who observe them. It's an impressive argument that no sophisticate can gainsay. By God's grace, the remnant not only stand up to pressures from without, but to pressures from within.

The three angels' messages are in verity the message of righteousness by faith. But righteousness by faith is not merely a theory, doctrine, or dogma. It is an experience—that experience which will characterize those who stand firmly on these great pillars of truth and allow Jesus to complete His work in them.

The everlasting gospel, as Paul tells us in Romans 1:16, is the power of God unto salvation. The good news is that we need not settle for partial salvation. Through the power of Christ and the Spirit, we can overcome sin in our lives. We can keep the commandments of God and the faith of Jesus.

To talk about keeping the commandments without adding the faith of Jesus gives the wrong impression. When we keep the faith through the same power Christ used to keep the faith, the Holy Spirit, we will vindicate God's law and character before a watching world. Ours will be the indisputable testimony that there is no excuse for failing to keep God's law. It can be done, and it must be done if the harvest is to follow.

The three angels' messages

The "everlasting gospel" is the basis of the three messages that the remnant presents as a final warning to the world. God always has had but one way of saving men and women—by faith in His gift provided through Christ. As they preach and live the three angels' messages, the remnant are to lift high the cross of Christ that all may look and live. The first angel's message challenges the world to be aware that the hour of God's pre-advent judgment already has come. It began on October 22, 1844, and soon will be completed. In calling the people of earth to "worship" the Creator, Revelation 14:6, 7 indicates that a significant part of preaching the "everlasting gospel" at this point in time involves keeping the seventh-day Sabbath.

The first angel announces the good news that is to prepare all who heed it for the second coming of Christ.

The second angel announces the fall of Babylon. The focus on the heavenly sanctuary in the first message calls in question the attacks of the little horn of Daniel 7 and 8 on the intercessory ministry of Christ. Babylon's focus on the earthly priestly system rather than on the work of Christ as our High Priest in heaven is judged and condemned by God. When first proclaimed, the first angel's message, with its clear upward look, caused many to see beyond the human counterfeit system on earth to the genuine ministry of humanity's only Priest in heaven. This broke the grip of Babylon over many people.

The third angel points to the ultimate showdown between Christ and His enemies at the second coming. The three messages set the stage for the final battle in the cosmic controversy. The mission of the remnant church is not only to warn the world that Christ is engaged in pre-advent judgment, which is soon to terminate, but also to make it clear that, when every living person has taken his or her stand for or against these messages, Christ will come to bring His reward with Him.

The other three angels of Revelation 14

You may not have noticed that there are *six* angels' messages in Revelation 14. The first three have to do with the preparation for the harvest. The last three announce the harvest. Often we fail to relate Revelation 14:6-12 with the rest of the chapter as we clearly should. Notice that there are three angels involved in the events that surround the second coming. Also there are two beings bearing sickles and two angels who announce to them that the time has come to reap. The chart on page 109 clarifies this relationship.

Note that two harvests are indicated in this chart—the grain harvest and the grape harvest. During the investigative judgment of the righteous, which began in 1844, the determination is made as to whose names will be retained in the Lamb's book of life. These make up the ripened grain that Jesus harvests at the second coming. Those whose names are not found in the book of life will be "cast . . . into the great winepress of the wrath of God" (Revelation 14:19; see also Revelation 20:15).

Recognizing that the harvest of the earth soon will be ripe, we must yield ourselves in total commitment to God in order that His Spirit may enable us to do our part in sowing the gospel seed and may bring our lives into conformity to God's will. Then we can wait in confident expectation of going home with Jesus when He reaps the grain harvest.

Contrast of Harvesters	Christ With Crown on His Head Carrying Sickle	"Another Angel" Carrying a Sharp Sickle
What are they doing?	Christ coming in the clouds at His second coming	Angel coming out of temple for judgment
From where did "another angel" come?	Out of the temple, crying with a loud voice to Christ	From the altar, crying with a loud voice to angel with sharp sickle
What did the angels invite the harvesters to do?	Thrust in the sickle and reap the (grain) harvest	Thrust in the sickle and gather clusters of grapes ready for the harvest
How did the harvesters respond?	Gathered ripened good grain—the righteous taken to heaven	Gathered fully ripened grapes for the wine-press—destruction of the wicked

Two significant challenges come to us from Ellen White. The first calls us to deeper study and understanding of the three angels' messages:

The third angel's message means far more than we take it to mean. We should search to find out all that is possible concerning this solemn message. The earth is to be lighted with its glory (*Letter* 1, October 12, 1875).

The second challenges us to more dedicated effort:

The Lord will not close up the period of probation until the warning message shall be more distinctly proclaimed. The trumpet must give a certain sound. The law of God is to be magnified. Its claims must be presented in their true, sacred character that the people may be brought to decide for or against the truth. Yet the work will be cut short in righteousness. The message of Christ's righteousness is to sound from one end of the world to the other. This is the glory of God which closes the work of the third angel (*Letter* 2c, December 21, 1892).

Chapter 13

"Blest Be the Tie That Binds"

John Fawcett was invited to pastor a small congregation at Wainsgate, England, in 1765. For seven years he tenderly cared for the spiritual needs of the people, diligently seeking to bind them together in united Christian fellowship. But his salary was insufficient for him and his wife to buy the necessities of life. The members of his congregation were so poor that they were not able adequately to supply the material needs of their pastor. Even so, he felt compensated by their faithfulness and the warmth of their fellowship.

Then Dr. Fawcett was invited to pastor a much larger church in London. While he was considering carefully and prayerfully, his parishioners pleaded with him to remain with them. But finally he decided to accept the invitation. As his few possessions were being packed into the wagon, many of his church members came to say goodbye and to offer one last plea for him to reconsider and stay with them.

John and his wife were so moved by the great outpouring of love that they began to weep. Overcome by the need of the people, Mrs. Fawcett exclaimed, "Oh John, I just can't bear this. They need us so badly here."

John replied, "God has spoken to my heart too! Tell them to unload the wagon! We cannot break these wonderful ties of fellowship."

Later, John wrote the beautiful hymn that has inspired Christians ever since:

Blest be the tie that binds
Our hearts in Christian love!
The fellowship of kindred minds
Is like to that above.

When we asunder part,
It gives us inward pain;
But we shall still be joined in heart,
And hope to meet again.

"Behold, how good and how pleasant it is for brethren to dwell together in unity!" (Psalm 133:1). But how can there be unity in the worldwide church when there are so many racial and cultural differences, such a diversity of educational levels among members, and such great differences of wealth and social standing? And how can there be unity of Christian belief and practice when there are so many conflicting ideas of what the Bible means on certain major subjects?

Jesus answered these questions in His teaching and in the manner in which He related to diverse cultures and opinions. He was aware of the destructive national chauvinism and prejudice against other races and cultures cherished by His disciples. When Jesus and the disciples were visiting the region of Tyre and Sidon, a Canaanite woman, whose daughter was "severely possessed by a demon" (Matthew 15:22, RSV), came to Him pleading that He would heal her.

The people of this district were of the old Canaanite race. They were idolaters, and were despised and hated by the Jews. To this class belonged the woman who now came to Jesus. She was a heathen, and was therefore excluded from the advantages which the Jews daily enjoyed (Ellen G. White, *The Desire of Ages*, p. 399).

To demonstrate to His disciples how cruel they were to treat such foreigners as outcasts, Jesus at first appeared to ignore the woman. But there must have been such sympathy and understanding in His look that she was not repulsed. She went on pleading, but the disciples had no compassion for her. To them, she was a heathen and an outcast. They exclaimed, " 'Send her away, for she is crying after us' " (Matthew 15:23, RSV).

When the woman persisted, Jesus replied, " 'I was sent only to the lost sheep of the house of Israel' " (verse 24, RSV). That was the attitude of His disciples, but not His attitude. The statement was diametrically opposed to the spirit of His entire ministry. He had taught Nicodemus, " 'God so loved the world that he gave his one and only Son, that *whoever* believes in him shall not perish but have eternal life' " (John 3:16, NIV, emphasis supplied). Later, Jesus exclaimed, " 'I, when I am lifted up from the earth, will draw *all* men to myself' " (John 12:32, NIV, emphasis supplied). There was no exclusiveness in Jesus' presentation of the good news of salvation. All may come; all are offered salvation; all may be His by right of adoption into the family of God.

The Canaanite woman must have detected by the tone of His voice that Jesus did not really mean what He said. She bowed at His feet, crying, "Lord, help me."

Again, Jesus gave the answer His disciples would have given: " 'It is not fair to take the children's bread and throw it to the dogs' " (Matthew 15:26, RSV). That answer might have discouraged her if she had not noticed Jesus' love and concern. "Beneath the apparent refusal of Jesus, she saw a compassion that He could not hide" (*The Desire of Ages*, p. 401).

She pressed her claim more earnestly: " 'Yes, Lord, yet even the dogs eat the crumbs that fall from their masters' table' " (verse 27, RSV). What an answer! "Yes," she admits, "I am a dog, but, because You are the master, and You would not deny a dog the crumbs that fall from Your table, please grant my request." Jesus' divine heart of love overflowed at that moment. The pent-up mercy of the Deity poured forth in a surging stream of pity and healing: " 'O woman, great is your faith! Be it done for you as you desire.' And her daughter was healed instantly" (verse 28, RSV).

What a lesson to the disciples—and to us! By simulating the prejudiced attitudes of the favored nation, Jesus demonstrated His equal love for all humankind, whatever the color, class, or creed.

Caste is hateful to God. He ignores everything of this character. In His sight the souls of all men are of equal value. He "hath made of one blood all nations of men for to dwell on all the face of the earth, and hath determined the times before appointed, and the bounds of their habitation; that they should seek the Lord, if haply they might feel after Him, and find Him, though He be not far from every one of us." Without distinction of age, or rank, or nationality, or religious privilege, all are invited to come unto Him and live. "Whosoever believeth on Him shall not be ashamed. For there is no difference." "There is neither Jew nor Greek, there is neither bond nor free." "The rich and poor meet together: the Lord is the Maker of them all." "The same Lord over all is rich unto all that call upon Him. For whosoever shall call upon the name of the Lord shall be saved." Acts 17:26, 27; Gal. 3:28; Prov. 22:2; Rom. 10:11-13 (Ellen G. White, *The Desire of Ages*, p. 403).

What is the tie that binds?
The fact that people of different races, speaking different languages, having different national and ethnic customs, and living under widely different political systems can be bound together in Christian love is a divine miracle. Christ is the tie that binds. When His Spirit lives in people's hearts, whatever their languages or cultural differences, they have the same basic purpose for living, the same loving concern to lead others to the Saviour, and the same hope of eternal life beyond the here and now. Their love for Christ and for all humanity transcends their cultural background and overcomes the divisive prejudices that may rule in their ethnic groups. They can cooperate with one another and with Christ's worldwide church because, above all else, they belong to Him and wish to reflect His character to one another and to the world.

Paul wrote to the Roman Christian church, which was becoming increasingly cosmopolitan:

As in one body we have many members, and all the members do not have the same function, so we, though many, are one body in Christ, and individually members one of another. Having gifts that differ according to the grace given to us, let us use them. . . . Let love be genuine; hate what is evil, hold fast to what is good; love one another with brotherly affection; outdo one another in showing honor. Never flag in zeal, be aglow with the Spirit, serve the Lord (Romans 12:4-11, RSV).

Paul sought to foster in the hearts of Christian believers everywhere the unity of love for which Jesus prayed just prior to His death.

"That they may all be one; even as thou, Father, art in me, and I in thee, that they also may be in us, so that the world may believe that thou hast sent me. . . . I in them and thou in me, that they may become perfectly one, so that the world may know that thou hast sent me and hast loved them even as thou hast loved me" (John 17:21, 23, RSV; compare Ephesians 4:4-6).

The unity of the Spirit among the followers of Jesus Christ is the greatest witness to the world of the truth of Christianity. When Jesus' prayer is completely fulfilled in the lives of His people, and His Spirit reigns with undisputed power in their hearts, the gospel will spread to all nations with unprecedented speed and effectiveness. "They will know us by our love."

"For just as the body is one and has many members, and all the members of the body, though many, are one body, so it is with Christ. For by one Spirit we were all baptized into one body— Jews or Greeks, slaves or free—and all were made to drink of one Spirit" (1 Corinthians 12:12, 13, RSV).

Why is doctrinal unity important?

Doctrines are the teachings of the Word of God—the beliefs that Christ would have us accept. It is impossible to separate Christ from the teachings of His Word. These teachings are so much a part of Christ that to accept Him involves accepting them. For a professed Christian to reject the doctrine of the second coming of Jesus is a contradiction (see Matthew 24). To claim belief in Christ while denying His full Deity and eternal pre-existence is actually to reject Him (see John 5:18; 8:58, 59; Colossians 2:9.)

It is not possible for Christians to establish genuine unity in Christ if they cannot agree on what the Bible teaches. Their understanding of God will be different, and they will not be worshiping the same divine Being.

That is why Paul wrote to the Galatians:

> I am astonished that you are so quickly deserting him who called you in the grace of Christ and turning to a different gospel—not that there is another gospel, but there are some who trouble you and want to pervert the gospel of Christ. But even if we, or an angel from heaven, should preach to you a gospel contrary to that which we preached to you, let him be accursed. As we have said before, so now I say again, If any one is preaching to you a gospel contrary to that which you received, let him be accursed (Galatians 1:6-9, RSV).

There is only *one* gospel of Jesus Christ. The only angel that would be likely to preach a different gospel is a *fallen* angel—one of Satan's demons. Unfortunately, the devil is very active, confusing Christians with false doctrines, prowling "around like a roaring lion, seeking some one to devour" (1 Peter 5:8, RSV). We are instructed to beware of him and his advocates: "Resist him, firm in your faith, knowing that the same experience of suffering is required of your brotherhood throughout the world" (verse 9).

In his Epistle to the Galatians, Paul sought to bring the believers back to the one true gospel. The Galatian Christians had been deceived by legalists who had convinced them that obedience to the law is the *means* of salvation. Paul taught, as Jesus did, that salvation is by grace alone through faith and that obedience to God's law is the *result* of the salvation experience (see Galatians 2:16; 3:1-3; compare Romans 3:19-31). Because the church of Galatia was divided over the issue, Christian unity was threatened.

Today, the same basic question is a source of great division among Christians: What is the gospel? The Bible answer is simple and direct: We are saved by Christ's grace when we choose to respond by believing in Him. And the result is obedience to His law. "For by grace you have been saved through faith; and this is not your own doing, it is the gift of God—not because of works, lest any man should boast. For we are his workmanship, created in Christ Jesus for good works, which God prepared beforehand, that we should walk in them" (Ephesians 2:8-10, RSV; compare Romans 3:31; 8:3, 4).

There need be no doctrinal divisions among us if we allow the Holy Spirit to guide us to truth as we study the Bible. For "he will guide you into all the truth" (John 16:13, RSV).

Does God expect all His people to have the same character?

Character is the sum total of the traits that form the individual nature of a person. Even though, inevitably, Christ's followers are vastly different in personality, the Bible teaches that their characters are to be like Christ's. When His Spirit is living in a person's heart, that person has the gift of righteousness (see Romans 8:9, 10). Righteousness is Christlikeness, and God wishes all His people to be like Christ in character (see Ephesians 3:16-21).

The gifts of the Holy Spirit are given to the church "for the perfecting of the saints, for the work of the ministry, for the edifying of the body of Christ: till we all come in the unity of the faith, and of the knowledge of the Son of God, unto a perfect man, unto the measure of the stature of the fulness of Christ" (Ephesians 4:12, 13).

The goal of every Christian is "the measure of the stature of the fulness of Christ." That is Christlikeness. When church members reflect Christ's character, inevitably, they will be united. Then "there cannot be Greek and Jew, circumcised and uncircumcised, barbarian, Scythian, slave, free man, but Christ is all, and in all" (Colossians 3:11, RSV).

Church unity is destroyed when some members reflect Christ's character and others do not. This is what happened among the disciples of Jesus. When pride and selfishness took the place of Christ's Spirit in their hearts, they argued bitterly over who was the most important man in the church (see Mark 9:33-37).

Similarly, when pride of opinion took the place of humility and love in the church of Corinth, the members became hopelessly divided (see 1 Corinthians 1:10-13). Inspired by the Holy Spirit, Paul sought to bring them back to the wonderful new-birth experience they had once enjoyed. "Do you not know that the unrighteous will not inherit the kingdom of God? . . . And such were some of you. But you were washed, you were sanctified, you were justified in the name of the Lord Jesus Christ and in the Spirit of our God" (1 Corinthians 6:9-11, RSV).

Will the church be thoroughly united before Jesus comes?

The Bible answers Yes. Jesus predicted that the church would be united before His second advent. " 'And I have other sheep, that are not of this fold; I must bring them also, and they will heed my voice. So there shall be one flock, one shepherd' " (John 10:16, RSV).

As the three angels' messages of Revelation 14:6-12 are preached in all the world before Jesus comes, those who are genuinely seeking for truth will join the remnant church. The great message of Revelation 18:1-4 will be proclaimed as heaven's last appeal to lost humanity. The other angel who comes down from heaven, making the earth "bright with his splendor," represents the Holy Spirit filling the hearts of God's people throughout the world.

The Holy Spirit is the One who bestows upon us the glory of the character of Jesus. When God's people, by faith in Jesus, put away sin and receive the final outpouring of the Holy Spirit spoken of in Joel 2:28, 29, then will be seen the fulfillment of Revelation 18:1. The glory of Christ's character will be proclaimed and demonstrated around the world. In the unity of the Spirit, Christ's followers will give the final warning that modern "Babylon" is spiritually fallen and morally degraded. Their great plea to all humanity will be, " 'Come out of her, my people, lest you take part in her sins, lest you share in her plagues' " (Revelation 18:4, RSV).

Then Christ's purpose for the church will be fulfilled: that He might "present the church to himself in splendor, without a spot or wrinkle or anything of the kind—yes, so that she may be holy and without blemish" (Ephesians 5:27, NRSV).

Then Old Testament prophecies that could have been fulfilled to ancient Israel had she remained faithful will be fulfilled for the remnant church of Jesus Christ.

> "In those days and in that time, says the Lord, the people of Israel and the people of Judah [representing repentant people all over the world] shall come together, weeping as they come; and they shall seek the Lord their God. They shall ask the way to Zion, with faces turned toward it, saying, 'Come, let us join ourselves to the Lord in an everlasting covenant which will never be forgotten'" (Jeremiah 50:4, 5, RSV; compare Isaiah 4:2-6; 11:12, 13).

Are you willing to enter into an everlasting covenant with the Lord in these final days of earth's history? Are you willing to join Christ's remnant people who are seeking Him earnestly for the spiritual power to give the last great appeal of Revelation 18:4 to the world? We pray that your response will be positive.

Chapter 14

Baptism
by Immersion

A visitor to the ruins of ancient Ephesus, if coming by ship, lands at the port of Kusadasi, Turkey. After being bused to the site of what was a great city in the apostle Paul's day, the visitor is impressed by the main thoroughfare known as the Arcadian Way. Running from the dock area of the ancient port, the marble-paved street leads slightly uphill for three-tenths of a mile to the ruins of the great amphitheater that once seated nearly 25,000 people. Taking the road to the left from this site, the visitor walks some distance to the sparse ruins of the Temple of Artemis. To the left of the ruins, at the top of a small hill, is found the remnants of the Basilica of St. John, built by Justinian in the sixth century on the hill where John's tomb was supposed to be located.

A fascinating cross-shaped baptistery is deep enough that only the head and top of the shoulders of someone standing in it are visible. This baptistery attests to the fact that baptism by immersion was practiced as late as the sixth century A.D. in that part of the Christian world. In Italy, there are no fewer than sixty-six such baptisteries constructed between the fourth and fourteenth centuries. All of these bear silent testimony to the practice of baptism by immersion in that area.

The fact that the biblical practice of baptism involved immersion should not come as a surprise, because the word itself comes from the Greek *baptizō*, which was used to describe the immersion of cloth in dye and the submerging of a vessel to fill it with water.

When did baptism originate? As a religious rite, it originated in pre-Christian times.

It was practiced by the Jews as a means of receiving proselytes to Judaism. [The legal status of such a proselyte was that of a newborn child.] . . . It is significant that the Jewish leaders did not question John concerning the validity of the rite of baptism, but only his authority to administer it (see Jn 1:19-28). Baptism was also practiced by the Essenes in connection with their religious rites. In *Khirbet Qumrân*, which was probably the center of the Essenes, several tanks with steps leading into them have been discovered. . . . These may have been used for baptismal rites, which apparently involved immersion, as did Jewish proselyte baptism (*SDA Bible Dictionary*, p. 113).

New Testament examples of baptism by immersion

Although Jesus and John the Baptist were cousins, they apparently had no direct acquaintance with each other. Jesus grew up in Nazareth, and John grew up in the wilderness of Judea. Therefore, it could not be claimed that they had conspired together to support each other's claims.

Apparently, John began his ministry about six months before Jesus responded to the Spirit's direction to begin His. John used the ordinance of baptism to symbolize confession for and repentance of sin. When Jesus came to him for baptism, John had no previous knowledge of who He was, but recognized in Him a purity of character that he had never before perceived in any man. John understood this to be the fulfillment of the promised sign that he would be the one to present the Messiah to the people.

When Jesus asked John to baptize Him, John shrank from doing so, exclaiming, " 'I need to be baptized by you, and do you come to me?' " (Matthew 3:14, NIV).

"Jesus replied, 'Let it be so now; it is proper for us to do this to fulfill all righteousness.' Then John consented" (verse 15, NIV). He led Jesus down into the water, where he baptized Him by immersion. Having never sinned, Jesus did not need to be baptized as a symbol of confession for sin. By being baptized He identified Himself with the sinner, who needs God's righteousness. He set an example for those who desire to confess their sins and be united with Him.

In Acts 8:26-39, we find the story of one of the seven deacons, Philip, baptizing an Ethiopian government official by immersion. Apparently this official was a Jewish proselyte who had gone to Jerusalem to worship. He had not come to an understanding as yet that Jesus was the Messiah. On his way home, he was studying the Old Testament book of Isaiah, reading the inspiring Messianic prophecies of the fifty-third chapter. He longed to understand their meaning.

Philip, an eminently successful missionary worker in Samaria, when directed to the Ethiopian by a heavenly messenger, opened to him the great truths of redemption that had come through the Messiah Isaiah had predicted. When the Ethiopian understood about Jesus, Philip must have revealed to him also what was present truth in his day—joining the developing Christian church and being baptized. The official inquired, " 'See, here is water! What is to prevent my being baptized?' And he [Philip] commanded the chariot to stop, and they both went down into the water, Philip and the eunuch, and he baptized him" (Acts 8:37, 38, RSV). This record provides another clear instance of baptism by immersion in the early church.

What baptism signifies

By baptism we (1) confess our faith in the death and resurrection of Jesus Christ, (2) testify of our death to sin and of our purpose to walk in newness of life, (3) acknowledge Christ as our Lord and Saviour, and (4) are received as members by His church.

Baptism is not an option to the converted Christian, nor is it to be taken lightly. Romans 6:3-10 elaborates on the above points by demonstrating that: we are immersed as a symbol of our death to the old man of sin, we are raised from the water in the likeness of Jesus' resurrection, and being freed from sin, we then live a new life unto God.

Baptism testifies that the Holy Spirit has taken up His abode with us. Through His guidance and work on our hearts, we have acknowledged and repented of our sins and desire to live a new life in Jesus. Baptism has no meaning unless it testifies publicly to what the Holy Spirit already has done in us to enable us to become members of the family of God. No one should seek to become a member of the church without baptism. Baptism attests to our union with Christ in the same way that the wedding service acknowledges publicly that two people have decided to devote their lives to each other. At baptism we take public vows that are just as sacred as wedding vows, testifying to the world that from that moment on, we belong to Christ and to His church family.

The purpose of this public witness is demonstrated by Mr. Peng, who attended evangelistic meetings held by Pastor Milton Lee in Taiwan. This Chinese gentleman was convinced that the Seventh-day Adventist Church was the true church but did not become a member.

A few months ago Mr. Peng learned he had cancer. It was felt he would only live about three months. He came to Taiwan Adventist Hospital for medical care. While there he met Mrs. Syau, a Bible worker. With tears streaming down his face, Mr. Peng declared his love for the Lord. "I should have been baptized years ago. I want God to forgive me. I want to be baptized now," he said.

Remembering that Elder Lee was visiting in Taiwan for a few weeks, Mrs. Syau invited him to visit Mr. Peng. Struggling for each breath, Mr. Peng told Elder Lee of his decision to be baptized.

Elder Lee shared the story of the thief on the cross and how God knew his heart even if he was not baptized. But in spite of his pain Mr. Peng persisted. "I want to be baptized."

Arrangements were made for the baptism. It was a touching service. A special peace now encircled Mr. Peng. His breathing became easier and his pain seemed to subside. His family noticed the difference. He seemed to rest in the assurance of God's love. The next day he closed his eyes in death.

At the funeral, Mrs. Peng, a devout Buddhist, said, "I

also want to be baptized before Elder Lee leaves this island." The son-in-law added, "Our whole family wants to be baptized."

Mr. Peng's example led his family to accept God's love and forgiveness for their sins. Now the entire Peng family is awaiting the return of the Life Giver (Carolyn Byers, "I Want to Be Baptized," Far Eastern Division *Outlook*, October 1987, p. 14).

Christ's death ratified the new covenant. By the terms of that covenant He will do for us what we cannot do for ourselves—write His laws on the fleshy tables of our hearts, making it possible for us to do His will. As Jesus does this for us, we enter into a covenant relationship with Him, receiving the fulfillment of His covenant promise that "I will be their God, and they shall be My people" (Jeremiah 31:33, NKJV). We are not our own. We belong to Him because He has paid the price of our salvation (see 1 Corinthians 6:19, 20). In every sense we have become His beloved sons and daughters and take upon ourselves the responsibility of demonstrating to the world about us what it means, by His help, to live as children of the royal family of the universe. They see that if we can do it by God's grace, they can too.

In Japan in the 1950s, much excitement was created when Crown Prince Akihito became engaged to Michiko Shoda. Their pictures were displayed everywhere. Magazines, newspapers, and television vied with one another to present the details of how this couple had met on a tennis court and fallen in love. For the first time a member of Japan's royal family was marrying a commoner. Those watching when Michiko's father was interviewed on television were surprised that he did not seem happy about what was happening. Although he was wealthy, he felt his daughter's upcoming marriage into the royal family and her future role as empress of Japan placed too much responsibility on his family. Even though Michiko had been educated in some of the best schools in Japan, she had to attend a special school for two years to learn how to properly represent her new family and serve as empress. Everything Michiko did was subjected to intense scrutiny to see whether she would measure up to her new responsibility.

We, too, are challenged after baptism, as adopted sons and daughters of the heavenly King, to live in a manner that befits our new royal status. It cost Christ everything to provide the crowns He earned for us. It will cost us something to wear them. We should be grateful and willing to live in such a way that we bring only honor and praise to heaven's royal family, of which we now are a part.

Our new status is outlined in 1 John 3:2: "Beloved, now are we the sons of God." As God's children we may be living on earth right now, but we belong in heaven as members of the royal family of the universe. This verse also promises, "We shall be like him; for we shall see him as he is." Verse 3 adds: "Every man that hath this hope in him purifieth himself, even as he is pure." The purpose of the atonement in heaven is not only to make us "at one" with God as members of the royal family, but to make us "at one" with Him in character. It is our privilege and responsibility as sons and daughters of God to uphold and vindicate His name and character before the universe.

The baptism of the Holy Spirit

The Adventist statement of fundamental belief says: "Baptism is a symbol of our union with Christ, the forgiveness of our sins, and our reception of the Holy Spirit." Matthew 3:16, 17 relates that at Jesus' baptism, the Holy Spirit descended upon Him in the form of a dove. We may not see the dove descending when we are baptized, but we should know that the Holy Spirit is being placed upon us as beloved sons and daughters of God, bringing us those gifts that will be necessary to our service for the Lord.

In John's report of Jesus' nighttime conversation with Nicodemus, the Saviour linked baptism by water with the baptism of the Spirit (see John 3:5-8). The baptism of the Holy Spirit is as essential as baptism by water. Why?

In the same way that the Spirit descended on Christ at His baptism to anoint and give Him special power for His assigned mission, at the time of our baptism, the Spirit brings us special power and gifts to fill the place God has ordained for us in the work of leading men and women to Christ and in helping to nourish them after they have united their lives to His.

When should people be baptized?

The statement of belief about baptism adds: It is "contingent on an affirmation of faith in Jesus and evidence of repentance of sin. It follows instruction in the Holy Scriptures and acceptance of their teachings."

Paul writes: "All of you who were baptized into Christ have clothed yourselves with Christ" (Galatians 3:27, NASB).

Baptism by immersion beautifully symbolizes a person's conversion experience. Involved in that experience are both sorrow for sin and turning away from it. The confessing sinner is forgiven and given new life in Christ. All these steps should precede baptism.

A newborn child cannot take these steps; therefore, Adventists do not believe in infant baptism or in the concept that underlies it—that babies are guilty of sin when they are born. We believe newborn infants have sinful natures, but they do not sin until they do so by conscious choice.

Adventists believe that a baptismal candidate should be instructed thoroughly in the basic precepts of the Adventist faith as outlined in this book. If this is not carried out, the new member cannot be expected conscientiously to practice the faith, for he or she has not received clear instruction as to what is expected of those who have been baptized.

What is the earliest age at which children should be baptized? At the age when they understand their accountability to God and are able to make an informed decision to give their lives to Him and join His church. Adventists have no fixed minimum age for baptism. Some children reach spiritual maturity before others do. When there is evidence that the child is mature enough to take responsibility for spiritual growth and character development and demonstrates a good understanding of what baptism means, we consider that child ready for this ordinance. When children are baptized, they become full-fledged members of the church, sharing all the privileges and responsibilities of membership.

What about rebaptism?

Sometimes college-age young people wonder whether they need to be rebaptized because they know so much more about Christ and His teachings than when they came into the church as children. Generally speaking, they need not be if theirs was a decision to be baptized because they loved Jesus and were sincere in their desire to give their lives to Him. If it were necessary to be baptized every time we realize we know much more about Christ and His truth than we once knew, most of us would have to be baptized quite often.

There is, however, a Bible precedent for rebaptism in the book of Acts (see Acts 19:1-5). In presenting the subject of rebaptism to those who have not up to this point been keeping the commandments of God fully, we need to allow the divine hand to lead them and the divine Spirit to impress their hearts as to what they ought to do.

But it is not necessary to be rebaptized every time we commit what seems to be a sin for which we have a hard time forgiving ourselves, because the ordinance of foot washing has been given as a rebaptismal service that cleanses us from the sins of our daily walk. Jesus' discussion with Peter in John 13:8-10 becomes particularly appropriate in this respect. Because the ordinance of foot washing is a rebaptismal service, Peter did not need to be immersed again for the forgiveness of his sins.

Just as baptism by water in the days of John the Baptist prepared people for Jesus' coming, baptism by water and the Spirit helps prepare Jesus' loved ones for His second coming. To those who have not as yet taken this step in their Christian experience, the Holy Spirit challenges, "And now why tarriest thou? arise, and be baptized, and wash away thy sins, calling on the name of the Lord" (Acts 22:16).

Chapter 15

The Humble Remember

How easy it is to forget that Jesus Christ is our Creator and Redeemer! Our tendency as humans is to imagine that we can craft our personalities and characters in the mold that we like best, with little awareness of our total dependence on a power beyond ourselves. One of the major teachings that Jesus attempted to impart to His disciples by both precept and example was that without Him they could never be productive servants of God and humanity.

When self-respect becomes pride, it not only destroys credibility but also cripples meaningful human relationships, undermining growth toward genuine usefulness. Only as we turn to Christ can we gain the capacity to evaluate our strengths and weaknesses realistically.

During his campaign for the presidency of the United States, Adlai Stevenson one day took a taxi to an airport. He introduced himself to the cabdriver and struck up a conversation with him.

"People say I talk over the head of the average man," Mr. Stevenson observed. "What do you think?"

The cabdriver thought for a few seconds and responded, "Well, Governor, I understand you, but I'm not sure about the average man."

Religious people who would not think of performing a wrong act are sometimes unduly enamored of their own goodness and humility. The late Professor Irwin Edman, of Columbia University, once had a conversation with a French monk. The monk complained that his order could not match the Jesuits for scholarship, nor could they equal the Trappists for silence and good works. "But," he added, "when it comes to humility, we're tops."

The truly great are always humble. There are many brilliant people whose contribution to their particular profession we much admire. But greatness is not synonymous with brilliance. Greatness is a matter of noble character, and, in the final analysis, greatness of character is a gift of God.

The genius of Copernicus revolutionized humankind's understanding of the universe. However, he viewed himself not as a great scholar and astronomer, but as a sinner in need of a Saviour. On his tombstone is carved the epitaph he wrote: "I do not seek a kindness equal to that given to Paul. Nor do I ask the grace granted to Peter. But that forgiveness which Thou didst grant to the robber—that, earnestly I crave!"

How is humility taught?

Humility is caught more effectively than it is taught. Jesus attempted to teach His disciples to be humble, and on a number of occasions He effectively illustrated it. But it was not until He gave them a personal demonstration that they caught on. Then they were so shamed by the contrast between their self-seeking and His unselfishness that their lives were changed.

Throughout Jesus' ministry, the disciples were persistently afflicted by an exaggerated impression of their own importance. They loved Jesus, believing sincerely that He was the Messiah and earnestly involving themselves in His ministry to their compatriots. But the lingering thought that He was about to become the ruler of an earthly kingdom kept alive for each of them the desire to be next to Him in authority. Each of them saw himself as a first-class prime minister.

As they approached Capernaum on one occasion, the disciples, lagging behind Jesus somewhat, were embroiled in a heated discussion as to who should occupy the highest position. "And they came to Capernaum; and when he was in the house he asked them, 'What were you discussing on the way?' But they were silent; for on the way they had discussed with one another who was the greatest" (Mark 9:33, 34, RSV). Jesus knew the subject of their conversation but wanted them to confess it.

Jesus called a child and took him in His arms. " 'Truly, I say to you,' " He said, " 'unless you turn and become like children, you will never enter the kingdom of heaven. Whoever humbles himself like this child, he is the greatest in the kingdom of heaven' " (Matthew 18:3, 4, RSV). Jesus was not urging them to become childish; His concern was that in attitude they should emulate the trusting dependence of a little child. If they could only be aware of their need of divine strength, they would have less confidence in their own capacity to lead and more confidence in Christ's ability to direct the affairs of His church. Distrust of self and total trust in Christ neutralize the desire to rise above others in status.

Unfortunately, the disciples did not assimilate the lesson. When the mother of James and John, with their full connivance, requested that they should sit one on Jesus' right and the other on His left in the kingdom, the rest of the disciples were indignant (see Matthew 20:20-24). Jesus could not make any such promise, even though the two brothers were confident that they were qualified to "drink" of the cup that Jesus was to drink of. How little they understood!

At that time Jesus stated a principle that should govern all our relationships within the Christian church:

"You know that the rulers of the Gentiles lord it over them, and their great men exercise authority over them. It shall not be so among you; but whoever would be great among you must be your servant, and whoever would be first among you must be your slave; even as the Son of man came not to be served but to serve, and to give his life as a ransom for many" (Matthew 20:25-28, RSV).

You see, Jesus' concept of greatness was willingness to render humble service. His ministry constantly demonstrated that principle. Kindness, acceptance, compassion, healing, and restoration were the watchwords of His ministry. But the disciples were slow to learn.

The night before He was crucified, Jesus ate the Passover with

His disciples and instituted the Lord's Supper. As they came into the dining room, the disciples could have expected a servant to pour water into a basin and wash their dusty feet. But there was no servant—except Jesus! He laid aside His outer garment, girded Himself with a towel, poured water into a basin, and washed the feet of each disciple in turn (see John 13:1-11).

Imagine their embarrassment! Jesus was the Messiah—God in human flesh. It was their role, not His, to act the part of a servant. But their pride had restrained them. No one who adopted such a role could be prime minister of the new kingdom—unless, of course, as they now discovered, the King regarded Himself as a servant. That put a new construction on the whole argument. If greatness consists of humility rather than status, then they wanted to be humble. Now, deploring their clamoring ambition, they saw their weakness exposed by Christ's greatness.

The ordinance of humility

Christ's practical example was reinforced by earnest counsel. What He had done, they were to do on a regular basis. " 'Do you know what I have done to you?' " He said. " 'You call me Teacher and Lord; and you are right, for so I am. If I then, your Lord and Teacher, have washed your feet, you also ought to wash one another's feet. For I have given you an example, that you also should do as I have done to you' " (John 13:12-15, RSV).

Jesus' point was not only that, in similar circumstances, the disciples should wash one another's feet but also that as a regular feature Christians should practice foot washing as an ordinance of humility. He added, " 'If you know these things, blessed are you if you do them' " (verse 17, RSV).

"More was meant than the washing of the feet of guests to remove the dust of travel. Christ was here instituting a religious service. By the act of our Lord this humiliating ceremony was made a consecrated ordinance. It was to be observed by the disciples, that they might ever keep in mind His lessons of humility and service" (Ellen G. White, *The Desire of Ages*, p. 650).

Jesus explained the meaning of the ordinance of humility while He was washing Peter's feet. Peter had objected to his

Lord's stooping to perform such a menial, humiliating task. But Jesus said, " 'If I do not wash you, you have no part in me' " (John 13:8, RSV). With characteristic forthrightness, Peter responded, " 'Lord, not my feet only, but also my hands and my head!' " (verse 9). But Jesus explained, " 'He who has bathed does not need to wash, except for his feet, but he is clean all over' " (verse 10, RSV).

Clearly the washing of Peter's feet symbolized a higher, spiritual washing. Unless he submitted to having his feet washed, Peter could have no part with Jesus, because the higher cleansing symbolized is absolutely essential to salvation. This is the "washing of rebirth and renewal by the Holy Spirit, whom he poured out on us generously through Jesus Christ our Savior, so that, having been justified by his grace, we might become heirs having the hope of eternal life" (Titus 3:5-7, NIV).

Before we approach the Lord's Supper, we enter into the ordinance of humility. The stains of sin need to be removed before we partake of the symbols of Christ's sacrifice. Our hearts need to be brought into union with Him and with our fellow believers. By humbling ourselves in service to others, our desire for status and honor is replaced by the love and gentleness of Jesus. As we copy Him, He takes possession of our hearts by the Holy Spirit, and we come to the Lord's Supper table purified vessels for His greater infilling.

The institution of the Lord's Supper

The Passover supper that Jesus and His disciples came together to celebrate the night before His crucifixion pointed back to God's deliverance of the Israelites from Egyptian slavery (see Exodus 12). It also pointed forward to the sacrificial death of the Messiah for the sins of the world. The Passover lamb represented Jesus, " 'the Lamb of God, who takes away the sin of the world!' " (John 1:29, RSV). The sprinkling of the blood of the Passover lamb on the two doorposts and the lintel of the Israelite houses in Egypt (see Exodus 12:7) symbolized the entire consecration of their hearts, and ours, to Christ. The blood protected them from the destroying angel as Christ's blood shelters us.

The unleavened bread the Israelites were to eat in the Passover celebration symbolized lives without sin. Leaven is a symbol of sin. Paul developed the symbolism: "Cleanse out the old leaven that you may be a new lump, as you really are unleavened. For Christ, our paschal lamb, has been sacrificed. Let us, therefore, celebrate the festival [the Lord's Supper], not with the old leaven, the leaven of malice and evil, but with the unleavened bread of sincerity and truth" (1 Corinthians 5:7, 8, RSV).

Jesus took some of the food that had been placed on the table for the Passover meal and used it to institute the Lord's Supper, the memorial of His sacrifice and a foretaste of the great marriage supper of the Lamb that will be celebrated in the heavenly kingdom (see Revelation 19:9). The Passover pointed back to the deliverance from Egypt and forward to Christ's death. The Lord's Supper points back to Christ's death and forward to His final redemption of His believing people.

"As they were eating, Jesus took bread, and blessed, and broke it, and gave it to the disciples and said, 'Take, eat; this is my body' " (Matthew 26:26, RSV). Notice that the bread Jesus took was already on the table. We know it was unleavened bread because that was the only kind of bread used in Passover celebrations. Paul underlined the importance of using only unleavened bread in the Lord's Supper when he urged that believers should celebrate the service "with the unleavened bread of sincerity and truth" (1 Corinthians 5:8, RSV). As sin has been put away during the ordinance of humility, so the symbol of sin is to be absent from the bread that we partake of in the Lord's Supper. Moreover, because the bread represents the body of our Lord, no symbol of sin should be present in it. It must be unleavened bread.

Next, Jesus "took a cup, and when he had given thanks he gave it to them, saying, 'Drink of it, all of you' " (Matthew 26:27, RSV). The wine that Jesus gave to His disciples was unfermented juice of the grape. In the time of Moses, God had instructed Aaron, the high priest, that he and his sons were not to drink wine or strong drink before approaching the tabernacle. "The Lord spoke to Aaron, saying, 'Drink no wine nor strong drink, you nor your sons with you, when you go into the tent of meeting, lest you die; it shall be a statute for ever throughout your generations' " (Leviticus 10:8, 9, RSV). In instituting the Lord's Supper, Jesus did not contradict the commands that He and His Father had given to the Israelite priests long before. As the Passover Sacrifice and the future High Priest, Jesus used unfermented wine.

The spiritual meaning of the Lord's Supper

When He gave the bread to His disciples, Jesus said, " 'Take, eat; this is my body' " (Matthew 26:26, RSV). When He gave the wine, He said, " 'This is my blood' " (verse 28). Medieval interpreters and some today think Jesus meant that the "substance" of His body and blood is literally present in the bread and wine. They think that when they partake of the Lord's Supper, they are eating the literal body and blood of Christ.

The difficulty, of course, is that Jesus was physically present when He gave the bread and the wine to the disciples. His flesh and blood were very much intact; the disciples were not partaking of it. Obviously they knew that the bread and wine were *symbols* of His spiritual presence in their hearts and of His sacrifice, even though at that time they did not understand that He was to die the next day. They could not have interpreted Jesus to mean that they should eat His literal flesh and drink His literal blood.

In explaining the significance of the wine, Jesus added: " 'This is my blood of the covenant, which is poured out for many for the forgiveness of sins' " (Matthew 26:28, RSV). The covenant is the everlasting covenant of righteousness by faith in Christ, made possible by His death upon the cross. For the believer, there are three parts to this covenant: (1) forgiveness for the past; (2) spiritual power for the present; and (3) eternal life in the future. By accepting Jesus as Saviour and Lord, we are forgiven for sin (see Acts 13:38, 39), given power to overcome sin (see 1 John 5:4), and granted the gift of eternal life (see John 3:36).

Jesus beautifully explained the meaning of the Lord's Supper in His teaching recorded in John, chapter 6. Jesus said, " 'Truly, truly, I say to you, unless you eat the flesh of the Son of man and drink his blood, you have no life in you; he who eats my flesh and drinks my blood has eternal life, and I will raise him up at the last day' " (verses 53, 54, RSV).

Jesus was not inviting His listeners to partake of His literal flesh and blood. He explained the symbolic nature of His sermon when He added: " 'It is the spirit that gives life, the flesh is of no avail; the words that I have spoken to you are spirit and life' " (John 6:63, RSV). We partake of Jesus' flesh and blood when we receive His words into our hearts. The Holy Spirit is the One who explains Jesus' words to us and writes them on our hearts. Jesus said, " 'He will guide you into all the truth' " (John 16:13, RSV). The Holy Spirit in our hearts is the presence of Christ in our hearts (see Romans 8:9, 10). And His presence is righteousness in our hearts.

When we come to the Lord's Supper, we come with rejoicing because our sins have been forgiven, and we are partaking of the symbols of Christ's presence in our hearts. We eat His flesh and drink His blood in a spiritual sense. Christ becomes our righteousness within because we remember His death and humbly accept Him as our ever-present Lord.

Have you found Jesus as the power for true humility? Have you committed your life to His care? Do you partake of His Word by receiving His Spirit into your heart every day and in the Lord's Supper service? Jesus' love for you and me is as infinite as was His love for His first disciples. Let us advance together in the Christian walk so that soon we can enjoy together the marriage supper of the Lamb (see Revelation 19:9).

Chapter 16

What More Can He Do?

Probably no Old Testament passage clarifies the extent of God's love for us more than His plaintive plea in Isaiah 5, "What more can I do?" It is found in the midst of a haunting passage:

Now will I sing to my well-beloved a song of my beloved touching his vineyard. My well-beloved hath a vineyard in a very fruitful hill: and he fenced it, and gathered out the stones thereof, and planted it with the choicest vine, and built a tower in the midst of it, and also made a winepress therein: and he looked that it should bring forth grapes, and it brought forth wild grapes. And now, O inhabitants of Jerusalem, and men of Judah, judge, I pray you, betwixt me and my vineyard. What could have been done more to my vineyard, that I have not done in it? wherefore, when I looked that it should bring forth grapes, brought it forth wild grapes? (Isaiah 5:1-4).

God's tender care not only led Israel into the Promised Land, but God had also given them every privilege and possibility. Yet they spurned what He had done and were captivated by the idolatry of their neighbors. How His heart yearned for them to turn to Him and gain all the blessings He was longing to bestow!

When Jesus retold the parable of the vineyard, He demonstrated that God *was* able to do something more for His people.

There was a certain householder, which planted a vineyard, and hedged it round about, and digged a winepress in it, and built a tower, and let it out to husbandmen, and went into a far country: and when the time of the fruit drew near, he sent his servants to the husbandmen, that they might receive the fruits of it. And the husbandmen took his servants, and beat one, and killed another, and stoned another. Again, he sent other servants more than the first: and they did unto them likewise. But last of all he sent unto them his son, saying, They will reverence my son. But when the husbandmen saw the son, they said among themselves, This is the heir; come, let us kill him, and let us seize on his inheritance. And they caught him, and cast him out of the vineyard, and slew him. When the lord therefore of the vineyard cometh, what will he do unto those husbandmen? (Matthew 21:33-40).

Notice the words *last of all*. It would seem that, after God had given His Son, He would have exhausted all that heaven could do for God's people on earth. He gave His dearly beloved Son to the human race, to be one of us for all eternity. What more can God do?

But even then, infinite mercy was not exhausted. Paul tells us that "when he ascended up on high, he led captivity captive, and gave gifts unto men" (Ephesians 4:8). What gifts? Later in the chapter the apostle enumerates some of the spiritual gifts. It is just not God's nature for there to be a limit to His giving. The only limit is our willingness and ability to receive.

More power available

Suppose you and a few of your friends had the privilege of meeting Christ, and He said to you, "What I want you to do is to carry the gospel to the entire world." What would you think? What would you do about it? His commission would seem impossible for a small group to accomplish, wouldn't it? But when He first gave that commission to a very small group of individuals, they took it seriously. They realized that they could not fulfill His commission on their own. But He had promised to give them the power of the Holy Spirit to do what seemed impossible.

There are so many more of us today. But do we sometimes throw up our hands at the seeming impossibility of world evangelism? We need not do so. Christ's promise of power to fulfill His commission was given just as much for us as it was for His early disciples. What is more, He has promised the special latter-rain power of the Holy Spirit to us to enable us to finish His work. Our problem is not a lack of power, but lack of faith to put it to work. God still has something *more* to give to His people.

When Christ left this world, He gave an overwhelming task to His church to accomplish. The work assigned would be impossible unless Christ gave some specific, spectacular, and miraculous means of fulfilling it. As indicated in Ephesians 4:8-11, Christ's plan was that everyone receiving the Holy Spirit would receive a spiritual gift that could be used for ministry.

Verse 11 contains a partial list of those gifts: "He gave some, apostles; and some, prophets; and some, evangelists; and some, pastors and teachers." God blesses His people with these gifts of ministry. The last one in the list usually is divided into two— pastor-teachers. Actually, the Greek lists this gift as being that given to "shepherds and teachers." The pastor or shepherd is necessarily a teacher, and the teacher also must be a shepherd or pastor of the flock God has given him or her to nurture.

Verse 12 is the heart of the entire message found in Ephesians 4. It is of great importance for us to understand what God is telling us here. Because the construction is somewhat awkward in the King James Version, this verse can be misleading. It suggests that Christ has three different reasons for giving the gifts of ministry to His church:

1. For perfecting of the saints.
2. For the work of ministry.
3. For edifying the body of Christ.

But there actually is just one reason spelled out here. Verse 12 literally says, "With a view to the mending of the saints for the purpose of the work of ministry unto the house building of the body of Christ."

Here we see that evangelism is the natural byproduct of discipleship. First, there must be the "perfecting of the saints," or, literally, the "mending." The word used here is most often used for mending of nets. It is a metaphor that carries the idea of restoring those overtaken in a fault. When the saints are restored to what Christ wants them to be, they will not only grow and mature in Christ but will also reach out to share what they have received with others.

"The work of the ministry" comes from the word for *deacons*. The kind of ministry being emphasized here is servant ministry. And it is pointed toward "edifying"—the Greek indicates "house building"—building up the body of Christ.

The implication of what we have just studied is that every member of the church is to be a "minister." We have different gifts but are to use them to minister for Christ.

In a fascinating article on this topic in the May/June 1986 issue of *Worker*, Floyd Bresee writes:

> The church is like an orchestra. Each member of the orchestra is gifted. You are not supposed to be in the orchestra unless you are gifted. People are not meant by our Lord to be in the church until they have the Holy Spirit which brings them gifts. These gifts are different. Just as the violin is different from the tympani, the gift of evangelism is different from the gift of hospitality. As a church we make a grave mistake when we develop the gift of evangelism but do nothing to develop the gift of hospitality. If evangelism brings people into the church but hospitality does not keep them there, there is not much sense in bringing them into the church in the first place.
>
> If we compare the church to an orchestra, the pastor is the conductor. It is not the business of the conductor to make the music. The conductor is to help each member of the orchestra play their instrument. Too many Adventist pastors are one-man bands. They want to make all the music. Then they wonder why the music does not attract. What is the conductor for? He does two things. (1) He inspires. The pastor should inspire the congregation. (2) The conductor coordinates. He says, "Tympani, now it is your turn. Violinist, it is your turn. We have too much trombone." Inspiring and coordinating the

members of the church are the work of the pastor.

The work of higher levels of church leadership is to train the gifted musicians and provide all the tools necessary for them to make music (p. 20).

The purpose of the gifts

Thus we see that God bestows on every member of His church some spiritual gift or gifts that the members are to employ in loving ministry for the church and for the world. These gifts are given to us through the agency of the Holy Spirit. The Spirit does not give everyone the same gifts, but apportions them to each member as He wills. Collectively, however, these gifts provide all the abilities and ministries needed by the church to fulfill the commission God has given to it.

The Scriptures list such gifts as faith, healing, prophecy, proclamation, teaching, administration, reconciliation, compassion, and self-sacrificing service and charity that will help and encourage people. Some members are called of God and endowed by the Spirit for those pastoral, evangelistic, apostolic, and teaching ministries that particularly are needed to equip the members for service, with a view to mending the saints for the work of ministry unto the house building of the body of Christ. They foster the unity of the faith and knowledge of God. When members employ these spiritual gifts properly, the church will be protected from the destructive influence of false doctrine and will be built up in faith and love.

Believers who fail to use the spiritual gifts God has given them will face the consequences of one of the great laws of life that God has given—use it or lose it. They also will be held accountable by God in the judgment for not using the talents God has given them (see Matthew 25:26-30).

Discovering our spiritual gifts

How do we discover which gift or gifts God has given us? The first step is to become acquainted with the gifts listed by Paul (see Romans 12:6-8; 1 Corinthians 12:4-11, 28-31; 13:1-3, 13; Ephesians 4:7-11). It probably would be helpful to form a small study group to share together the study of the biblical topic of spiritual gifts.

The following list briefly explains what these gifts are:

1. Gifted People:

Apostles. Although this title is not used in our church today, it means "sent-out one," referring especially to those commissioned to represent the church in a broader ministry. It could be applied to church leaders and others called to minister to the world field.

Missionaries. Those given the ability to minister across cultures.

Prophets. A special and unique gift given to about eighty people in the history of the world. God speaks through persons specially selected by the Holy Spirit, giving them messages for His church.

Evangelists. Those given the ability to persuasively present the gospel in a way that leads others to become disciples of Christ.

Pastor-teachers. Those given the ability to shepherd, counsel, and encourage believers, and to search out and validate truth effectively and teach God's Word clearly.

2. Gifts:

Knowledge. The ability to recall a fund of knowledge from God's Word to meet particular needs.

Wisdom. The ability to penetrate into a matter, seeing the larger relationships, and to impart wise counsel.

Healing. The ability to call upon the healing power of God in such a way that persons in need receive physical, mental, social, and spiritual healing.

Discernment of spirits. The ability to distinguish between truth and error and the influence of good and evil angels.

Giving, helps, sacrifice. The ability to share what God has given us joyfully and eagerly with those in need.

Administration, leadership. The ability to organize, plan, and lead the body of Christ toward its divinely appointed goals.

Showing mercy, comfort, compassion. The ability to identify with, comfort, and help those who are in trouble or distress.

Willingness to serve under others. The ability to be a loyal and supportive follower of those chosen to lead.

Miracles. The ability to perform supernatural acts that glorify God through His power.

Tongues. The ability to speak in a foreign language not previously learned.

Interpretation of tongues. The ability to interpret the above so that people will be edified.

3. Abiding (Lasting) Gifts:

Faith. Special, unswerving confidence in God.

Hope. An anchor to the soul.

Love. God's kind of agape love.

As you go through this list, you and those studying with you will want to ask yourselves which gift or gifts the Spirit most likely has given you. When you have your personal list, you will need to look for affirmation from other Spirit-led church members. If God has called and gifted you for some area of service, others will notice and probably will confirm your gift.

However, if you receive no such affirmation or find drudgery in putting what you consider to be your gift to work, perhaps you need to rethink the question of what gifts you have been given.

"God equips His Spirit-filled people to be the channels through whom He can pour the rich resources of heaven upon those in need—in the church and out. One of the most thrilling discoveries a Christian can make is to see God's kingdom extended and humbly acknowledge, 'God used me there' " (Don Jacobsen, "What Spiritual Gifts Mean to Me," *Adventist Review*, 25 December 1986, pp. 12, 13).

The Lord has given each of us special gifts to use for His service. What a joy it is to discover these gifts and to put them to use in a way that He can bless!

Chapter 17

A True Prophet

Seventh-day Adventists accept Ellen G. White (1827-1915) as a genuine modern prophet because she passes all the Bible tests and specifications. Nevertheless, throughout the history of the Seventh-day Adventist Church, Ellen White's claim to receive special revelations from the Lord has been violently attacked, and her life and character have been subjected to close, and often unfair, criticism. Many have questioned whether her interpretations of Scripture can be trusted. Others charge that Seventh-day Adventists' doctrinal beliefs and prophetic interpretations cannot be substantiated from Scripture alone. Without Ellen White's writings, they say, Adventism as a theological system cannot be demonstrated.

Yet every one of the Bible doctrines discussed in this volume is taught by Ellen White. Not only are her writings entirely consistent with Scripture, they are specifically designed to lead the reader to turn to the Bible for salvation and spiritual guidance.

Every major criticism directed at Ellen White may also be leveled at Bible writers. Although she was a person of irreproachable character, she was a faulty human being; so were the Bible writers. Her writings contain some discrepancies; so do theirs. She sometimes misunderstood God's communications to her; so did they. She used uninspired literary sources to help her convey her messages; so did they. She did not always acknowledge the sources that she used in writing her books; nor did they.

Every doctrine taught in the writings of Ellen White is found in the Bible. The influence of her work and writings has always been spiritually positive. Her prophetic forecasts have been and are being fulfilled. Ellen White's writings encourage full acceptance of the Christian message by exalting the genuine Deity and full humanity of Jesus Christ and the enormous significance of Calvary for the salvation of humanity.

There is no substitute for reading Ellen White's books for oneself. Accepting people's criticisms without reading the author's works yourself is to be ruled by prejudice. The only fair way to judge the effectiveness, Christian consistency, and doctrinal purity of any author is to read his or her works personally. Read carefully *Steps to Christ*, *Christ's Object Lessons*, and *Thoughts From the Mount of Blessing*. Compare them with the Bible. Read the Conflict of the Ages Series: *Patriarchs and Prophets*, *Prophets and Kings*, *The Desire of Ages*, *The Acts of the Apostles*, and *The Great Controversy*. You will discover, as many have, that these books contain the hallmarks of inspiration.

Let us now compare Ellen White's life and work with that of Bible prophets. We will demonstrate that, although she taught that her writings are not an addition to the sacred canon, nor are they to be used as a substitute for it, her claim that they came directly from God for the instruction and guidance of His people in these final days of earth's history is thoroughly reasonable.

Later inspired prophets are authoritative interpreters of earlier prophets

The evidence from Scripture demonstrates conclusively that prophets who were chosen by God in later centuries provided inspired interpretations of earlier prophetic writings. We accept these interpretations because they came from the Holy Spirit (see 2 Peter 1:20, 21).

Study Paul's interpretation of Moses' statements regarding works and faith (see Romans 10:5-8; Galatians 3:12; Leviticus 18:5; Deuteronomy 30:11-14). The apostle Paul twice quoted the statement found in Leviticus 18:5 that the person who obeys God's laws "shall live in them." Both Moses and Paul knew that anyone who always obeys all God's laws will have continuing life. But continuing life by law keeping is possible only if the law is never broken. Therefore, obtaining eternal life by law keeping is not possible for Israel, or any other earthly people, because all have sinned (see Romans 3:23).

Referring to God's laws, Moses, Ezekiel, and Nehemiah (see Leviticus 18:5; Nehemiah 9:29; Ezekiel 20:11, 13, 21) stated: "Which if a man do, he shall live in them." They meant that God wants His people, because of their faith in Him and covenant relationship with Him, to obey His laws. They meant that we will have spiritual life in the present, and eternal life, if we will obey God by faith. Their statement is not referring to righteousness by works but to the obedience expected by God on the part of His people who are living by faith in Him.

Paul relates Moses' statement to the righteousness-by-works problem of ancient Israel: "Moses describeth the righteousness which is of the law, That the man which doeth those things shall live by them" (Romans 10:5). Since achieving righteousness by keeping the law is impossible for fallen human beings, "Israel, which followed after the law of righteousness, hath not attained to the law of righteousness" (Romans 9:31). Paul's teaching is thoroughly consistent with the rest of Scripture. But he has given a different application than that given by Moses of the principle stated in Leviticus 18:5. When Moses said of God's laws, "Which if a man do, he shall live in them," he was not speaking of the attempt to earn salvation by human works. Moses meant that a person who lives by faith can keep God's laws, and that person will have life. Paul pointed out that the Israelites were trying to "live in them" (God's laws) without having faith. They were, therefore, failing to obey God's laws. The solution is to obey by faith in Jesus Christ.

No one who believes in the inspiration of Paul's writings doubts that his interpretation of Leviticus 18:5 is trustworthy and true, even though he used the principle stated there somewhat differently from the way it is used in the Old Testament. The Holy Spirit, speaking through the apostle Paul, has a perfect right to give applications to Bible passages that He deems appropriate. Because "holy men of God spake as they were moved by the Holy Ghost" (2 Peter 1:21), we can assume that Paul's use of Old Testament Scripture is consistent with the will of the Holy Spirit, even if it is not strictly in agreement with the original context of the Old Testament statement.

Because some contemporaries of Paul had serious doubts about his apostolic authority and the inspiration of his utterances, he was obliged to explain that his messages came from special revelations given by God (see 2 Corinthians 12:1-12). No doubt there were those who thought that accepting Paul's interpretations of Scripture would involve surrendering their own Spirit-directed capacity to draw conclusions regarding the meaning of the Old Testament. Careful thought would reveal to them that (1) the Holy Spirit never contradicts Himself, (2) Paul's interpretation of a passage was not presented as the only possible one, and (3) for them to reject Paul's interpretation as false would be to contradict, not man, but God.

Were the early Christians, therefore, in the position of having to regard Paul as a kind of pope? No. The pope of the Roman Catholic Church claims that his interpretations of the Bible are infallible when he speaks *ex cathedra*. He claims infallibility in determining the meaning of any theological work. By contrast, Paul did not deny the teaching ministry of the Holy Spirit for the individual Bible student. He did not claim, for example, that his interpretation of Leviticus 18:5 is the only possible one. The pope demands that Roman Catholics accept his scriptural interpretations and doctrinal pronouncements, even if they contradict the teachings of Bible writers. Paul's inspired utterances are always consistent with the rest of Scripture. Even when a canonical author under the inspiration of the Holy Spirit goes beyond the teaching of earlier prophets, he never discounts or contradicts their teachings. We accept Paul's claim to special revelation from God, but we do not accept the pope's.

In Romans 10:6-8, Paul quoted the Septuagint version (Greek Old Testament) of Deuteronomy 30:11-14, applying the passage to his righteousness-by-faith message. Paul's point is that, when Moses taught that God's law should be written on the human heart, he was teaching the same message of righteousness by faith that Paul proclaimed. Paul's interpretation is thoroughly correct. Moses emphasized that the law can be kept if it is written on the heart (see Deuteronomy 30:14), and elsewhere he taught that such an experience is possible only to the person who has faith in God (see Genesis 15:6; Deuteronomy 6:4-6).

Paul's doctrine of righteousness by faith (see Romans 1:16, 17) is supported by an accurate application of Habakkuk 2:4. "The just shall live by faith" is as much an Old Testament doctrine as a New Testament one.

In 1 Corinthians 9:9, Paul quotes Deuteronomy 25:4: " 'You shall not muzzle an ox when it is treading out the grain' " (RSV). Paul is giving inspired instruction that the ministry of the church should be supported financially and materially by the church members. But the Old Testament statement had a much more literal application. Mosaic law stipulated that oxen were to be permitted to eat the grain as they walked round and round in the threshing process. Paul uses the statement as an allegory. The oxen represent the ministry of the church. As the oxen were to be allowed to eat the grain that was the property of the owner, so the church's clergy are to be supported by receiving a percentage of the members' income. Paul does not contradict the original meaning of the passage, but his figurative application provides a convenient sermon illustration.

(For further New Testament uses of Old Testament passages, compare Galatians 4:22-24 with Genesis 16; 21. Compare Matthew 24:15 with Daniel 8:13; 9:27; 11:31. Compare Acts 2:17-21 with Joel 2:28-32. Compare Acts 2:25-28 with Psalm 16:8-11.)

The New Testament is, in part, an interpretation of the Old Testament. Later prophets received from the Holy Spirit interpretations of statements made by earlier prophets. We accept these applications, not because they conform strictly to the original interpretations, but because they were inspired by the Holy Spirit.

The relevance for the writings of Ellen G. White

Ellen White emphasized the Protestant doctrine that the Bible alone is the rule of our faith and practice.

The word of God is the standard by which all teaching and experience must be tested (*The Great Controversy*, p. vii).

God will have a people upon the earth to maintain the Bible, and the Bible only, as the standard of all doctrines and the basis of all reforms. The opinions of learned men, the deductions of science, the creeds or decisions of ecclesiastical councils, as numerous and discordant as are the churches which they represent, the voice of the majority— not one nor all of these should be regarded as evidence for or against any point of religious faith (*The Great Controversy*, p. 595).

The Bible, and the Bible alone, is to be our creed, the sole bond of union; all who bow to this Holy Word will be in harmony. Our own views and ideas must not control our efforts. Man is fallible, but God's Word is infallible. Instead of wrangling with one another, let men exalt the Lord. Let us meet all opposition as did our Master, saying, "It is written." Let us lift up the banner on which is inscribed, The Bible our rule of faith and discipline (*Selected Messages*, bk. 1, p. 416).

Let all prove their positions from the Scriptures and substantiate every point they claim as truth from the revealed Word of God (*Evangelism*, p. 256).

Ellen White never put her writings ahead of the Bible, nor did she regard herself as a canonical prophet whose writings should be regarded as an addition to the sacred canon.

The testimonies of Sister White should not be carried to the front. God's Word is the unerring standard. The Testimonies are not to take the place of the Word. . . .
Never do we want any soul to bring in the Testimonies ahead of the Bible. . . .
Little heed is given to the Bible, and the Lord has given a lesser light to lead men and women to the greater light (*Evangelism*, pp. 256, 257).

In His word the Lord has plainly revealed His will to

those who have riches. But because His direct commands have been slighted, He mercifully presents their dangers before them through the *Testimonies* [her writings]. He does not give new light, but calls their attention to the light that has already been revealed in His word (*Testimonies*, vol. 2, pp. 660, 661).

Even so, Ellen White regarded her writings as providing inspired interpretations of Scripture.

How many have read carefully *Patriarchs and Prophets*, *The Great Controversy*, and *The Desire of Ages*? I wish all to understand that my confidence in the light that God has given stands firm, because I know that the Holy Spirit's power magnified the truth, and made it honorable, saying: "This is the way, walk ye in it." In my books, the truth is stated, barricaded by a "Thus said the Lord." The Holy Spirit traced these truths upon my heart and mind as indelibly as the law was traced by the finger of God, upon the tables of stone, which are now in the ark, to be brought forth in that great day when sentence will be pronounced against every evil, seducing science produced by the father of lies. . . .

God would be pleased to see *The Desire of Ages* in every home. In this book is contained the light He has given upon His word (*Colporteur Ministry*, p. 126).

This is my work—to open the Scriptures to others as God has opened them to me (*Testimonies*, vol. 8, p. 236).

The testimonies God has given His people are in harmony with His word (*Testimonies to Ministers and Gospel Workers*, p. 402).

Describing how early in the history of the church she received interpretations of Scripture in vision, Ellen White wrote:

The power of God would come upon me, and I was

enabled clearly to define what is truth and what is error.

As the points of our faith were thus established, our feet were placed upon a solid foundation. We accepted the truth point by point, under the demonstration of the Holy Spirit (*Gospel Workers*, p. 302).

The Spirit of God would come upon me, I would be taken off in vision, and a clear explanation of the passage we had been studying would be given me. . . .

A line of truth extending from that time to the time when we shall enter the city of God, was plainly marked out before me (*This Day With God*, p. 317).

We can summarize the relevant points of her statements as follows:

1. Ellen White's interpretations of Scripture, like Paul's, were inspired by the Holy Spirit. Therefore, they are authoritative.

2. This does not mean that other interpretations of some passages, different from those of Ellen White's, may not also be correct. Paul undoubtedly would have accepted an interpretation of Deuteronomy 25:4 that was different from the one he presented in 1 Corinthians 9:9. Some passages of Scripture may be interpreted in a number of ways. Sometimes an inspired author provides interpretations that would not have occurred to us.

3. Like Paul, Ellen White sometimes takes passages of Scripture out of context and gives them meanings that would not result from a strict application of ordinary principles of exegesis or interpretation. Like the Bible writers, she sometimes adapts passages from other inspired authors or merely borrows their language as a convenient means of conveying her message (see, for example, her use of 1 Corinthians 2:9 in *Fundamentals of Christian Education*, page 49, and in *The Story of Redemption*, pages 430, 431).

4. Like Paul, Ellen White does not attempt to interpret the entire Scriptures, even though her teachings are consistent with it. In other words, there is still plenty of room for the

teaching ministry of the Holy Spirit to function in individual hearts and minds.

5. To deny the truthfulness of a particular scriptural interpretation given by Ellen White is to reject the teaching ministry of the Holy Spirit. Understandings given to Paul and Ellen White by the Spirit are inspired truth.

6. This does not mean that we have exalted Ellen White's authority above the Bible or that we have made her a pope. The pope claims he has the right to declare new doctrines that are not in the Bible. He also interprets Scripture consistently with the doctrinal understandings of the Catholic Church, even though the interpretations may be contradicted by inspired Bible writers. Ellen White's interpretations, like those of Paul, are in agreement with Scripture throughout, and never are her doctrinal statements a contradiction of previously revealed truth.

7. Because Paul was a canonical writer, it is acceptable for him to teach new doctrine given him by the Holy Spirit. On the other hand, the Bible records that there were many noncanonical prophets who, like Ellen White, were given inspired counsels that were not intended to be part of the sacred canon and yet were thoroughly consistent with it. Elijah, Elisha, Nathan, Gad, Deborah, and Huldah are typical examples. Some of these noncanonical prophets even wrote books that were accepted by Bible writers as authoritative (see 1 Chronicles 29:29; 2 Chronicles 9:29).

8. Like earlier noncanonical prophets, Ellen White has all of the same inspired authority that Paul possessed, except that she was not chosen to present any new doctrine. She was commissioned by the Lord to present Spirit-inspired interpretations of that which has long been revealed in the canonical Scriptures. Surely any message that comes directly from the Holy Spirit is authoritative truth. Such were the messages given to Ellen White.

Do prophets ever sin or make mistakes in their personal lives? Do they need to be corrected by the Lord?

Consider the sins of which David was guilty (see 2 Samuel

11:2-17; 12:7-9; 1 Chronicles 21:1-14). Read of Solomon's sin (see 1 Kings 11:1-14). Note how Peter sinned after the resurrection of Jesus (see Galatians 2:11-14). The apostle John taught that sin exists in the experience of every human being (see 1 John 1:8; compare Romans 3:23).

Commenting on the sins in the lives of these Bible writers, Ellen White wrote:

If they had been without foible they would have been more than human, and our sinful natures would despair of ever reaching such a point of excellence. But seeing where they struggled and fell, where they took heart again and conquered through the grace of God, we are encouraged, and led to press over the obstacles that degenerate nature places in our way (*Testimonies*, vol. 4, p. 12).

Writing of her own character weaknesses, Ellen White said:

I do not claim infallibility, or even perfection of Christian character. I am not free from mistakes and errors in my life. Had I followed my Saviour more closely, I should not have to mourn so much my unlikeness to His dear image (Letter 27, 1876 [quoted in Robert W. Olson, *One Hundred and One Questions on the Sanctuary and on Ellen White* (Washington, D.C.: General Conference, E. G. White Estate, 1981) p. 47]).

Ellen White was a godly woman whose character was often praised by those who did not believe in her prophetic role. Yet she was a faulty human being. Like Bible prophets, she grew spiritually by reliance on the Lord Jesus Christ.

Do the writings of prophets contain some mistakes in detail?

Although the divine truth they presented was infallible, Bible writers sometimes made mistakes in factual details that were not revealed by the Holy Spirit. (These discrepancies also may have been produced by copyists.) For example, the writer of the book of Judges identified Moses' father-in-law as Hobab (see Judges 4:11), whereas Hobab was Moses' brother-in-law. Moses' father-in-law was Reuel (see Exodus 2:16-21), or Raguel (see Numbers 10:29, KJV). No such minor discrepancy changes the teachings of the Bible one iota, nor does it have any bearing on the special message of the passage in which it is contained. The Holy Spirit gave the prophet an inspired message, which the prophet wrote in his own words. Obviously, there was room for human error.

Ellen White sometimes made mistakes, which in no way detracted from the inspired message she presented. *The Great Controversy* was not written as a history book. Historical details are used to contribute to the overall message. The *message* was given by the Lord, not the historical details. To criticize the book on the basis of certain historical discrepancies is to be diverted from the saving message of the book. In the introduction to *The Great Controversy*, Ellen White wrote:

As the Spirit of God has opened to my mind the great truths of His word, and the scenes of the past and the future, I have been bidden to make known to others that which has thus been revealed—to trace the history of the controversy in past ages, and especially so to present it as to shed a light on the fast-approaching struggle of the future (p. xi).

Ellen White's son, W. C. White, who worked with her for years, explained:

The framework of the great temple of truth sustained by her writings was presented to her clearly in vision. In some features of this work, information was given in detail. Regarding some features of the revelation, such as the features of prophetic chronology, as regards the ministration in the sanctuary and the changes that took place in 1844, the matter was presented to her many times and in detail many times, and this enabled her to speak very clearly and very positively regarding the foundation pillars of our faith.

In some of the historical matters such as are brought out in *Patriarchs and Prophets* and in *Acts of the Apostles*, and in *Great Controversy*, the main outlines were made very clear and plain to her, and when she came to write up these topics, she was left to study the Bible and history to get dates and geographical relations and to perfect her description of details (Letter to L. E. Froom, 13 December 1934, quoted in Appendix C of *Selected Messages*, bk. 3, p. 462).

Do prophets sometimes misunderstand the inspired messages given to them?

Because they are fallible human beings, it would be unusual if prophets did not sometimes misunderstand. For example, the vision of Daniel 8 was given in "the third year of the reign of king Belshazzar" (verse 1), the year 551 B.C. The events of Daniel 9 occurred in "the first year of Darius," or 538 B.C. Hence, there were thirteen years between the two visions. The first part of Daniel 9 indicates that Daniel had not understood the Daniel 8 vision. He could not reconcile the time prophecy of that vision with the seventy years of captivity predicted by Jeremiah (see Jeremiah 25:11). Daniel prayed to the Lord for understanding. The answer is recorded in Daniel 9:21-27. Gabriel came to explain to him the Daniel 8 vision. It is doubtful that even then Daniel understood fully the real significance of the time prophecies. Later he was told that his book would be sealed "even to the time of the end" (Daniel 12:4). Only then would the time prophecies identifying the time of the end be understood. The indications are that for at least thirteen years Daniel did not understand the significance of a vision that he had received from God, and it is possible that he never did understand it fully.

Acts 10:9-17 tells us that Peter did not at first understand the vision of the unclean animals that he was commanded to kill and eat. There are many in our world today who still do not understand the vision. The Lord was not telling Peter that now he had permission to eat unclean meats. He was using the animals as a symbol of the Gentiles, whom the Jews rejected, but whom He was leading to enjoy His cleansing grace.

The disciples of Jesus consistently misunderstood the nature of the kingdom He was establishing (see Mark 9:31, 32; Luke 24:21, 25, 26; John 20:8, 9; Acts 1:6). They hoped for an earthly kingdom, with Israel as the leading nation. They could not grasp the significance of His predicted death and did not understand when He told them that He would rise the third day. When they preached, " 'The kingdom of heaven is at hand' " (Matthew 10:7), they meant something quite different from what Jesus intended (see Matthew 4:17). They did not realize that the kingdom then at hand was solely the kingdom of grace and that the kingdom of glory would come only later. They were so enamored with the concept of national glory that they could not understand Christ's message.

Ellen White at first misunderstood the correct time to commence the Sabbath. She had been told in vision, "From even unto even, shall ye celebrate your sabbath" (Leviticus 23:32), but for a time she thought that "even" was six o'clock, as Joseph Bates taught. Later, after thorough Bible study by J. N. Andrews had established the biblical position, she received a vision confirming the understanding that "even" is sunset (see R. W. Olson, *One Hundred and One Questions*, pp. 54, 55).

For a few years after 1844, Ellen White misinterpreted her first vision. She thought the door of mercy had been shut for the entire world. But subsequent revelations from God opened her understanding. By January 1850, it was clear to her that, even though the door of mercy had closed for some persons, it had not for the world at large. Years later she wrote, "With my brethren and sisters, after the time passed in forty-four [1844] I did believe no more sinners would be converted. But I never had a vision that no more sinners would be converted" (*Selected Messages*, bk. 1, p. 74).

She explained that it sometimes took several visions from the Lord to clarify a point in her mind: "Often representations are given me which at first I do not understand, but after a time they are made plain by a repeated presentation of those things that I did not at first comprehend, and in ways that make their meaning clear and unmistakable" (*Selected Messages*, bk. 3, p. 56).

Do inspired prophets use other sources to help them present their messages?

There is a great deal of evidence that Bible writers borrowed from literary sources—sometimes uninspired sources—in the process of preparing their books. Usually they did not acknowledge the sources from which they received their materials. For example, the wording of the synoptic Gospels (Matthew, Mark, and Luke) is identical in many passages. Even grammatical features are copied. The parenthetical clause in Mark 2:10 is virtually identical in Matthew 9:6 and Luke 5:24. Most scholars agree that Matthew and Luke copied from Mark, as well as from another source common to them both. Whether this suggested solution to the synoptic problem is correct, the fact remains that the Gospel writers copied heavily from sources in writing their books. Mark is the shortest of the synoptics, consisting of 661 verses. Almost all of Mark's material occurs in Matthew and Luke. Only about thirty of Mark's verses appear exclusively in Mark. Not only is there close agreement in the arrangement of the material in the synoptic Gospels, but many passages also show close similarity in wording.

R. W. Olson comments on the borrowing of Bible writers: "Paul quoted the Greek poets Aratus (Acts 17:28), Epimenides (Titus 1:12), and Menander (1 Corinthians 15:33). Jude quoted the so-called 'book of Enoch' (Jude 14, 15). John the Revelator apparently drew many lines from the book of Enoch" (*One Hundred and One Questions*, p. 106).

In explaining why Ellen White borrowed from other writers, Dr. Olson makes four points:

First, it was to help her express well what she had seen and heard in vision. . . .

Second, she borrowed historical, geographical, chronological, and other details not revealed to her in vision. . . .

Third, at times the Lord led her to the discovery and use of beautiful gems of truth in the works of other authors. . . .

Fourth, she appropriated some of the doctrinal writings of her fellow-workers, since they had developed their doctrinal concepts by mutual study (ibid., pp. 71, 72).

The Bible presents a magnificently symmetrical and coordinated body of truth. Not only does it identify our era as the final one before the second coming of Jesus, but it also enables us to understand the means by which we can be prepared spiritually to meet our returning Lord. The inspired messages given by Ellen G. White were neither intended to replace the Bible nor to be an addition to the sacred canon. They were given to us by God to clarify divine truth and provide further comfort and guidance through the stormy days just prior to the second appearing of Christ.

Chapter 18

The Law
of Love

The only truly safe and happy way for us to travel is along the path on which we can walk hand in hand with Jesus. One day on Market Street in San Francisco, five-year-old twin brothers were walking with their parents, who were window shopping. Because the streets were crowded, the parents insisted that the twins stay close to them. But because five-year-olds like to feel independent, the boys were sure that they could get along nicely without holding their parents' hands. Disobeying instructions, they ran far ahead several times. Their parents decided to teach them a lesson. The next time the boys ran ahead, Mom and Dad stepped into the entryway of a store where they could still see the twins through the glass but the boys could not see them. A moment later, the twins turned to see where their parents were but could not find them. Two of the widest mouths ever opened on Market Street gave vent to their feelings of insecurity. I am sure you know what happened next. When the parents revealed themselves, the children clung tightly to their hands the rest of the way home.

What about the way we walk with our heavenly Parent? "Our only safety is in walking with Christ, our hand in His, our hearts filled with perfect trust" (Ellen G. White, *Selected Messages*, bk. 1, p. 79).

What many Christians fail to understand is that the pathway along which Christ walked and on which He leads us is the path of obedience. Because God's instructions and laws are intended for our good, our only safety is in following the path He has

161

marked for us. Through His laws He has spelled out for us in great detail how to get the most out of life.

God knows what is best for us, and the major principles are embodied in the Ten Commandments and exemplified in the life of Christ. The Decalogue expresses God's love, will, and purposes concerning human conduct and relationships. Because of that, the principles outlined in God's laws are intended to bless and benefit all people in every age. Through the agency of the Holy Spirit, God's laws point out sin and awaken a sense of need for a Saviour.

A St. Louis woman noticed a few bees buzzing around the attic of her home. She did not pay much attention, for there were only a few. She remained unconcerned throughout the summer as more and more bees flew in and out of the attic vent. But the entire attic became a huge hive. Finally, the ceiling of her second-floor bedroom caved in under the weight of hundreds of pounds of honey. We ignore sin only at the risk of having the ceiling cave in on us from the weight of accumulated, sweet-smelling sins. It is God's law that makes us aware of what sin is and how harmful it is.

One common saying advises: "Sin causes the cup of joy to spring a leak." In fact, "sin," in the sense of violating the God-given laws of life and health, fills our cup with sadness and sorrow rather than with the happiness God wants us to experience.

The basis of morality

At the time of this writing, it is apparent that we have come to a strange pass in our world. While former godless Communists are looking to religious values to help overcome crime and restore authority, here in the United States, Ted Turner recently passed off the Ten Commandments as outmoded and irrelevant for people today—merely ten suggestions. In contrast, in the fall of 1991, a group of nineteen evangelical ministers were invited by the Russian Supreme Soviet to visit Moscow and share with them thoughts on how to rebuild the moral values of Christianity. The vice-chairman of the KGB told them, "There can be no *perestroika* apart from repentance.

The time has come to repent of . . . [our] past. We have broken the Ten Commandments, and for this we pay today." Later he added, "What good is a path that doesn't lead to repentance, to the Ten Commandments?" (Philip Yancey, "Praying With the KGB," *Christianity Today*, 13 January 1992, p. 18).

When something goes wrong with the car, we reach for the manufacturer's manual. When something goes wrong with our lives, it is time to reach for the Manufacturer's manual too. And there is enough in our world now that unsettles and even terrifies us to cause us to reach for that manual—the Bible and God's laws. Most of what is wrong in our world can be traced to sin, disobedience of God's laws of life and health.

Their natural bias to sin leads people everywhere to disobey the revealed will of God. It is not just an understanding of God's will that we need to set the record straight. What we need more than anything are new hearts and minds that are attuned to what God tells us we must do to straighten out the problems in our lives. In Hebrews 10:16, 17, God promises to do just that for us, saying: "This is the covenant that I will make with them after those days, saith the Lord, I will put my laws into their hearts, and in their minds will I write them; and their sins and iniquities will I remember no more." It is God's grace that makes true obedience possible. Without His grace we can no more obey God than can the leopard exchange its spotted coat for a striped one.

Because salvation is all of grace and not of works, keeping the law cannot save us—only Christ does that—but the fact is, we cannot be saved without keeping the law. The fruitage of true faith is obedience to the commandments. This obedience develops Christian character, transforms our lives, and results in a sense of well-being. It is evidence of our love for the Lord and our concern for those about us.

Law and grace

One of the truly thrilling aspects of God's grace is His ability to deal with our sins and straighten out the records of our lawlessness because Christ paid the price of disobedience for us. Isaiah, chapter 40 begins with these words: "Comfort ye, comfort ye my people, saith your God. Speak ye comfortably to Jerusalem, and cry unto her, that her warfare is accomplished, that her iniquity is pardoned: for she hath received of the Lord's hand double for all her sins" (verses 1, 2).

The idea of receiving double for your sins may not appeal to you. Perhaps you see in it a threat on God's part to double your punishment. But that concept doesn't fit the poetic style of this verse. In order to understand what God means, we have to go back to a most interesting custom of Bible times. The word *double* in Hebrew is *kephal*. It means "to fold over." In other words, God's people have received a folding over of their sins.

What this means can be illustrated with this imaginary story. Jonah, a man living in Jerusalem during Isaiah's day, has gotten himself into so much debt that he cannot possibly repay it. So what do the creditors do? They write out the record of what the debtor owes them on a large sheet of papyrus and hang the record on his door during the night. The next morning when Jonah is leaving his house to go to work, he sees the sheet there on his door. It is the demand of his creditors. He is not allowed to tear it down but must leave it hanging there all day for all his neighbors and friends to view.

As Jonah reads the bill of particulars, he learns, to his horror, that if he cannot settle these debts in one week, all he owns will be sold, including his family members. They will go into slavery for seven years.

Each morning as Jonah goes out, he sees the notice still hanging on his door. He is becoming desperate. The list frightens and condemns him. Finally, the last day dawns. It has been a sleepless night for Jonah and his family. Their only expectation is that the new day will be the worst day of their lives—bringing the loss of all they own and separation from one another.

But it doesn't happen. Why not? During the night, when no one else was around, a benefactor folded over the bill of particulars hanging on Jonah's door. In addition, he wrote on the back, "I will pay all of these debts for Jonah."

Tremblingly, early the next morning, Jonah goes out to look at that horrible record of his debts for the last time. But with great joy and thankfulness he rushes in to share the good news with the family. They, too, rush out to see for themselves what has happened. And you will have no difficulty imagining what happens next—the tears of rejoicing, the celebration, the rush to express their gratitude to their benefactor.

That's the comforting news that chapter 40 of Isaiah brings to us. The debt is paid. The record of our iniquity and guilt has been doubled back, folded over. In His own blood Jesus has written on the back, "I will pay all of it." We did not ask Him to come to Calvary and do so. But He has done it because He loves us so much.

My sin—O the joy of this glorious thought—
    My sin, not in part, but the whole,
Is nailed to the cross, and I bear it no more:
    Praise the Lord, praise the Lord, O my soul!
(Horatio G. Spafford, "It Is Well With My Soul," *Seventh-day Adventist Hymnal*, no. 530).

But equally as thrilling as the good news of forgiveness is the good news that the One who has forgiven our sins has power to enable us to overcome our sins and live in accordance with His laws of life. His grace is not limited to forgiveness. The same power that created the world can create in us new hearts that "delight to do" God's will (see Psalm 40:8).

Some find Paul's teachings on faith and works in Galatians confusing. What Paul comes out so strongly against in Galatians is not the law of God but its misuse by those who thought that they were made righteous by the works of the law. Notice how strongly he takes this position in Galatians 3:

Are ye so foolish? having begun in the Spirit, are ye now made perfect by the flesh? . . . He therefore that ministereth to you the Spirit, and worketh miracles among you, doeth he it by the works of the law, or by the hearing of faith? . . . For as many as are of the works of the law are under the curse: for it is written, Cursed is every one that continueth not in all things which are written in the book of the law to do them (verses 3-10).

What is legalism?

Just as they later did with Paul, many of Jesus' contemporaries, particularly the religious leaders of His day, considered Him to be a lawbreaker. But if Jesus were here today, many religionists would call Him a legalist. Why? Because we have come to a strange moment in the history of Christianity, when those who love their Lord so much that they seek to bring their lives into conformity to His will as expressed in His Word are accused of being legalists because of their ethical convictions.

What a travesty of Christlikeness this provides! Those Christians who seek to follow as closely as possible the example that Jesus set are often ridiculed by fellow Christians for being "too strict" or "too rigid" in their lifestyle. It is long past time to set the record straight. It is time to pinpoint what legalism actually is. The Jewish legalism that Jesus rejected consisted of mere outward conformity to the law. The Jewish legalists kept the Sabbath while putting Christ to death!

In those days, whether a Jew kept the spirit of the law or merely conformed to it externally apparently did not matter to those judging his religious life. Conformity to the letter of the law was considered a virtuous fulfillment of duty and was thought to earn the law keeper the right to salvation. Jesus valued the law as much as, if not more than, did the legalists, and taught His followers to give heed to every jot and tittle. But He pointed to the strict outward conformity of the Pharisees as worse than worthless because it substituted the letter for the spirit.

Jesus realized that there was no merit earned toward salvation by obedience to the law. Instead, only conformity resulting from heartfelt gratitude to God indicates that the love of God fills the lives of those completely committed to the Lord. Such obedience has no merit in itself but signals clearly that those keeping the law enjoy a true relationship with God that extends to a commitment to follow His expressed will in every detail. The Jews of Jesus' day and the Jewish Christians who attacked Paul certainly were orthodox, but orthodoxy is not enough. When the letter of the law is followed strictly, but the spirit of loving obedience is missing, legalism bursts out in full bloom.

And that is what Jesus and Paul found fault with. Both Jesus and Paul kept the law conscientiously but did so out of a loving desire to follow God's will in every respect.

Paul did his best to make it clear that legalism is a false approach to salvation. Yet we must be sure that we understand what legalism is and what it is not. Some have come to suppose that the opposite of legalism is illegalism. What is illegalism? If legalism is an attempt to be saved by works, illegalism is an attempt to be saved without works, and that doesn't work.

Faith works by love

Ellen White's favorite description of righteousness by faith is that it is a faith that works by love and purifies the soul. The painting of the motto for the 1947 Washington Conference camp meeting was assigned to a local shop. The word *faith* was supposed to be placed on one side of the main theme and the word *works* on the other. Misunderstanding his instructions, the sign painter put these words at the center bottom portion of the banner, so that it read, "Faith works." Although that was not what was intended, it made a most appropriate motto, for faith does not stand alone, isolated by itself. Wherever genuine faith is manifested, it is a faith that works by love and purifies the soul.

Righteousness involves not only right-being but also right-doing. If we have Christ's love in our hearts, we will keep Christ's law. In the first table of the law we see that

if man love God in all the breadth and beauty suggested by the words "with all thy heart, and with all thy soul, and with all thy mind," he cannot possibly find room for another God, and so the first word is kept. If man love God supremely, he will not suffer anything to stand between him and God, thus the graven image is broken to pieces, and swept away by the force of a stronger affection. Out of love will spring that hallowing of the name of God which will dry the springs of blasphemy, and make the double dealing of the hypocrite an impossibility. The Sabbath will be eagerly welcomed, and all its privileges earnestly and gladly appropriated when it is a season in which love may find its way into the attitude of worship, and the acts of service following therefrom.

Passing to the second table, and looking now at love in its working toward others, it will at once be seen that the only sufficient power for obedience and honor rendered to parents is that of love. There will be no thought of murder until the awful moment has arrived in which the flame of love has died out upon the altar. Unchastity of every description is love's sure destruction, growing gross upon the very death of that which it so vilely personates. All theft is rendered impossible by true love for one's neighbor. Love sits as a sentinel at the portal of the lips, and arrests the faintest whisper of false witness against a neighbor; nay, rather dwells within the heart, and slays the thought that might have inspired the whisper. It is love and love alone that, finding satisfaction in God, satisfies the heart's hunger, and prevents all coveting (G. Campbell Morgan, *The Ten Commandments* [New York: Fleming H. Revell Company, 1901], pp. 120, 121).

Righteousness by faith not only applies to God's forgiveness for our past sins but also involves what the Lord does to keep us from falling into sin.

Sanctification is a state of holiness, without and within, being holy and without reserve the Lord's, not in form, but in truth. Every impurity of thought, every lustful passion, separates the soul from God; for Christ can never put His robe of righteousness upon a sinner, to hide his deformity. . . . There must be a progressive work of triumph over evil, of sympathy with good, a reflection of the character of Jesus (Ellen G. White, *Our High Calling*, p. 214).

The pure white robe of Christ's righteousness is not given us to cover up deformity and sin. Only when we empty ourselves of self and sin, giving them to God so that He may forgive us and give us power to overcome, can we become pure and clean, covered by Christ's robe of righteousness. Faith works by appropriating the salvation that Christ provided on the cross and enables us to live Christ's kind of life—obedience to all that God requires and makes possible for us.

Salvation is all of grace and not of works, but its fruitage is obedience to the commandments. This loving commitment results in the development of Christian character and a sense of well-being and happiness.

Chapter 19

Why Should Christians Observe the Bible Sabbath?

Creation week was drawing to a close. By presenting Adam with his beautiful bride, God established earth's first home. Then the Creator introduced the most appropriate conclusion to a week of exciting fulfillment—a day of rest and rejoicing! As Adam and Eve gloried in the perfect relationship God had given them, He focused their attention on the Source of all their joy. Together Deity and humanity exalted in the beauty of creation; in the supreme love of God, who gave humankind such an unsurpassed home; and in the holiness of life that results from close fellowship between humankind and God.

Here was the pattern for all future homes and Sabbaths. God loved, He created, He bonded our first parents, and He led them in worship and adoration of their Creator. No wonder the Sabbath is depicted throughout the Bible as the most important day of the week! No wonder God preserved it throughout the ages, despite human unwillingness to acknowledge His love and creative power! The Sabbath remains as the timeless memorial of divine love, a day of joyous worship, a day for communion with and praise of our Creator, a day to strengthen home's ties and the forces that unite believers in loving fellowship.

Christians should observe the Bible Sabbath because it is a

Christian institution. Jesus Christ is the Creator. "All things were made by him" (John 1:3). "By him were all things created, that are in heaven, and that are in earth, visible and invisible, whether they be thrones, or dominions, or principalities, or powers: all things were created by him, and for him: and he is before all things, and by him all things consist" (Colossians 1:16, 17). God "hath in these last days spoken unto us by his Son, whom he hath appointed heir of all things, by whom also he made the worlds" (Hebrews 1:2). As the Creator, Christ instituted the Sabbath on the seventh day of Creation week and set it apart as a perpetual reminder of His creative work (see Genesis 2:1-3).

Christ did not rest on the seventh day because He was physically weary, nor did the perfect human beings He had created become weary as we do today. But Christ, the Creator, wanted every seventh day to be a time of special fellowship and communion between Himself and the beautiful persons He had placed in the perfect garden called Eden. They were to worship God every day as they tended the garden and savored the sights, sounds, tastes, and perfumes that their lovely home had to offer. But Christ saw that they needed a weekly change of focus—from the beauties of earth to the glories of heaven, from daily physical and emotional satisfactions to the greater spiritual fulfillment of a day spent in communion with Him and with heaven's angels. So "God blessed the seventh day, and sanctified it: because that in it he had rested from all his work which God created and made" (Genesis 2:3).

The same Christ who created the world and instituted the Sabbath during Creation week accompanied His faithful people through the long centuries after humanity's fall into sin. Abraham's faith in the Messiah (Christ) who would come to die for all human sin is upheld in the New Testament as the example for all to follow (see Galatians 3:7). When the gospel was preached to Abraham (see verse 8), he "believed God, and it was accounted to him for righteousness" (verse 6, quoting Genesis 15:6). Yet Abraham, who is upheld as the great example of righteousness and salvation by faith in Christ, "obeyed my [God's] voice, and kept my charge, my commandments, my statutes, and my laws" (Genesis 26:5). One way Abraham remembered his Creator was by observing the seventh-day Sabbath as a memorial of His creative works.

Christ led the Israelites out of Egypt. He accompanied them in their desert wanderings, manifesting Himself through the pillar of cloud by day and the pillar of fire by night: "They drank of that spiritual Rock that followed [Greek: accompanied] them: and that Rock was Christ" (1 Corinthians 10:4). Christ reminded the Israelite ex-slaves whom He had led out of Egypt that the seventh day was His holy Sabbath day—a day for spiritual rest and refreshment; a day free from secular work; a day for worship of, and fellowship with, God; a day to remember their Creator and their Deliverer from the bondage of Egypt. Christ drama- tized the importance of observing the Sabbath by raining manna from heaven six days a week, with twice as much on the sixth day, but none at all on the seventh day (see Exodus 16:21-23).

When Christ spoke His law from Mt. Sinai, He did not give the Israelites a system of works as the means of their salvation. The covenant (agreement) He had made with Abraham was a cov- enant of grace, involving the free gift of salvation because of God's love for those who believe in Him. Abraham " '*believed* God, and it was reckoned to him as righteousness' " (Galatians 3:6, RSV, emphasis supplied). God promised that the same covenant of righteousness and salvation by grace would be given to all Abraham's descendants (see Genesis 17:7, 9, 19). That is why the covenant God offered Israel at Sinai was the same covenant of grace that He had made with Abraham. "The law, which came four hundred and thirty years afterward, does not annul a covenant previously ratified [confirmed] by God, so as to make the promise void" (Galatians 3:17, RSV). Thus, God made avail- able also at Sinai, 430 years after Abraham's day, the Abrahamic covenant of salvation by Christ's grace. Hence, when God pro- claimed His Ten Commandments from Sinai, placing the Sab- bath commandment in the heart of His law, He was asking His people, who were to be saved by grace, to obey His laws, including the Sabbath law, as Abraham had done before them. It was not God's fault that the people disobeyed and broke the covenant. He had offered them exactly the same means of salvation He had offered Abraham—salvation by grace, which results in obedience to His law. God's grace always precedes man's obedience.

The New Testament teaches that the same Ten Commandment law given to Israel is to be written on the hearts of Christians today when they believe in Christ as Abraham did. Christ wants "the blessing of Abraham" to "come on the Gentiles . . . that we might receive the promise of the Spirit through faith" (Galatians 3:14). After Israel had long ignored the covenant relationship with God, the prophet Jeremiah told them that the Lord would renew His covenant with those willing to be faithful, writing His law upon their hearts (see Jeremiah 31:31-34). The New Testament Epistle to the Hebrews quotes Jeremiah, emphasizing that the same Ten Commandment law, of which Jeremiah spoke, is to be written on the hearts of faithful Christians. " 'This is the covenant that I will make with the house of Israel after those days, says the Lord: I will put my laws into their minds, and write them on their hearts, and I will be their God, and they shall be my people' " (Hebrews 8:10, RSV). Christ gave the everlasting covenant to His ancient people, and He gives it to us today. If we believe in Him, He grants us salvation by His grace and the power to obey His law—the same law kept by Abraham and his faithful descendants, the law proclaimed from Sinai and extolled by Jeremiah.

The seventh-day Sabbath is the heart of this law. A secondary reason Israelites were to observe the Sabbath is that it was to remind them of their deliverance from slavery in Egypt (see Deuteronomy 5:15). But the primary purpose of Sabbath observance was to remind God's people of His creative works.

Remember the sabbath day, to keep it holy. Six days shalt thou labour, and do all thy work: but the seventh day is the sabbath of the Lord thy God: in it thou shalt not do any work, thou, nor thy son, nor thy daughter, thy manservant, nor thy maidservant, nor thy cattle, nor thy stranger that is within thy gates: *for in six days the Lord made heaven and earth, the sea, and all that in them is, and rested the seventh day: wherefore the Lord blessed the sabbath day, and hallowed it* (Exodus 20:8-11, emphasis supplied).

This law, along with the other nine of the Ten Commandments, is to be written on the hearts of Christians who, by faith, are enjoying the everlasting covenant of salvation by Christ's grace (see Hebrews 8:8-12; 10:16, 17). It is not surprising, therefore, that the book of Revelation presents the Sabbath message as a key element in the "everlasting gospel" to be preached throughout the whole world immediately before the second coming of Jesus: "I saw another angel fly in the midst of heaven, having the *everlasting gospel* to preach unto them that dwell on the earth, and to every nation, and kindred, and tongue, and people, saying with a loud voice, Fear God, and give glory to him; for the hour of his judgment is come: *and worship him that made heaven, and earth, and the sea, and the fountains of waters*" (Revelation 14:6, 7, emphasis supplied).

As we have seen, Christ "made heaven, and earth, and the sea, and the fountains of waters." We are to worship Him as the Creator. Notice the connection between Revelation 14:7 and the fourth commandment:

Exodus 20:11	**Revelation 14:7**
"In six days the Lord made heaven and earth, the sea, and all that in them is, and rested the seventh day."	"Worship him that made heaven, and earth, and the sea, and the fountains of waters."

The first angel's message (see Revelation 14:6, 7) is one of the last three messages to be given to the world before Jesus returns. It points us back to the fourth commandment, the Sabbath command. The day He blessed and sanctified at the end of Creation week, the day He reminded Israel to observe as a memorial of His creative works, is the day we are to observe as we allow the everlasting gospel to have full reign in our lives while we faithfully prepare to meet our returning Lord.

There is no doubt at all that the seventh day today is the same seventh day Abraham kept and the same day the Jews have observed since the time of the Exodus. Throughout history, despite changes in the calendar, the weekly cycle has never changed. The seventh day we observe as the Sabbath today is the day on which Christ rested at the end of Creation week.

Jesus observed the Sabbath and urged His followers to do likewise

Luke records of Jesus: "He came to Nazareth, where he had been brought up: and, as his custom was, he went into the synagogue on the sabbath day, and stood up for to read" (Luke 4:16). Jesus was reared in Nazareth by Jewish parents. You would expect that He would customarily keep the Sabbath. Even during His ministry He continued observing it. Writing years after Jesus' death and resurrection, Luke gives not the slightest hint that Jesus ever changed His custom of Sabbath observance or suggested that His followers should change the day.

In fact, Jesus made it thoroughly clear that He wanted His disciples to continue observing the Sabbath after His death. In predicting both the fall of Jerusalem and His second advent, Jesus instructed that, when it is necessary for His followers to flee from their enemies, they are to pray that their "flight be not in the winter, neither on the sabbath day" (Matthew 24:20). Of course, fleeing from the enemy in the winter would involve considerable suffering. Fleeing on the Sabbath day would render it impossible to enter into the rest and spiritual communion that the Sabbath is designed to foster. Jesus was speaking of His followers in Judea (see verse 16) fleeing just before the destruction of Jerusalem in A.D. 70. He wanted them to be careful in observing the Sabbath almost forty years after His death and resurrection.

Why did Jesus not mention that after His resurrection the Sabbath of the fourth commandment would be changed and Sunday substituted as the memorial of His resurrection? Obviously, because He had no intention of changing the fourth commandment or of exalting Sunday as a day of worship. In recording Jesus' words, why did not Matthew inform Christian believers that, since Jesus' death and resurrection, a change had been made in the day of worship? Obviously Christ never made any such change.

The context of Jesus' instruction recorded in Matthew 24:20 is His prediction of events that would occur not only at the destruction of Jerusalem, but also of events immediately prior to His second coming. His people are to flee in response to the "abomination of desolation, spoken of by Daniel the prophet" (verse 15). Jesus is referring to the "transgression of desolation," the work of the "little horn" power mentioned in Daniel 8:9, 13. This power is to be the enemy of God's people until the end of time. It is to "be broken without hand" (verse 25) at the second coming of Jesus. Before Jesus comes, His faithful people will be forced to flee, as the believers in Judea fled before the destruction of Jerusalem. Matthew 24:20 applies as much to God's last-day people as it did to His people in A.D. 70. He wants us to pray that, however extreme our circumstances, we will be able to observe His holy Sabbath day right down to His second advent.

The apostles observed the Sabbath

Jesus was crucified on the sixth day of the week. "That day was the preparation, and the sabbath drew on" (Luke 23:54). The Greek word translated "preparation" refers to the sixth day of the week, the day on which preparation was to be made for the Sabbath. Arndt and Gingrich's Greek lexicon says that the word for *preparation* (*paraskeue*) means "Friday, on which day everything had to be prepared for the Sabbath, when no work was permitted" (p. 627). The word may also refer to the preparation day for the annual Passover, which occurred on different days of the week. But in the year in which Jesus was crucified, the Passover preparation day and the preparation day for the weekly Sabbath were the same day.

On the day after the preparation day, Jesus' followers "rested the sabbath day according to the commandment" (Luke 23:56). The day after the Sabbath, on "the first day of the week, very early in the morning" (Luke 24:1), Jesus rose from the dead. Mark records: "Jesus was risen early the first day of the week" (Mark 16:9). This was the "third day" (Luke 24:7; 1 Corinthians 15:4).

It is apparent, then, that the day on which Jesus rested in the tomb and on which His disciples observed the Sabbath "according to the commandment" (Luke 23:56) was the day after Friday and the day before Sunday. How appropriate that Jesus should rest on the Sabbath day at the end of His ministry and after His great sacrificial atonement for all human sin had been made! The Sabbath memorializes not only Christ's work of creation but also His work of redemption. And how appropriate that His disciples should observe the Sabbath when their Lord was resting on the seventh day after His intense labors and sufferings!

We have not the slightest hint in any of the New Testament apostolic writings that, because Jesus rose from the dead on the first day of the week, therefore we should now replace the Sabbath with Sunday as the memorial of the resurrection. In the eight references to the first day of the week in the New Testament, there is no mention that it is now to be regarded as a day of worship because it is the memorial of Christ's resurrection (see Matthew 28:1; Mark 16:1, 2, 9; Luke 24:1; John 20:1, 19; Acts 20:7; 1 Corinthians 16:1, 2).

The fact that Paul met with the believers at Troas on the first day of the week (see Acts 20:7) proves only that the early Christians met on various days of the week to eat and worship together. Later in the same chapter, we have recorded a service conducted by Paul on Wednesday or Thursday. First Corinthians 16:1, 2 records instruction for the believers in Corinth to put aside money at home on the first day of the week so that they would have offerings to give Paul when he arrived. It is not referring to Sunday worship services.

The apostles consistently observed the seventh-day Sabbath (see Acts 13:14, 15, 42-44; 16:13-15; 17:1, 2; 18:1, 4). They met in synagogues on the Sabbath day, not merely because this was a convenient means of reaching Jews with the gospel, but because the Sabbath was also their day of worship. In Philippi, Paul and his associates met for worship on the Sabbath day "by a river side, where we thought [supposed, assumed] there was a place of prayer" (Acts 16:13, literally translated). They found a quiet place to pray, worship, and witness on the Sabbath day.

The suggestion by some Bible interpreters that Paul's message of righteousness and salvation by faith led him to reject the Sabbath is thoroughly unfounded. Paul taught that obedience to the Ten Commandments is the mandatory result and evidence of salvation by faith in Christ (see Romans 3:31; 7:7, 12, 14; 8:3, 4). Romans 14:1-7 does not discuss the weekly Sabbath. The subject seems to be eating or not eating certain foods (fasting) on particular days. A similar concern of some early Christians is reflected in chapter 8 of the *Didache*, an early Christian document, which instructs Christians to fast on Wednesday and Friday rather than on Monday and Thursday, as did the Jews (see Raoul Dederern, "On Esteeming One Day as Better Than Another," in *The Sabbath in Scripture and History*, ed. Kenneth A. Strand [Washington, D.C.: Review and Herald, 1982], pp. 333-337). Another suggestion is that the days referred to (see Romans 14:5, 6) are the annual ceremonial sabbaths of the Jews, with possible additions made by the Essenes. Jewish Christians had great difficulty giving up their ceremonial observances, including festival days, which were established during the Exodus (see Leviticus 23).

Paul instructed the Colossians that no one is to pass judgment on Christian believers "with regard to a festival or a new moon or a sabbath. These are only a shadow of what is to come; but the substance belongs to Christ" (Colossians 2:16, 17, RSV). The point is that the Old Testament consistently uses the phrase, "a festival, a new moon, a sabbath" (or some variation of it) to refer to *the ceremonial aspects of the law, whether practiced weekly, monthly, or yearly* (see 1 Chronicles 23:31; 2 Chronicles 2:3, 4; 8:12, 13; 31:3; Nehemiah 10:33; Ezekiel 45:17; compare Numbers 28, 29). The sanctuary sacrifices, whenever they were offered, foreshadowed the death and heavenly ministry of Jesus Christ and ceased to be significant at the cross (see Hebrews 7-10). What Paul is saying, then, is that no Christian is to be judged as failing in his duty because he refuses to take part in sanctuary ceremonial services that have been superseded by the death and ministry of Christ, to which they pointed. The seventh-day Sabbath never was a shadow of what is to come. Thus it is still binding on Christians who desire to follow the example of Jesus.

The Epistle to the Hebrews presents the weekly Sabbath rest as a symbol of the spiritual rest God grants to those willing to enter into fellowship with Him (see Hebrews 4:1-11). Ancient Israel largely failed to enter into God's spiritual rest, and they tended to ignore the Sabbath observance that symbolized it. Christians are admonished to accept the spiritual rest of which the weekly Sabbath is the symbol. "So then, there remains a sabbath rest for the people of God; for whoever enters God's rest also ceases from his labors as God did from his" (Hebrews 4:9, 10, RSV).

The message of the Epistle to the Hebrews underlines the Old Testament emphasis on Sabbath observance as a sign of holiness (see Exodus 31:13; Ezekiel 20:12). God's people are to be holy in all their conduct, "since it is written, 'You shall be holy, for I am holy' " (1 Peter 1:15, 16, RSV). Sabbath observance is the sign of their holy relationship with Christ, and it is the means by which this relationship is enriched. Significantly, the people who respond positively to the three angels' messages of Revelation 14, including the Sabbath truth clearly implied in Hebrews 4:7, are recipients of God's character and are to be spiritually spotless (see Revelation 14:1, 5). They have received the end-time seal of God (compare Revelation 7:1-3 with 14:1). Sabbath observance is an integral part of their total commitment to Christ.

How should we observe the Sabbath?

The fourth commandment instructs that we, and any others who are part of our households and businesses, should refrain from work on the Sabbath day (see Exodus 20:8-11). Isaiah explains that true Sabbath observance involves refraining from not " 'going your own ways, or seeking your own pleasure, or talking idly.' " God will bless those who " 'call the sabbath a delight,' " honoring it as His holy day. " 'Then you shall take delight in the Lord, and I will make you ride upon the heights of the earth; I will feed you with the heritage of Jacob your father, for the mouth of the Lord has spoken' " (Isaiah 58:13, 14, RSV).

While here on earth, Jesus observed the Sabbath, but He rejected the man-made, legalistic restrictions with which the rabbis had invested it. Contrary to the stipulations of the Israelite leaders, Jesus healed the sick on the Sabbath day (see Mark 3:1-6). As "lord of the Sabbath" (Mark 2:28), He taught that the satisfaction of basic human needs was not inconsistent with correct Sabbath observance (see verses 23-27). " 'So it is lawful to do good on the sabbath' " (Matthew 12:12, RSV) by assisting a neighbor who is confronted by an emergency situation.

In response to the teaching of Scripture, Seventh-day Adventists refrain from business and secular pleasure on the Sabbath day. Whatever detracts from wholehearted fellowship with Christ and His people is regarded as inconsistent with acceptable Sabbath observance. But care of the sick and performance of essential home and church duties are considered to be consistent with the true spirit of the Sabbath day. The Sabbath is a delightful day of rest from weekly activities, of fellowship with those of like faith, and of communion with God and witnessing for Him.

Are you observing the day that Christ instituted at Creation and invites His people to honor? Jesus said, " 'If you love me, you will keep my commandments' " (John 14:15, RSV). To follow Jesus is to do what He asks, gratefully accepting the wonderful blessings that He offers to the faithful Sabbath keeper.

Chapter 20

It Takes More Than a Label

An antique dealer was rummaging through the contents of an attic of an old home. Among the musty, dusty things that had been stored and forgotten, he found a battered violin case. In the dim light he saw that it contained an old violin. Downstairs, in better light, he examined the instrument more closely and discovered a label inside, bearing the name Stradivarius. Here was a fortune.

Leaving the rest of the attic's contents for the time being, he hastened to the shop of a musical-instruments dealer who was an expert on violins. Trying to conceal his excitement, he inquired as to the worth of his find. The musician put strings on the violin, took a bow from a hook on the wall, tightened it, and rubbed it over a piece of resin a time or two. Then he played a few notes on the old, long-silent instrument.

"It's worth about five dollars," he said as he loosened the bow, hung it back in its place, and laid the violin down.

The finder was amazed. "But you must be mistaken," he said. "Look at that label. That's a Stradivarius."

Without a word, the musician again took the bow and carefully played a classic melody. Then, shaking his head, he said deliberately, "It takes more than a label to make a Stradivarius violin." How true! It also takes more than the label "Christian" to enable us to be committed fully to God and to His will for us.

All that we have belongs to God. We are His stewards— managers entrusted by Him with time and opportunities, abilities, possessions, and the blessings of the earth and its resources.

We are responsible to Him for their proper use. We acknowledge God's ownership of all we have by faithful service to Him and those about us. We consider it a God-given privilege to be able to use all that He has provided to nurture in love those to whom He leads us. The Lord's plan of stewardship is designed to help us gain the victory over selfishness and covetousness.

A Bible example of faithful stewardship

In the world in which we live, we are most likely to think of a steward as someone who takes care of us on an airplane. To find what stewardship is all about, let us look at a classic Bible example. *Eliezer* means "my God is a helper." That was an appropriate name for one who did so much to help Abraham and, faithfully, to manage all that he owned. Eliezer had come to Abraham from Damascus, probably as a young man, and had made himself indispensable to his master. Abraham trusted him so much that he placed him in charge of "all that he had" (Genesis 24:2).

At one time Abraham had considered Eliezer to be his heir (see Genesis 15:2). Now Eliezer had been displaced by the son of Abraham's old age. Yet this faithful steward demonstrated the caliber of his commitment to his master by dedicated service to the needs of the heir who had replaced him. When Isaac was forty years old, Abraham sent Eliezer on a mission to find a suitable wife for his son. Commenting on Abraham's choice of one to carry out this most significant and delicate task, Ellen White tells us that Eliezer was "a man of piety, experience, and sound judgment, who had rendered [Abraham] long and faithful service" (*Patriarchs and Prophets*, p. 172).

Although stewardship involves the faithful and efficient management of everything entrusted to us by God, in its larger dimensions it "involves the wise and unselfish use of life" (Paul G. Smith, *Managing God's Goods* [Nashville: Southern Publishing Association, 1973], p. 21).

The fifth happiness

The basic principle that underlies stewardship can be found in the Beatitudes in Matthew 5. These have been called the "Be-

happy-attitudes" because the word *blessed* also means "happy."
In the fifth happy blessing, Jesus pronounced, "Blessed are the
merciful: for they shall obtain mercy" (verse 7). More than the
spirit of mercy or forgiveness is intended. When Christ fills our
heart, it overflows with His beneficence. We cannot help sharing
all that we have with those about us. Thus begins a chain of
mercy and benevolence that keeps on growing. To give is to gain.
The more we share, the more we receive in return.

According to Ellen White, this rule makes up the law of life for
the universe.

In the light from Calvary it will be seen that the law of
self-renouncing love is the law of life for earth and heaven;
that the love which "seeketh not her own" has its source in
the heart of God; and that in the meek and lowly One is
manifested the character of Him who dwelleth in the light
which no man can approach unto. . . .

Looking unto Jesus we see that it is the glory of our God
to give. "I do nothing of Myself," said Christ; "the living
Father hath sent Me, and I live by the Father." "I seek not
mine own glory," but the glory of Him that sent Me. John
8:28; 6:57; 8:50, 7:18. In these words is set forth the great
principle which is the law of life for the universe. All things
Christ received from God, but He took to give. So in the
heavenly courts, in His ministry for all created beings:
through the beloved Son, the Father's life flows out to all;
through the Son it returns, in praise and joyous service, a
tide of love, to the great Source of all. And thus through
Christ the circuit of beneficence is complete, representing
the character of the great Giver, the law of life (*The Desire
of Ages*, pp. 20, 21).

Later in the book, Ellen White restates the principle this way:
"We can impart only that which we receive from Christ; and we
can receive only as we impart to others. As we continue imparting, we continue to receive; and the more we impart, the more we
shall receive. Thus we may be constantly believing, trusting,
receiving, and imparting" (p. 370).

Too often in the church, stewardship has been measured by what we do with our money—our tithes and offerings. But there is much more to it than that. It involves the faithful and wise use of everything we have—physically, mentally, socially, and spiritually. In faithfully managing all our assets, we glorify God and demonstrate our appreciation of what He has done for us.

The tithe (10 percent of our gain) and the offerings God asks us to bring into His storehouse, the church (see Malachi 3:8-12), and the keeping of the Sabbath (one-seventh of our time) are only suggested minimums. What God really wants is for us to commit all we have and are to Him without any reservations.

The forerunner

The important thing for us to realize in this respect is that God does not expect us to do any more for Him than He already has done for us. The basis for all stewardship is an appreciation of the fact that because of what He has done, we have a tremendous hope. That hope is stated in Hebrews 6:19, 20: "Which hope we have as an anchor of the soul, both sure and stedfast, and which entereth into that within the veil; whither the forerunner is for us entered, even Jesus, made an high priest for ever after the order of Melchisedec." There is more in the text than we usually recognize. Adventist pioneer S. N. Haskell explains:

The Saviour gave His life a sacrifice for sin here upon the earth; and as He entered the heavenly sanctuary as High Priest, He is called the "Forerunner." Under no circumstances, except as He enters "within the veil" of the heavenly sanctuary, is that name applied to the Saviour (*The Cross and Its Shadow* [South Lancaster, Mass.: South Lancaster Printing Co., 1914], p. 70).

Elder Haskell indicates that the forerunner is a familiar character in those countries which have monarchical forms of government.

In gorgeous uniform, with waving plumes, he [the forerunner] rides before and announces the approach of the royal carriage. While he is always hailed with joy by the waiting crowds, yet he is not the center of attraction; their eyes do not follow him as he passes on, but are turned down the road whence he came to get the first glimpse of the royal personage of whom he is the forerunner (ibid).

In Philippians 2, Paul outlines the condescension of Christ when He emptied Himself for us by coming to this world as a human being and dying a criminal's death on the cross. But here we find another step in Christ's emptying Himself for us:

> When He entered heaven a mighty Conqueror over death and the grave, before the entire heavenly host and representatives of other worlds, He entered a forerunner for us. He presented the "wave sheaf," those brought forth from the graves at the time of His resurrection, as a sample of the race He had died to redeem, thus directing the attention of that wonderful assemblage down the road whence He came to watch—for royalty?—yes, for royalty made so by His precious blood. It is only a company of poor, frail mortals stumbling along and often falling by the way; but when they reach the heavenly gate, they will enter "heirs of God, and joint-heirs with Christ" (ibid., pp. 70, 71).

What Christ is pictured doing as our forerunner not only describes what He will do for us in the future, but what He *already has done*. The last several paragraphs in the magnificent book *The Desire of Ages* describe the scene of Christ's joyful reentry into heaven. It would be helpful for you to read the entire section on pages 833-835. We can only summarize it here.

Jesus entered heaven as a conqueror over sin and death as all heaven was waiting to honor and welcome Him. But as they rushed forward to pay homage to Him, He waved them back. He had yet to do the work of the Forerunner. The explanation is given:

> He cannot now receive the coronet of glory and the royal robe. He enters into the presence of His Father. He points

to His wounded head, the pierced side, the marred feet; He lifts His hands, bearing the print of nails. He points to the tokens of His triumph; He presents to God the wave sheaf, those raised with Him as representatives of that great multitude who shall come forth from the grave at His second coming. . . . He declares: Father, it is finished. I have done Thy will, O My God. I have completed the work of redemption. If Thy justice is satisfied, "I will that they also, whom Thou hast given Me, be with Me where I am." . . .

The voice of God is heard proclaiming that justice is satisfied. Satan is vanquished. Christ's toiling, struggling ones on earth are "accepted in the Beloved." Eph. 1:6. Before the heavenly angels and the representatives of unfallen worlds, they are declared justified. Where He is, there His church shall be (*The Desire of Ages*, p. 834).

Having completed the work of the Forerunner, Jesus then was able to receive the homage, glory, and honor due to the God who for our sake became forever linked with the human race. But we should not minimize what it meant for Him to be accepted and welcomed in heaven on the day He returned with the "wave sheaf" as our representative.

After describing that amazing scene, Ellen White adds:

Songs of triumph mingle with the music from angel harps, till heaven seems to overflow with joy and praise. Love has conquered. The lost is found. . . .

From that scene of heavenly joy, there comes back to us on earth the echo of Christ's wonderful words, "I ascend unto My Father, and your Father; and to My God, and your God." John 20:17. The family of heaven and the family of earth are one. For us our Lord ascended, and for us He lives (ibid., p. 835).

When the Father eagerly stepped down from the throne and, in the greatest exhibition of His love ever recorded, threw His arms around His returning Son—our Forerunner, He encircled each one of us with all the enthusiastic love with which He welcomed Jesus home. *We are* accepted in the Beloved. None of us need ever wonder again about God's being willing to accept us. The only question that remains is, Are we willing to be accepted?

When we allow God to do what He wants to do—accept us as His children and heirs of the kingdom—we will follow our Lord's example and empty ourselves completely, giving all we have and are to Him. We recognize that all with which He has entrusted us is given us to employ in His service. With hearts full of gratitude for all He has done, we do what little we can in exchange by committing all we have and are fully to Him. When we do this, we recognize that He has given us the responsibility of doing our best as faithful stewards to manage all that He has shared with us.

Then we will know from experience that "God planned the system of beneficence, in order that man might become like his Creator, benevolent and unselfish in character, and finally be a partaker with Christ of the eternal, glorious reward" (Ellen G. White, *Counsels on Stewardship*, p. 15).

Chapter 21

Why Are Standards of Conduct Important?

Love changes the way we think. The story is told of a young woman who read a book and, having completed it, remarked that it was one of the dullest books she had ever read. A short time later, she began dating a young man with whom she fell in love and to whom she became engaged. One day when he was visiting her home, she remarked, "I have a book in my library that was written by a man whose name is the same as yours. Isn't that a coincidence!"

She showed him the book, and he commented, "No, it's not a coincidence; I wrote that book."

That night the young woman sat up until the early morning hours reading the book again. The next day she declared that it was the most interesting book she had ever read.

Why the change in attitude? She now knew and loved the author. What a change it makes in our attitude to the Bible and the manner of life it upholds when we become personally acquainted with the Author! Love for Jesus changes the way we think, speak, and act. Because we do not wish to wound Him any further by living contrary to His will, we stop doing some things and begin doing other things. The pleasures we seek and the company we keep often change dramatically, and we are more concerned about our physical health and mental efficiency than we were before. We do not want to do anything that interferes with our ability to enjoy Jesus' company, and we give much greater attention to His will for our lives.

The Bible does not discuss every practice current in our world today, telling us specifically which ones are right and which are wrong. Many of these practices did not exist in the same form when the Bible was written. But the Bible does provide adequate principles to guide us in every situation of life. These principles direct our decisions regarding such matters as dress, entertainment, diet, and work practices. Faithful Christians search the Bible for these principles. The question they ask is not so much, "What is wrong with what I want to do?" but "What would Jesus have me do, and why?" The purpose of the Christian is to prepare for heaven. If that means forsaking some modes of behavior, some kinds of dress, and some kinds of entertainment, the person who loves Christ does not hesitate for a moment. His or her relationship with Christ is more important than anything else.

The Bible invites us to love God with all our heart, soul, and might (see Deuteronomy 6:5). His love filling our hearts is the motivation for Christian conduct. A little boy once said that he loved his mother "with all his strength." When asked to explain what he meant, he said, "You see, we live on the fourth floor of this apartment building; and there's no elevator, and the coal is kept down in the basement. Mother is busy all the time, and she isn't very strong; so I see to it that the coal bin is never empty. I lug the coal up four flights of stairs all by myself. And it's a pretty big bin. It takes all my strength to get it up here. Now, isn't that loving my mother with all my strength?" That is exactly what Jesus meant when He said, " 'If you love me, you will keep my commandments' " (John 14:15, RSV). " 'You are my friends if you do what I command you' " (John 15:14, RSV).

Basic principles

To love and serve Jesus in this manner involves allowing Him to control our minds. "As he [a person] thinketh in his heart, so is he" (Proverbs 23:7). "The thought of foolishness is sin" (Proverbs 24:9). "Out of the heart proceed evil thoughts, murders, adulteries, fornications, thefts, false witness, blasphemies" (Matthew 15:19). Conduct that Jesus regards as sin begins in the mind. That is why the Bible instructs: "Let this mind be in you, which was also in Christ Jesus" (Philippians 2:5). Jesus' love for His Father and His unselfish love for others motivated Him to do only noble, pure deeds. All His thoughts, words, and actions were holy. He "did no sin, neither was guile found in his mouth" (1 Peter 2:22).

Because of the transforming, controlling work of the Holy Spirit in his life and in the lives of his fellow Christians, Paul was able to say, "We have the mind of Christ" (1 Corinthians 2:16). The Holy Spirit dwelling in their hearts had imparted to them the righteous principles of thought that were characteristic of Christ. Christ's plan is that His Spirit will direct the thoughts of His disciples in pure, holy channels. "For the weapons of our warfare are not worldly but have divine power to destroy strongholds. We destroy arguments and every proud obstacle to the knowledge of God, *and take every thought captive to obey Christ*" (2 Corinthians 10:4, 5, RSV, emphasis supplied).

Christian believers who submit to the Lordship of Christ over their minds have built-in control of their feelings, emotions, words, and actions. When tempted to allow their thoughts to run in impure channels, they turn to Christ for strength, and by the power of the Holy Spirit, He gives them deliverance. Such people are not consumed by the desire for sinful pleasures or for extravagant modes of dress or for such emotional crutches as alcohol and drugs. Their desires are directed and controlled by a higher Power to whom they have given total allegiance.

Another principle spelled out in Scripture is that Christ is the owner of our lives. "Do you not know that your body is a temple of the Holy Spirit within you, which you have from God? You are not your own; you were bought with a price. So glorify God in your body" (1 Corinthians 6:19, 20, RSV). A similar thought is expressed in 1 Corinthians 3:16, 17 (RSV): "Do you not know that you are God's temple and that God's Spirit dwells in you? If any one destroys God's temple, God will destroy him. For God's temple is holy, and that temple you are."

That being the case, a major priority for Christians is to keep the temple of their mind and body pure and undefiled so that Christ, by the presence of the Holy Spirit, will always wish to dwell there. This principle excludes reading and television programs that defile the mind, exciting emotions and passions contrary to Christ's will. It also excludes eating and drinking practices that are harmful to health, and drug use that destroys both mental and physical efficiency. If the Holy Spirit is to continue occupancy of our soul temple, we must cooperate with Him by rejecting every practice that defiles the temple and drives Him from it.

What does the Bible teach about personal adornment?

The Bible principles are clearly presented in a number of passages so that no one need be in doubt. The specific application of those principles must be made by the Spirit-directed believer.

God wants the character of each believer "to be conformed to the image of his Son" (Romans 8:29, RSV). Persons who receive Christ are now partakers of the divine nature (see 2 Peter 1:4). Their old self has been replaced by the indwelling Holy Spirit, who imparts a new heart and manner of life (see Romans 8:9-17; Ephesians 4:22-24). The new person, who reflects the love and purity of Christ, wishes to think, speak, and act like his Lord. Because Christ is living out His life through the individual (see Galatians 2:20), he or she dresses and acts in ways that Christ approves, and the Holy Spirit brings the person progressively nearer to Christ's image (see 2 Corinthians 3:18).

Two significant passages in the New Testament speak to the dress issue: 1 Timothy 2:9, 10; 1 Peter 3:3-5. Although women are being discussed, the counsel is equally appropriate for men. The two salient principles are (1) modesty and (2) modes of dress that reflect purity of heart. Obviously, applying these principles will involve avoiding many kinds of dress (or undress) that are not mentioned in the Bible. The wearing of jewelry is specifically ruled out, as are extravagant clothing and hairstyles more designed to attract to oneself than to the beauty of Christian character (see Isaiah 3:16-24).

Is dancing right or wrong for the Christian?

What are the principles at stake in a discussion of dancing? Because the supreme concern of Christians is to be taken to heaven with Christ at His second advent, they wish to follow the

Bible instruction of doing all things to the glory of God (see 1 Corinthians 10:31-33). Is the kind of dancing that is current today for the glory of God? The Lord has told us clearly that physical proximity between the sexes leads to problems (see 1 Corinthians 7:1-5). Everyone who has had anything to do with modern dancing knows that it involves considerable temptation to immorality. The Bible warns us against immorality of all kinds (see 1 Thessalonians 4:1-7; Titus 2:2-8).

When ancient Israelites rebelled against God after their exodus from Egypt, they danced promiscuously around the golden calf (see Exodus 32:4, 6, 19). Herod made a fool of himself when, under the influence of alcohol, he had Herodias's daughter dance before him and his court (see Mark 6:22, 23). His passions were stirred, and he made a promise that he afterward regretted.

Victory over all sin, made possible by the infilling of the Holy Spirit, is the goal of Christians who intend to live with Christ for eternity (see Revelation 3:2-5; 19:7, 8). When the righteousness of Christ lives in their hearts, they will not wish to engage in any kind of dancing that would take them away from their Lord.

What about gambling?

The Bible presents principles that adequately answer this question. The apostle Paul emphasizes that "the love of money is the root of all evils; it is through this craving that some have wandered away from the faith and pierced their hearts with many pangs" (1 Timothy 6:10, RSV). By contrast, the goal of existence for the Christian is "righteousness, godliness, faith, love, steadfastness, gentleness" (verse 11, RSV).

Gambling is based on the love of money and the attempt to get rich quickly. The Bible warns that "he that maketh haste to be rich shall not be innocent" (Proverbs 28:20). Jesus pointed out how difficult it is for a rich person to enter heaven (see Matthew 19:23), not because God cannot save them, but because they tend to depend on their own resources instead of on Christ.

The gambler ignores Jesus' counsel that, rather than seeking earthly riches, we should seek His righteousness and His kingdom (see Matthew 6:19-34). God is well able to supply all our material needs when we follow the plan of life He maps out for us.

Gambling demonstrates a lack of trust in God's willingness to provide for our needs.

The gambler also contradicts the Bible instruction that every able person should work for his or her living. The Christian is counseled to "work with your own hands" (1 Thessalonians 4:11). Paul instructed that "if any would not work, neither should he eat" (2 Thessalonians 3:10).

Gamblers may argue that they do it for fun, not specifically for money. They may be otherwise hard-working persons. But if they are thoroughly honest with themselves, they will admit that the fun is in the unexpected making of money. Before long, the desire for money takes precedence, and they find themselves completely out of line with Bible principle. Gambling involves risking valuable money that the Lord has enabled someone to earn, and all for the sake of rapidly winning money that the gambler has not earned (see Judges 14:11-20).

What about tobacco, alcohol, and other drugs?

It has been scientifically proved and publicly announced many times that tobacco is a poison that destroys health and takes the lives of multitudes annually. Significantly, in the nineteenth century, the Lord gave Ellen White special counsel regarding the use of tobacco. It has taken about a century for science to verify her statement. In 1875 she wrote: "Tobacco is a slow, insidious poison, and its effects are more difficult to cleanse from the system than those of liquor" (*Temperance*, p. 55).

Most people have some knowledge of what alcohol and drugs do to the human body and mind. Even drinkers who ignore the danger signals are aware that alcohol destroys their physical, mental, and spiritual efficiency. The crucial issue for a Christian is to know God's will regarding alcohol and other drugs and to be willing, by His indwelling power, to turn away from them. Only by Christ's power can such problems be entirely eliminated from the life.

In Scripture, the Hebrew and Greek words for *wine* are used for both alcoholic and nonalcoholic wine. This is why in some passages wine is condemned and in others it is not. Alcoholic drink is listed in Scripture among the greatest dangers to humankind. The Bible says only a little about the use of wine as a medicine (see 1 Timothy 5:23), but it strongly condemns the use of alcohol (see Proverbs 20:1; 23:20, 29-35).

Among the strongest condemnations of alcohol and other drugs are the passages in the book of Revelation that list the kinds of people whom God will exclude from His kingdom. The "sorcerers" (see Revelation 21:8; 22:15) (Greek: *pharmakoi*) are "mixers of poisons," or "poisoners." These people who use drugs for wrong purposes will be among those cast into the lake of fire at the end of the millennium. They will be classed among murderers, adulterers, and idolaters. When we observe the tragic effects of drug use on body and mind, we can understand why those who are defiling the temple of the Holy Spirit in this way cannot inherit the kingdom of God. Christ calls them to repent and turn to Him so that He can transform their lives.

Why is diet important?

No one who has bought a new car would think of putting faulty oil or gasoline into it. Why are we so concerned about what we put into our cars and often so careless about what we put into our bodies? The original diet God gave humankind consisted of vegetables, fruits, nuts, and grains (see Genesis 1:29).

God permitted a diet of flesh food after the Flood because all of earth's vegetation had been destroyed (see Genesis 9:3). Later, when new crops and orchards were productive, the Lord allowed the continued eating of flesh food under certain conditions: (1) Only flesh without blood was to be eaten; no blood was ever to be eaten (see Genesis 9:4). (2) Only certain kinds of animal, fish, and bird were to be regarded as clean and fit for food. The clean and unclean varieties are listed in Leviticus, chapter 11, and Deuteronomy, chapter 14.

Guided by the Lord's counsels given through Ellen White, for years Adventists have pointed out the disadvantages of a flesh-food diet. There is considerable disease in animals, poultry, and fish used for food. The cholesterol content of flesh foods is very high. Cholesterol is one of the main causes of arteriosclerosis (hardening of the arteries) that leads to heart disease. (For more information, see Ellen G. White's *Counsels on Diet and Foods*;

Counsels on Health; *The Ministry of Healing*; *Medical Ministry*; *Temperance*.)

The Christian approach to health matters involves a total abstinence from things that are harmful and a moderate, judicious use of things that are good. By following this principle, we can know that we are not defiling our body temples and that God will bless us.

Chapter 22

Marriage and the Family

Carol's day had been unusually frustrating, but in spite of everything that had gone wrong, she took time to bake Jim his favorite dessert—apple pie. When Jim arrived home, it was apparent that Carol was in a bad mood. Jim had had a hard day too, and was upset that Carol seemed irritable all through dinner. When it came time to eat dessert, Jim seemed pleased about the apple pie, but when he tasted it he frowned. However, he didn't say anything. Carol happened to see him frown, so she asked, "What's wrong?"

"Oh, the pie seems kind of sour," Jim answered.

The next day when Jim returned home, he found Carol in a much sweeter mood. After dinner she served some of the leftover pie. Jim was surprised that it tasted much better than it did the night before. Of course, Carol had not done a thing to the pie. It was the sweeter atmosphere with which it was served that made it taste better. Such experiences help us discover the truth of the Bible statement that "pleasant words are as an honeycomb, sweet to the soul, and health to the bones" (Proverbs 16:24).

Marriage was divinely established in Eden and affirmed by Jesus to be a lifelong union between a man and a woman in loving companionship. Yet, even in the best marriages, there are times when one or the other of the partners, and sometimes both, undergoes stresses that strain their relationship. But the love of Christ, when cherished in the hearts of both partners, can put the ordinary stresses and strains that are bound to occur in their proper perspective. When that happens, stresses tend not to become disruptive.

In Eden, God gave Adam and Eve the blessing of the Sabbath. It memorialized the loving relation between them and God. Another gift God gave in Eden—marriage and the home—was intended to bring to the newly formed pair a sense of belonging and of loving companionship. In fact, marriage was the first of these two Edenic institutions. It was performed on the last day of Creation week in order that earth's first married couple could spend their first day together celebrating the Sabbath with their Creator.

The first marriage helps us understand that, for the Christian, a marriage commitment is to God as well as to the spouse. For that reason, it can be most effective when entered into between partners who share a common faith in and love for God. Their mutual love for God leads to love, honor, and respect for each other. For this reason, the Bible teaches that this relationship is to reflect the love, sanctity, closeness, and permanence of the relationship between Christ and His church (see Ephesians 5:21-32).

Although some family relationships may fall short of God's ideal, when marriage partners fully commit themselves to each other in Christ, they will work together to achieve a more loving and happy union. But they cannot achieve the kind of agape love God outlines in 1 Corinthians 13 through their own combined efforts. That kind of love comes as the gift of the Holy Spirit and must be constantly nurtured by the Spirit. Through the ministry of the Spirit in their individual hearts, spouses can assist each other in an ever-growing love relationship toward each other and toward God.

Three steps in forming a lifelong bond

Genesis 2:24 suggests that three steps are involved in forming a lifelong bond in marriage—leaving, cleaving, and becoming one flesh. It tells us that the first step is separation from the parent-child relationship that has been the primary tie before marriage. Many marriages fail because those involved do not find it possible to give priority to the new relationship rather than to the old natural ties. The old ties should not be broken, but neither should they be given first place.

The idea of "cleaving" is to stick together, hold on to. Anything that forms the kind of close tie that marriage does cannot be dissolved without harm to those so bound. One thing that binds is the marriage vow both have freely taken. It is a solemn vow before God that the couple will love and cherish each other no matter how difficult things become in their life together, or how pleasant. It is a lifetime vow.

The union that results is so close that the couple is said to become "one flesh." That applies to the physical, social, mental, emotional, and spiritual dimensions of their lives. Anything or anyone allowed to come between the two, except, of course, their allegiance to the God who blessed the marriage, violates the marriage bond and helps destroy the union. However, this close union does not keep marriage partners from exercising individuality. What it should do is encourage them to develop their individuality within the security that belonging to each other unconditionally provides. Each partner in the ideal marriage will find freedom to take full responsibility for his or her own actions. As they spend time together in seeking the Lord and dedicating themselves to Him, they will find that their individual relationship to God will become stronger and that it will serve as a source of strength and encouragement in their relationship.

Marriage and family responsibility

According to God's instruction to the first pair in Genesis 1:28, marriage was intended for procreation, as well as pleasure. That is one reason why the Bible makes it plain that sexual activity is to be enjoyed only within the marriage union. Any other sexual relationship denigrates the blessing God intended to be reserved for and practiced by married partners.

Parents have the responsibility of teaching their children to love and obey the Lord. By their example and their words, they are to teach them that Christ is a loving disciplinarian, ever tender and caring, who wants them to become members of His body, the family of God. Increasing family closeness is one of the earmarks of the final gospel message. Part of the Elijah message of Malachi 4 reads, " 'He will turn the hearts of the fathers to their children, and the hearts of the children to their fathers' " (Malachi 4:6, NIV). This has special application to God's remnant people in the end time. A Christian home, where the love of Christ reigns supreme, is a powerful witness to the effectiveness of the gospel of Jesus Christ.

Parents assume a solemn responsibility when they have children. Children are a precious gift of God. They are not our property, but younger members of the Lord's family to be loved and led to Him. The parents' first responsibility to the children is to live consecrated Christian lives before them.

There are many who, for one reason or another, come to believe that they no longer can stay married. Divorce has come to be common in some parts of the world. Regarding divorce, Jesus taught that the only acceptable reason for divorce is sexual infidelity (see Matthew 5:32; 19:9). Even such unfaithfulness does not mean that divorce is mandatory. God can help the injured spouse to forgive when the guilty spouse is truly repentant, and His grace can lead to a reconciliation if both parties are sincere in seeking such.

There are home and family situations that are far from ideal. That makes this question of divorce one for which there are no simple answers. Yet consider the spiritual implications of divorce. It is the severing of a relationship between persons whom God has joined together. It involves breaking not only vows made to another person but vows made to God. Even in a civil ceremony in a registry office, where vows are not made to God, promises are made mutually that are sacred. Paul's burden in 1 Corinthians 7:10, 11 seems to be that everything should be done that can be done to hold a marriage together. It should be observed, however, that a marriage partner should not remain in a situation that threatens his or her life.

Singleness in the family of God

Whether by choice or by circumstances, many find themselves single. Often they look upon themselves as singing solo in a duet world. At times they feel a bit out of step with those about them. If you should be in this category, you may be the only single at a party where everyone else is married. Perhaps someone is even so unkind as to suggest that you should consider getting married soon. At times you may have longed for someone close with whom you could share your intimate thoughts and ideas—someone you could trust who would not be critical. Perhaps you feel discriminated against when others are given financial advantage because they are married. And some of you who have been married miss tremendously the closeness you once shared with another person. There are, of course, some advantages that at times make you thank the Lord for your singleness. But many times you feel a little at odds because you are singing solo in a duet world.

Probably you have been told that you're not alone in this situation, that, in fact, the greatest Person who ever lived, the Master Teacher, the Son of God, who could have arranged whatever circumstances He wanted before He came to this world, chose to be single. Theologians have speculated on why He made that choice. Some have suggested that there would have been enormous consequences in the years that followed if He had fathered children. Others have pointed to the fact that pressures and diversions would have interfered with His total commitment to His calling. Still others have suggested that it would not have been fair for Him to choose a life companion when He knew that He would die as a young man. Whatever the reason, the Great Exemplar, the Model Man, chose to sing solo in what was even then a duet world. And by doing so, He established special ties with those who find themselves following His example in this respect.

Was Jesus lonely and misunderstood? Of course He was. Undoubtedly more so than anyone. Even His family did not appreciate what He was or what He was doing, and they attempted to pressure Him into being what they considered "more normal." There were times when He longed intensely for understanding and companionship—such as in the Garden of Gethsemane. How it must have hurt Him when His best friends and companions deserted Him en masse as He was being led captive out of that garden! When we feel lonely, deserted, and unappreciated, it comforts us to know that the One who chose to be our Elder Brother experienced the same emotions and feelings. We have a dear Friend in heaven who understands us completely and loves us because He has been in the same circumstances we are in.

Actually, if you're in this category, you really never do sing solo, not when you have Jesus. You have the most precious and talented Partner of all—One who stands ready at any moment to supply your need when you're looking for someone with whom to sing a duet. What all of us need to understand is how much He cares for us and to appreciate how much He already is doing for us. If you are single, consider yourself to be in a special way a member of the family of God in heaven and on earth. You, too, face the challenge of being a responsible member of God's family.

Keys to successful human relationships

The Bible presents many keys to successful and happy relationships, including that of marriage. We'll present just four of these:

1. *Matthew 5:44, 45. Pray for one another.* In this scripture we find Jesus counseling: "Love your enemies, bless them that curse you, do good to them that hate you, and pray for them which despitefully use you, and persecute you; that ye may be the children of your Father which is in heaven." Praying for those about us helps us understand them better and helps remove whatever bitterness and anger we may feel toward them. It is fascinating to read that "the Lord turned the captivity of Job, when he prayed for his friends" (Job 42:10). His prayer is not recorded, but it must have been filled with the confidence and humility he learned through his dialogue with God.

   Prayer is sharing with God just what we are and the way we feel. God is not burdened by our prayers. He loves to have us converse with Him. We can present our petitions knowing that our loving Father is more than willing to provide all we need (see Philippians 4:19).

   When we unite our hearts in shared prayer with those we love, we cannot help but draw closer to them as we mutually draw closer to God. Shared prayer also enables us to understand better what those with whom we are praying feel and think, and to understand better how God can use us to minister to their needs.

2. *Matthew 7:1-5. Do not judge or condemn.* Jesus instructed: "Judge not, that ye be not judged. For with what judgment ye judge, ye shall be judged: and with what measure ye mete, it shall be measured to you again. And why beholdest thou the mote that is in thy brother's eye, but considerest not the beam that is in thine own eye? Or how wilt thou say to thy brother, Let me pull out the mote out of thine eye; and, behold, a beam is in thine own eye? Thou hypocrite, first cast out the beam out of thine own eye; and then shalt thou see clearly to cast out the mote out of thy brother's eye." We may sense some intended humor in Christ's illustration, but the point He made is a serious one.

3. *Romans 12:10. Prefer one another.* Paul counsels: "Be kindly affectioned one to another with brotherly love; in honour preferring one another." We need to give the benefit of the doubt to others. This becomes easier when we realize that "every association of life calls for the exercise of self-control, forbearance, and sympathy. We differ so widely in disposition, habits, education, that our ways of looking at things vary. We judge differently. Our understanding of truth, our ideas in regard to the conduct of life, are not in all respects the same. There are no two whose experience is alike in every particular. The trials of one are not the trials of another. The duties that one finds light are to another most difficult and perplexing. So frail, so ignorant, so liable to misconception is human nature, that each should be careful in the estimate he places upon another" (Ellen G. White, *The Ministry of Healing*, p. 483).

We also need to be careful about what we say. One reason is that when we express something, it is easy to convince ourselves that what we said is true, even if it is not. Ellen White wrote: "The words are more than an indication of character; they have power to react on the character. Men are influenced by their own words. Often under a momentary impulse, prompted by Satan, they give utterance to jealousy or evil surmising, expressing that which they do not really believe; but the expression reacts on the thoughts. They are deceived by their words, and come to believe that true which was spoken at Satan's instigation" (*The Desire of Ages*, p. 323).

4. *Ephesians 4:32. Be kind and forgiving.* Paul also states: "Be kind one to another, tenderhearted, forgiving one another, even as God for Christ's sake hath forgiven you." When God forgives, He forgets. But that is difficult for us to do. We say we are willing to forgive, but we find it hard to keep from remembering what others have done to hurt us, even though they have tried to make it right. It takes God's kind of love in our hearts to be truly forgiving and tenderhearted to others. His kind of love is unselfish. It reaches out to the needs of others and makes us more concerned about healing their hurts than about our own feelings.

"Kind words at home are blessed sunshine. The husband needs them, the wife needs them, the children need them. . . . It ought to be the desire of every heart to make as much heaven below as possible" (Ellen G. White, *Our Father Cares*, p. 35).

These keys to happy relationships should, above all, be used to make for happy homes. In the home, feelings of belonging, identity, and personal worth are developed. It also is the training ground for developing the grace and love of Christ, a place where the principles of real Christianity are put into practice. Our families deserve the very best from each of us. By living for Christ in the home, we develop those positive Christian characteristics that will enable those about us to see Jesus in us.

Chapter 23

Good News— Ancient and Modern

The good news is that Christ made forgiveness and salvation possible when He endured our punishment for sin. On the cross He "bore our sins in his body . . . that we might die to sin and live to righteousness" (1 Peter 2:24, RSV). There is no greater news than that! We are not irrevocably lost because we have sinned. We are mercifully saved when we believe.

That truth is exciting for us because we are living this side of the cross. Looking back, we can rejoice in an accomplished fact. But what about people who lived before the time of Christ? How could they understand forgiveness and salvation? How could they know about the atoning work of Jesus Christ? God loves all people equally; He has given everyone, irrespective of his place in history, the same opportunity to be saved by grace. Knowing this increases our joyful wonder and strengthens our faith in our heavenly Father.

As we study the ancient Israelite sanctuary, we become impressed that the messages, experiences, and services given to God's people before the time of Christ improve our understanding of the good news revealed in the New Testament. Old Testament examples and symbols improve our grasp of the New Testament message. And the New Testament reciprocates by throwing light on the meaning of Old Testament symbolism.

The ancient Israelite sanctuary

When the ancient Israelites were traveling from Egypt to the Promised Land, Moses was commanded by the Lord to build a sanctuary that would be His dwelling place, as well as a place of worship for the people (see Exodus 25:8). God revealed to Moses all the specifications for the tabernacle (see verse 9). This tabernacle, or sanctuary, was not the same as a modern church. The tent or tabernacle itself, surrounded by a courtyard, contained two rooms, one twice the size of the other. The larger room was called the Holy Place, and the smaller one the Most Holy Place.

The court surrounding the tabernacle was one hundred cubits long by fifty cubits wide (approximately 172 feet by 86 feet, assuming the Israelites used the Egyptian cubit; see Exodus 27:9-19). The tabernacle within the court was thirty cubits long, ten cubits wide, and ten cubits high (approximately 52 feet long by 17 feet wide and high; see Exodus 26:1-29 for a detailed description of the tabernacle).

There were two items of furniture in the court: the altar of burnt offering and the laver (see Exodus 27:1-8; 30:18-21). The altar of burnt offering was an outdoor fireplace, or grill, on which the remains of animals could be burnt as sacrifices to God. The laver was a large washbasin from which the priests drew water to wash their hands and feet before entering the tabernacle to minister.

The Holy Place of the tabernacle, or sanctuary, contained three items of furniture: (1) a candlestick with seven branches (the *menorah*), (2) a table on which twelve loaves of bread were placed each Sabbath, and (3) an altar, on which incense was burned every morning and evening (see Exodus 25:23-32; 30:1, 7, 8).

The Most Holy Place contained the ark of the covenant, a relatively small box containing the tables of stone on which God had written the Ten Commandments. Across the top of the ark was a slab of gold, which the New Testament calls the mercy seat. At either end of the ark were the cherubim, or likenesses of angels (see Exodus 25:10, 16-20). The ark was a symbol of the throne of God because the divine presence of the Lord was manifested above the mercy seat (see Numbers 7:89; 1 Samuel 4:4; 2 Kings 19:15).

The court containing the altar of burnt offering was the place for animal sacrifices. The services conducted in the Holy Place represented priestly intercession or mediation. The Most Holy

Place was where God dwelt. Here each Day of Atonement (the tenth day of the seventh month) the high priest conducted a ministry that was an important part of the cleansing of the sanctuary. The Day of Atonement was the judgment day for the past religious year. Sacrifice, mediation, and judgment are the three great ministries provided by Jesus Christ to save repentant, believing sinners. The services of the sanctuary symbolized the earthly sacrifice of Christ followed by His heavenly mediation and judgment ministries.

The court—sacrifice

Various kinds of ceremonial rituals were conducted in the court of the sanctuary. Among them were offerings by which individuals received purification from sin. Sin offerings were brought to the court of the sanctuary by Israelites who wished to have God's forgiveness. Different kinds of sacrificial offerings were brought by different people (see Leviticus 4-6). The sins of priests and rulers were regarded as more serious because, in view of their exalted office, they exercised greater influence.

The plan was for the sinner to place his hand on the head of the animal that he had brought as a sin offering. He was then to take the life of the animal. The priest would collect the blood and sprinkle some of it on some part of the sanctuary. In the case of the sin offering for the high priest, the blood was daubed in the Holy Place, "seven times before the Lord in front of the veil of the sanctuary" (Leviticus 4:6, RSV). This was the veil that separated the Holy Place from the Most Holy Place. The blood was also daubed "on the horns of the altar of fragrant incense before the Lord" (verse 7, RSV).

The blood of the sin offering for rulers and common persons was daubed on the horns of the altar of burnt offering in the court (see Leviticus 4:25, 30, 34). Then the priest cooked some of the flesh of the sacrifice for the ruler or common person and ate it in the court of the sanctuary (see Leviticus 6:24-30).

The Bible says, "The priest shall make atonement for him for his sin, and he shall be forgiven" (Leviticus 4:26, RSV; see also verses 20, 31, 35). Sins of the penitent sinner were transferred to the sanctuary, and he or she was forgiven when (1) the sinner presented the sin offering in the court, symbolizing confession of sin; (2) an animal was sacrificed; (3) the priest daubed blood at the altar. Exceptions were made for the very poor, but they too were required to bring sin offerings to the sanctuary (see Leviticus 5:11-13).

The entire service of offering animal sacrifices for sins symbolized the sacrifice and high priestly ministry of Jesus Christ. Christ's one sacrifice took the place of all animal sacrifices in the ancient sanctuary (see Hebrews 7:27; 9:28; 10:11, 12; 1 John 3:5). God dramatized the end of the earthly sanctuary services (or ceremonial law) by rending the veil of the temple in Jerusalem when Jesus died (see Matthew 27:50, 51). At that point, the symbol met its reality, type met antitype, the Old Testament earthly ministry was to be replaced by the heavenly ministry of Christ our High Priest in the sanctuary above (see Hebrews 8:1, 2).

That was good news for both Old and New Testament believers! Those who died before the cross, believing in the Messiah to come, will be raised at the second coming of Jesus, because He died for their sins. If Jesus had not died and risen again, there would have been no hope for the faithful dead to rise again (see 1 Corinthians 15:17-23). Animal sacrifices could save no one (see Hebrews 10:1). Only the death and resurrection of Jesus could make forgiveness available (see Hebrews 9:15).

But even the infinite suffering of Jesus, centrally important though that is, could not fulfill all the divine requirements for forgiveness. You and I must confess our sin by virtue of Jesus' death (see 1 John 1:9), as the ancient sinner confessed by placing his hand on the head of the sacrifice. Moreover, there must be high priestly ministry in heaven. Just as the earthly priest sprinkled the blood of the sacrifice in some part of the sanctuary, so Jesus applies the merits of His shed blood for us when we confess our sins to Him (see 1 Timothy 2:5; Hebrews 9:11-14, 24, 25; 1 John 2:1). As the earthly priests ate some of the flesh of the sin offering, so Christ "bore our sins in his body on the tree, that we might die to sin and live to righteousness" (1 Peter 2:24, RSV; compare Leviticus 10:16-18). Christ provides *atonement* for our sins in the Bible sense, following three events: (1) Christ's perfect sacrifice; (2) our confession of sin; (3) Christ's mediation for sin in the heavenly sanctuary.

The Holy Place—mediation

The furniture and ministry of the earthly Holy Place symbolized Christ's constant ministry for us in the Holy Place of the heavenly sanctuary. In the earthly example the officiating priests daubed or sprinkled the blood of the sin offerings on some part of the sanctuary (on the altar of burnt offering or in the Holy Place). They also ministered in the Holy Place daily, trimming the lamps and offering incense morning and evening. Every Sabbath day they placed fresh bread on the table.

In the fulfillment to which the earthly ministry pointed, Christ shed His blood for the sins of the whole world (see 1 John 2:2), taking upon Himself all human guilt (see Isaiah 53:6; 2 Corinthians 5:21; Peter 2:24). Then He ascended to the heavenly sanctuary, where He constantly pleads the merits of His sacrifice for sinners.

The "shewbread" (KJV) or "bread of the Presence" (RSV) placed on the table in the Holy Place every Sabbath represented Christ, the true spiritual Bread of Life (see Exodus 25:30; Leviticus 24:5-9; John 6:32-35, 48-58, 63). As we prayerfully study His Word and invite Him to come into our hearts by the Holy Spirit, we are partaking of the Bread of Life. "We are made partakers of Christ, if we hold the beginning of our confidence stedfast unto the end" (Hebrews 3:14).

Also within the Holy Place of the sanctuary was a candlestick with six branches (see Exodus 25:31, 32, 37). On top of each of the seven lampstands was an oil lamp. The lamps were trimmed every day so that the light would shine forth continually (see Leviticus 24:2). The oil in the lamps symbolizes the Holy Spirit (see Zechariah 4:1-6). The light of the candlesticks represents Christ, the light of the world (see John 8:12), and His believing people, who are to reflect the glory of His character (see Matthew 5:14).

The altar of incense was placed in the Holy Place before the veil that separated the two apartments of the sanctuary (see Exodus 30:1, 6). The burning of incense on this altar every morning and evening represented our prayers ascending to God, mingled with the merits of Christ's intercession for us (see Psalm 141:2; Revelation 5:8; 8:3, 4). Our prayers are acceptable to God because of Jesus' death and ministry on our behalf.

The Most Holy Place—judgment

The ark of the testimony, with its various attachments, was the one item of furniture in the Most Holy Place of the earthly sanctuary. It was a representation of the throne of God (see Exodus 25:10, 21, 22).

The ark, made of acacia wood, was two and one-half cubits long and one and one-half cubits wide and high; approximately four and one-half feet long and two and one-half feet wide and high. It was overlaid with gold within and without. The "testimony," God's law written on tables of stone, was placed inside the ark (see Exodus 25:21; 31:18). Hence, it was called the "ark of the testimony," and the sanctuary was called "the tabernacle of testimony" (Exodus 38:21).

The only time any human being entered the presence of God in the Most Holy Place was when the high priest entered there on the Day of Atonement. The cleansing of the sanctuary on the Day of Atonement, representing judgment ministry, is described in Leviticus, chapter 16.

Two goats were selected by God when the high priest cast lots, one representing Christ and the other representing Satan. The goat that represented Christ was slain and its blood applied upon the mercy seat and before the mercy seat in the Most Holy Place, on the horns of the altar of incense in the Holy Place, and on the horns of the altar of burnt offering in the court. Thus every part of the sanctuary was symbolically cleansed on the Day of Atonement.

The purpose of the service is described as follows: "On this day shall atonement be made for you, to cleanse you; from all your sins you shall be clean before the Lord. . . . He [the priest] shall make atonement for the sanctuary [Most Holy Place], and he shall make atonement for the tent of meeting [Holy Place] and for the altar [altar of burnt offering], and he shall make atonement for the priests and for all the people of the assembly" (Leviticus 16:30, 33, RSV). All Israelites were to "afflict" themselves, examining their hearts to be sure they were not resisting the cleansing work that the Lord was doing for them (see verse 29). Anyone who refused to be spiritually cleansed on the Day of Atonement was to be cut off from the camp of Israel (see Leviticus 23:27-32).

The Day of Atonement services symbolized the court session that is now occurring in the Most Holy Place of the heavenly sanctuary—the final judgment ministry of Christ before His second advent. Daniel describes this heavenly judgment (see Daniel 7:9-14). The chapter speaks of the "little horn" power that opposed God's truth and people for centuries. Only after the lapse of those centuries did the judgment in heaven begin (see Daniel 7:21, 22, 25, 26). We know that it is an investigative court session because Daniel 7:10 says that after God and the angels had taken their places, "the books were opened." This is a court session in which the books of record are looked into as the basis of the verdict.

Christ is the "son of man" spoken of in Daniel 7:13. He is the lawyer or advocate in the heavenly court session. Just as the earthly high priest on the Day of Atonement daubed or sprinkled blood in all three parts of the sanctuary, symbolizing that both the sanctuary and sinners were finally cleansed, so during the antitypical Day of Atonement Jesus pleads the merits of His sacrifice on behalf of believers who are putting away sin and daily maintaining their walk with Him.

Daniel 8:14 is parallel with Daniel 7:9-14. The cleansing of the sanctuary of Daniel 8:14, which began in 1844 at the end of the 2,300 years, is the heavenly court session of Daniel 7. The Lord is revealing to the heavenly court who is right with Him and who is not. Of course, He Himself knows that already, but the period of the court session is designed to give people on earth a last opportunity to put away sin. Those who do will have their names *retained* in the book of life (see Daniel 12:1; Revelation 3:5). Those who refuse to reject sin will have their names *removed* from the book of life.

Only believers in Christ have had their names recorded in the book of life in the first place (see Luke 10:20; Hebrews 12:23). In the pre-advent judgment this heavenly book is edited; the names of those believers who have failed to maintain their born-again relationship with Jesus are taken out of the book of life. These are the modern counterparts of the Israelites whom God rejected because they refused to put away sin on the Day of Atonement (see Leviticus 23:27-29). The editing of the book of life and the final blotting out of the record of sins that have been pardoned is the cleansing of the heavenly sanctuary spoken of in Daniel 8:14.

One of the vital results of the pre-advent judgment is the vindication of the character of God before the entire universe. God is not on trial in the judgment; humankind is on trial. But the display of the records of every human life before the universe demonstrates without doubt that God has been perfectly just in the manner in which He has treated every human soul. "To the intent that now unto the principalities and powers in heavenly places might be known by the church the manifold wisdom of God, according to the eternal purpose which he purposed in Christ Jesus our Lord" (Ephesians 3:10, 11).

John foresaw this same heavenly pre-advent judgment when he wrote, "The hour of his judgment is come" (Revelation 14:7). This message announcing that the pre-advent judgment is now in progress is one of three end-time messages that John foresaw would go into the world a short time before the coming of Jesus (see verses 6-12).

At the end of the pre-advent heavenly court session, Jesus is depicted symbolically as casting the censer into the earth (see Revelation 8:5). His heavenly intercession for sinners is then concluded and the proclamation is made, "He that is unjust, let him be unjust still . . . and he that is righteous, let him be righteous still" (Revelation 22:11). This is when Michael (Christ) stands up (see Daniel 12:1) and probation closes because God has finally declared who will be saved and who will not.

As the scapegoat carried the sins of Israel out of the camp (see Leviticus 16:10, 21), so at the end of time Satan will carry responsibility for all the sins he has tempted God's people to commit. Satan is not our sin bearer! Only Jesus Christ died for our sins! The blood of the scapegoat was not shed on the Day of Atonement; only the blood of the goat symbolizing Christ was shed. "Without the shedding of blood there is no forgiveness of sins" (Hebrews 9:22, RSV). But there is a dual responsibility for sin. Satan suffers because our sins are also his sins. He is the evil mastermind who leads us into sin; he is responsible along with us; in fact, he is more responsible because he is the instigator. As the real scapegoat, Satan is confined to the desolate, unpopulated earth for one thousand years, and then meets his final punishment in the fires of the last great day (see Revelation 20). Satan's followers are destroyed with him. But God's people, whose walk with Jesus was demonstrated to the heavenly court, will enjoy an eternal life of perfect happiness in a universe finally purged of all sin and suffering.

Praise God for Christ's Most Holy Place ministry! It means that believers who are delivered from guilt and condemnation now (see Romans 8:1), who continue to put away sin and persevere till the end (see Matthew 24:13), will be judged worthy of eternal life. Their names will be retained in the book of life. They will be sealed at the end of the judgment (see Revelation 7:3; 14:1-5) and protected during the final great time of trouble (see Daniel 12:1). Just as the Israelite was forgiven for sin in the daily services during the year (see Leviticus 4), so we are forgiven when we come to Jesus and confess our sins (see 1 John 1:9). We are finally declared eternally free by the heavenly court because of the victorious Christian life we have been habitually enjoying. The Day of Atonement was a yearly cleansing from sin. The end-time Day of Atonement is final cleansing from sin for eternity. The spiritual victory over sin that God's people will enjoy is His gift to them by the Holy Spirit.

Chapter 24

Wanting
Jesus to Come

Queen Victoria one day listened to a stirring sermon on the second coming of Christ presented by her chaplain, Dean Farrar. As she was leaving the chapel she grasped his hand, saying, "Oh, I want so much to see Jesus come!"

Noticing the tears in her eyes, the pastor inquired, "Why is that, Your Majesty?"

The queen answered, "Because I long to take off my crown and lay it at Jesus' feet."

How do we respond to the biblical teaching that Jesus will come soon? Do we long with all our hearts for His return?

The second coming of Christ is the blessed hope of the church, the grand climax of the gospel. "The grace of God that bringeth salvation hath appeared to all men, teaching us that, denying ungodliness and worldly lusts, we should live soberly, right-eously, and godly, in this present world; looking for that blessed hope, and the glorious appearing of the great God and our Saviour Jesus Christ" (Titus 2:11-13).

Christ's second coming is mentioned 318 times in the New Testament. One Bible writer who looked forward eagerly to Jesus' return was John, the beloved disciple. He reported Jesus' promise: "I go to prepare a place for you. And if I go and prepare a place for you, I will come again, and receive you unto myself; that where I am, there ye may be also" (John 14:2, 3). John also heard and recorded Jesus' last promise to return, "Surely I come quickly," and responded enthusiastically, "Even so, come, Lord Jesus" (Revelation 22:20).

217

Many Old Testament passages (including Job 19:25-27; Psalm 50:3-5; Daniel 2:44, 45) contribute to our understanding of the second coming of Christ. Christians who love Jesus live for the fulfillment of these prophecies. If they die before Jesus comes, they do so with this hope in their hearts. Why do these prophecies mean so much to them? Because of their love and commitment to Jesus, they long to be with Him. They also recognize that, in turn, Jesus loves His human brothers and sisters and very much wants them to be with Him.

Victory over death depends on the return of Jesus

Hebrews 9:28 is the one text in the Bible that links the term *second* with Christ's return. When Christ comes the second time, He will take His beloved to heaven with Him—including those who have died and are resurrected when He comes (see 1 Thessalonians 4:16, 17). Three important concepts concerning the resurrection can be found in 1 Corinthians 15:19-23. First, Paul holds out hope for all who accept Christ. That hope reaches beyond this life to include the life the righteous will receive on the resurrection day. Second, Paul argues that if there is no second coming of Christ, then there can be no resurrection of the dead. In that case, our belief, hope, and trust in Christ would be quite futile. Third, Paul emphasizes the fact that the resurrection definitely takes place at Christ's coming.

Notice in 1 Corinthians 15:51-54 that, whether righteous people are dead or living when Christ returns, the glorious gift of immortality is bestowed on them. Never again are they to be haunted by the fear of death. Death will have lost its sting. The grave will have been robbed of the victory it has claimed.

In 1 Thessalonians 4:13-17, it is made quite clear that the Saviour's coming will be literal, personal, and visible. Matthew 24:24-30 adds to this understanding, and Revelation 1:7 states that when He comes with clouds, "every eye shall see Him." According to 1 Thessalonians 4:13-17, the righteous dead will be resurrected. Then, together with the righteous living, they will be glorified and taken to heaven; but the unrighteous will die, destroyed by the brightness of His coming (see 2 Thessalonians 2:8).

We are living in the last moments of time

Another Bible description of what will take place when Christ comes is found in Revelation 11:18: "The nations were angry, and thy wrath is come, and the time of the dead, that they should be judged, and that thou shouldest give reward unto thy servants the prophets, and to the saints, and them that fear thy name, small and great; and shouldest destroy them which destroy the earth." In this age of unprecedented build-up of nuclear weapons and the environmental hazards imposed by pollution of all kinds, we certainly have arrived at a time when human beings are capable of destroying the earth. Scientists warn that unless something drastic is done soon, the earth will not last long.

No wonder, then, that thinking people everywhere, especially those attuned to Bible prophecy, are convinced that we are living in the end of time and that Christ is soon to return. One of the most startling events of the last half of the twentieth century took place on December 1, 1989, when Soviet president Mikhail Gorbachev, president of what was then the Soviet Union, met at a Vatican summit with Pope John Paul II. One newspaper reported that a priest in the Vatican remarked: "The lion is lying down with the lamb, but in this case it's hard to tell who is playing which role." Subsequent events have shed some light on which of the two came out on top.

Not long after, and probably due more than we realize to what happened at that meeting, a sudden whirlwind of startling events swept through Eastern Europe. The Berlin Wall was torn down, and Russian troops and arms were removed from territories they had dominated since World War II. The Soviet empire itself was fractured into several independent or loosely confederated states.

For decades it had been difficult to see how the whole world could wonder after the beast, with so much of it being dominated by atheistic Communism. Now we suddenly are confronted with the clear possibility that the long-predicted event will take place in the immediate future. As Ellen White wrote long ago in *Testimonies*, vol. 9: "The final movements will be rapid ones" (p. 11).

The unprecedented intensity in the increase of the traditional signs of Christ's return lead many today to realize that it will not be long before the little cloud, about half the size of a man's hand, heralds the great day when Jesus will come (see *The Great Controversy*, p. 640).

The almost complete fulfillment of most of the great lines of prophecy found in Daniel and Revelation, together with the present condition of the world, indicates that Christ's coming is imminent. Because the time of that event has not been revealed, we are exhorted to be ready at all times.

What it means to be ready

In Matthew 24 and 25, Jesus gave seven parables designed to teach us how to be ready for His second coming:

1. *Parable of the fig tree (Matthew 24:32-35).* Here is a call to an awareness of the nearness of Christ's return. Today we see events taking place that turn our minds to the prediction that the United States will fill a major role in setting up the "image to the beast" in the last moments of time (see Revelation 13:11-15).

   During the long period known as the "cold war," some of us believed that the time would come when the USSR would have to be overthrown in order for the United States to fulfill its predicted role. Many of those holding this conviction wondered whether it would take a massive nuclear war to bring this about. But now we find the United States unexpectedly has become the lone superpower.

2. *As in the days of Noah (Matthew 24:36-42).* This parable warns us concerning the unexpectedness of the close of probation that will precede the second coming. The people who were warned of the Flood scoffed at such an idea. It didn't fit into their concepts of science and philosophy. A flood of false ideas contributes to many ignoring God's warnings today. According to recent polls, 58 percent of Americans say that they believe in reincarnation. Of these, 21 percent are Protestants and 25 percent are Roman Catholics. This has come about largely because of what is

called "New Age" teaching. It emphasizes a "new world order" that will control our world. Satan still is convincing people that God was wrong when He warned Adam and Eve that sin would bring death. According to New Age philosophy, you do not die when you die—you just move on into another life. One woman commenting on this concept gushed, "I believe in reincarnation. When I come back, I'm going to be wealthy and skinny." Shirley MacLaine, who is considered the high priestess of this movement, when holding her newborn daughter, wondered, "Had she, in fact, been my mother?" Nonsense! you say. But a large number of people around the world believe this satanic lie, which eliminates the need for a Saviour.

We're thrilled by the accounts coming out of Russia and Eastern Europe describing people's desire for Christian values and morality. But, without an understanding of the Scriptures, they are unable to discriminate between the false and the true. Many are turning to New Age teachings. Long ago, Ellen White warned: "As we near the close of time, there will be greater and still greater external parade of heathen power; heathen deities will manifest their signal power, and will exhibit themselves before the cities of the world; and this delineation has already begun to be fulfilled" (*Testimonies to Ministers*, pp. 117, 118).

When you understand the roots of the New Age movement in Hinduism and the Eastern mystery religions, you can see how this prediction is being fulfilled.

3. *The thief in the night (Matthew 24:43, 44).* This parable emphasizes readiness and watchfulness. Ordinarily, those who have had a burglar break into their house spend the next day doing everything they can to secure their premises more efficiently than before. The challenge here is to do so *before* you have to undergo the experience in order to prevent the burglary. Christ is not depicting Himself as a thief, but is urging the same state of alertness and care toward His coming that we would take to protect ourselves if we knew a burglar was about to select our residence as a target.

4. *The two types of servants (Matthew 24:45-51)*. Here we learn a lesson about responsibility and faithfulness in the light of our Master's soon return. We need a new sense of urgency. Whether we have put it in these words or not, so much of what we have been doing says, "My Lord delayeth His coming." The challenge is to recognize what we are doing and to look forward so much to Christ's return that we will do all in our power to hasten His coming.

5. *The ten virgins (Matthew 25:1-13)*. This parable calls us to spiritual concern and dedication. In his book *The Keys of This Blood*, Malachi Martin, formerly a Jesuit professor at the Vatican's Pontifical Biblical Institute, makes it clear that a millennial end game is going on in our world. Governments are contending for leadership of what they perceive to be the new world order. He states: "The chosen purpose of John Paul's pontificate—the engine that drives his papal grand policy and that determines his day-by-day, year-by-year strategy—is to be the victor in the competition now well under way" (p. 17). Revelation 13 predicts that the papacy will achieve that goal. The papacy is completely committed to filling the place prophecy tells us it will fill. Shouldn't we be as intent on meeting our challenge to prepare the world for Christ's soon return?

6. *Talents (Matthew 25:14-30)*. This parable challenges us to diligent stewardship of the gifts God has given. If we become fully aware of the fact that we are living in the very last remnants of time, we cannot expect to carry on business as usual. There are exciting times ahead for the people of God. In this final harvesttime, God's people will unite with heavenly agencies in reaching out to every city, town, and person in the world in order to prepare those who respond for the second coming of Christ. The work will spread like fire in the stubble. But it will be God's work, not ours. Yet God cannot accomplish this work unless He has our cooperation. If we do not faithfully and unselfishly commit ourselves to this task, the coming of Christ will be delayed.

7. *The sheep and the goats (Matthew 25:31-46)*. Here is a call to love as Christ loved. Only Christ's kind of love filling our

hearts and souls can provide us with the right motivation to get ready to meet Him soon. Peter was one of the privileged few who heard Jesus speak these words on the Mount of Olives. He adds: "The end of all things is at hand: be ye therefore sober, and watch unto prayer" (1 Peter 4:7). We need to pray that God will lead us individually to forsake our pet sins and yield ourselves to Him as empty vessels that can be filled to the full with the Holy Spirit. We need to pray for unity in the church, and for each other, as well as for the finishing of God's work on earth. Before we can reflect the love of Jesus fully to the world, He must be invited to take over our hearts and lives.

Setting our faces to go to the New Jerusalem

Revelation 3:20 introduces Jesus knocking at the door, urging us to let Him come in. It is true that He knocks at the door of our hearts. But what exactly is the door in Revelation 3? Isn't it the door to the Laodicean church? Christ longs now to come into our church, bringing the final outpouring of the Holy Spirit in the latter rain. "Behold," He calls out, "I stand at the door, and knock." How long are we going to rudely keep Him waiting there?

Luke 9:51 records that, when Jesus knew the time had come for Him to sacrifice His life for us, He "stedfastly set his face to go to Jerusalem."

The time has come for us to set our faces to go to the New Jerusalem.

The end is near! God calls upon the church to set in order the things that remain. . . .

The upbuilding of the kingdom of God is retarded or urged forward according to the unfaithfulness or fidelity of human agencies. The work is hindered by the failure of the human to co-operate with the divine. Men may pray, "Thy kingdom come. Thy will be done in earth, as it is in heaven;" but if they fail of acting out this prayer in their lives, their petitions will be fruitless. . . .

If you would go forth to do Christ's work, angels of God would open the way before you, preparing hearts to receive the gospel. Were every one of you a living missionary, the message for this time would speedily be proclaimed in all countries, to every people and nation and tongue. This is the work that must be done before Christ shall come in power and great glory. I call upon the church to pray earnestly that you may understand your responsibilities. Are you individually laborers together with God? If not, why not? When do you mean to do your heaven-appointed work? (Ellen G. White, *Testimonies*, vol. 6, pp. 436-438).

In the light of this challenge, isn't it time for us to make a full and final commitment to do what we must to finish God's work? Jesus waited until He knew the time had come for Him to finish His work on earth. Then He set His face steadfastly to go up to Jerusalem. Nothing could sway Him from His commitment to God's purpose for His life—not even the certain knowledge that betrayal and crucifixion lay ahead. When it was time, He went. Do we have any doubt that now is the time for us to finish the work God has given us to do?

Opening the heart's door to Jesus in order that He may come quickly means being completely, unconditionally yielded to Him so that He can use us as He wishes in these last moments of time.

It is intriguing how many times the word *come* is used in the book of Revelation. Some form of the word appears at least sixty-three times. Several passages use *come* in the passive sense. The book of Revelation speaks of the coming of salvation, the hour of judgment, the day of wrath, the marriage of the Lamb, the hour of temptation, and the New Jerusalem. But none of these comings of judgment are intended to scare us into getting ready for the events of the last day.

The shortness of time is frequently urged as an incentive for seeking righteousness and making Christ our friend. This should not be the great motive with us; for it savors of selfishness. Is it necessary that the terrors of the day of God should be held before us, that we may be compelled to right action through fear? It ought not to be so. Jesus is attractive. He is full of love, mercy, and compassion. . . .

He has a right to command our love, but He invites us to give Him our heart. . . . His invitation to us is a call to a pure, holy, and happy life—a life of peace and rest, of liberty and love—and to a rich inheritance in the future, immortal life (Ellen G. White, *Lift Him Up*, p. 98).

The *comes* of Revelation also focus on Christ's second coming in such passages as Revelation 1:7; 2:5, 25; 14:15; and 16:15. Our response to these promises should be that of the apostle John. He was so eager to see his Lord again that he responded enthusiastically to Christ's four-time promise to come quickly with the prayer, "Even so, come, Lord Jesus" (Revelation 22:20). Shouldn't that be our prayer today?

Chapter 25

Hope
Beyond the Grave

During His earthly ministry, Jesus had no place to call home. His lot was to trudge the dusty roads of Palestine to bring healing to the sick and salvation to the sinful. But there was one home where Jesus found refuge from the pressure of His demanding ministry and from the sting of pharisaical criticism—the home of Mary, Martha, and Lazarus of Bethany. The record says that Jesus loved these folk, and they loved Him too, and depended on Him for spiritual encouragement.

Sorrow entered this peaceful Bethany home. Lazarus was stricken with a sudden illness, and Mary and Martha sent to Jesus the message, " 'Lord, he whom you love is ill' " (John 11:3, RSV). They assumed that Jesus would be sympathetic and would be with them just as soon as He could reach Bethany. But Jesus did not come. The days passed, and finally Lazarus died. Naturally, Mary and Martha were heartbroken; they could not understand why Jesus had not come.

For two days after receiving the news of Lazarus's illness, Jesus remained in the same place. Then He said to His disciples, " 'Let us go into Judea again' " (John 11:7, RSV). He explained to them why He wanted to return to Judea. He said, " 'Our friend Lazarus has fallen asleep, but I go to awake him out of sleep' " (verse 11, RSV).

The disciples responded, " 'Lord, if he has fallen asleep, he will recover' " (verse 12, RSV). They did not understand that Jesus was talking about Lazarus's death. They could not see why it was necessary to be concerned about a man who was enjoying a good sleep.

Jesus explained Himself. "Lazarus is dead" (verse 14).

Then the disciples realized that it was necessary for them to go to Bethany to offer the comfort and encouragement that Mary and Martha needed so much. They followed Jesus as He made His way back to Jerusalem and Bethany.

As Jesus approached Bethany, Martha went out to meet Him. She saw in His face the same tenderness and love that had always been there.

"Martha said to Jesus, 'Lord, if you had been here, my brother would not have died. And even now I know that whatever you ask from God, God will give you' " (verses 21, 22, RSV).

Jesus replied, " 'Your brother will rise again' " (verse 23, RSV).

Martha answered, " 'I know that he will rise again in the resurrection at the last day' " (verse 24, RSV).

Jesus responded, " 'I am the resurrection and the life; he who believes in me, though he die, yet shall he live' " (verse 25, RSV).

Accompanying Martha, Mary, and the mourners to the tomb of Lazarus, who had been dead four days, Jesus commanded that they take away the huge stone that had been placed at the entrance to the tomb. Then in a loud voice He commanded, " 'Lazarus, come out' " (verse 43, RSV). "The dead man came out, his hands and feet bound with bandages, and his face wrapped with a cloth. Jesus said to them, 'Unbind him, and let him go' " (verse 44, RSV). Imagine how the sorrow of those mourning loved ones was suddenly changed into enormous surprise and overwhelming joy!

Where was Lazarus during those four days? Obviously, his body was in the tomb, but where was his soul? Jesus said that Lazarus was sleeping. Does that mean that he was unconscious, or was his most important part living somewhere else?

What happens when a person dies? Does the soul go to heaven? Or to hell? Or does it stay in the grave? Does the dead person know what is happening on earth? Can he or she, as many people believe, communicate with living loved ones? Where are the dead? Will their circumstances ever change, or is death the end of it all? Is there life immediately after death? Later? Never?

Philosophers have come up with theories of all kinds on this subject. The doctrine of the immortality of the soul taught by the ancient Greek philosopher Plato (about 427-347 B.C.) greatly influenced Jewish thought in the Hellenistic period (fourth century through the first century B.C.). The Jewish Pharisees believed in the immortality of the soul. The Alexandrian Jew, Philo, who wrote in the first century A.D., had accepted this doctrine and influenced early Christian theologians. Origen (about A.D. 185-254) and others passed on the concept of the soul's immortality to the Christian church. The result was that Greek philosophical teaching was largely accepted by Christians. Does the Bible teach that doctrine? Because only God knows the true condition of those who have died, we turn to His Word for the answer.

Death is a sleep

In both the Old and New Testaments death is represented as sleep. As sleep is a state of unconsciousness, so is death. Shortly before Moses' death, the Lord said to him, " 'Behold, you are about to sleep with your fathers' " (Deuteronomy 31:16, RSV). Anticipating death, Job said, "Now shall I sleep in the dust" (Job 7:21). Daniel wrote of the dead as "those who sleep in the dust of the earth" (Daniel 12:2, RSV). Matthew wrote of the "bodies of the saints who had fallen asleep" (Matthew 27:52, RSV). Speaking of a dead girl, Jesus said, " 'The child is not dead but sleeping' " (Mark 5:39, RSV). In describing the death of Stephen, Luke declared simply, "He fell asleep" (Acts 7:60). Writing of the condition of believers before the second coming of Jesus, the apostle Paul stated, "We shall not all sleep" (1 Corinthians 15:51).

Never do the Bible writers suggest that part of a human being sleeps at death while another part goes on living in a conscious state. Never do they imply that death is not, like sleep, a state of unconsciousness. As Bible writers faced death, they did not expect to be conscious, living beings again until, by a divine miracle, their existence was restored.

What is the "spirit" in humankind?

"The Lord God formed man of dust from the ground, and

breathed into his nostrils the breath of life; and man became a living being" (Genesis 2:7, RSV). The breath of life that God breathed into man's nostrils was the life principle, or life force, that gave existence to the individual. In death, the opposite process takes place. The breath of life (spirit) goes back to God, and the body goes back to the dust of the earth (see Psalm 146:4; Ecclesiastes 12:7). The word *spirit* in these verses is a translation of the Hebrew word *ruach*; the Greek equivalent is *pneuma*.

Kittel's *Theological Dictionary of the New Testament* (ed. Gerhard Friedrich, vol. 6, pp. 359-362) gives these meanings of the Hebrew word *spirit* (*ruach*): (1) breath of the mouth (see Psalm 33:6); (2) breath of air, soft breeze, strong wind (see Exodus 14:21); (3) the principle that gives life to the body (see Genesis 6:17; 7:15); (4) the seat of the emotions, intellectual functions, and attitudes of the will (see Genesis 41:8; Deuteronomy 34:9).

Never in the Bible is the "spirit" of humankind said to survive the death of the body as an immortal, conscious entity. The spirit is simply the life force implanted by God at Creation and shared by every breathing, living thing, whether human being or animal.

> For the fate of the sons of men and the fate of beasts is the same; as one dies, so dies the other. They all have the same breath, and man has no advantage over the beasts; for all is vanity. All go to one place; all are from the dust, and all turn to dust again. Who knows whether the spirit of man goes upward and the spirit of the beast goes down to the earth? (Ecclesiastes 3:19-21, RSV).

Some Bible interpreters attempt to prove from Ecclesiastes 12:7 that the immortal spirits of good people go to heaven when they die. The text reads, "The dust returns to the earth as it was, and the spirit returns to God who gave it" (RSV). This is the opposite process of the one that occurred at Creation (see Genesis 2:7). If the "spirit" in Ecclesiastes 12:7 is immortal, surviving the death of the body, then the souls of *all* people, good and bad, must go to heaven when they die. But no one believes that the spirits of evil people ascend to heaven, and the Bible never suggests that they do. The text is simply telling us that the life principle given by God to all people is taken back by God when they die. The doctrine of the immortality of the soul is not even implied.

Both the Old and New Testaments sometimes use the word *spirit* to refer to the mind of humans, their capacity to reason, as well as their ability to feel and choose (see Daniel 2:1; 5:12; Matthew 26:41; Romans 1:9). Such intellectual and emotional faculties never survive the death of the body. The Bible does not depict the spirit as the real self that goes on living after the body has died. In this sense, the spirit is the inner life of human beings that is totally dependent upon the existence of the body.

What is a "soul"? Is it immortal?

"The Lord God formed man of the dust of the ground, and breathed into his nostrils the breath of life; and man became *a living soul*" (Genesis 2:7, emphasis supplied). Man did not become an immortal soul; he became a *living* soul. The obvious implication of the text is that if the breath of life were removed, man would become a dead soul. Because souls can die, they cannot be regarded as immortal; immortality is total immunity from death.

Ezekiel wrote that "the soul that sinneth, it shall die" (Ezekiel 18:4). Writing of the Nazarite vow, Moses commanded, "All the days that he separateth himself unto the Lord he shall come at no dead body [Hebrew: soul]" (Numbers 6:6). Thus, in the Bible a dead soul is a corpse. Predicting the end-time plagues, John wrote, "Every living soul died in the sea" (Revelation 16:3).

Because souls can die, they are not immortal. When the breath of life is taken from a soul, it ceases to be a living soul. Jesus taught that eventually, wicked souls will be destroyed in hell (see Matthew 10:28). That being so, the doctrine of an ever-burning hell cannot be true. The idea of eternal suffering in hell for lost souls depends on the doctrine of the immortality of the soul. Since the soul can die, it is not immortal, and since God plans to destroy wicked mortal souls in hell, they cannot suffer for eternity.

The Hebrew word for soul is *nephesh*; the Greek equivalent is *psuche*. In the King James Version the word *creature* is used to translate the Hebrew *nephesh* in the following verses: Genesis 1:20, 24; 2:19; 9:10, 12, 15, 16. In all of these passages, animals are spoken of as "souls" (compare Genesis 1:30). God made the animals living souls, even though they are spiritually, mentally, and emotionally inferior to humankind. God formed the animals from the dust and breathed into their nostrils the breath of life, and they became living souls. Like humankind, when they die, they are dead souls.

Comparing humankind with God, the Bible says unequivocally that God "only hath immortality" (1 Timothy 6:16). That being so, human souls are not immortal. The death of the body is the death of the soul.

Kittel's *Theological Dictionary of the New Testament*, edited by Gerhard Friedrich, comments on the Hebrew word for *soul* (*nephesh*). The soul

> has no existence apart from the body. Hence the best translation in many instances is "person" comprised in corporeal reality. The person can be marked off and counted, Gn. 12:5; 46:18; Jos. 10:28; 11:11. Each individual is a [*nephesh*], and when the texts speak of a single [*nephesh*] for a totality, the totality is viewed as a single person, a "corporate personality." Hence [*nephesh*] can denote what is most individual in human nature, namely, the ego, and it can become a synonym of the personal pronoun, Gn. 27:25 (vol. 9, p. 620).

The New Testament Greek word for *soul* (*psuche*) has meanings similar to those of the Old Testament word *nephesh*. It is often best translated "life." A human life is a "soul" (see Mark 3:4; 8:35).

Nowhere in the Scriptures is the *soul* spoken of as disembodied or immortal, in heaven or hell. The word may refer to the total personality or to part of it. Sometimes the reference is to the spiritual self or the intellectual or emotional self. But these aspects of soul are not conceived as entities separate from the physical self. When the body dies, so do the other faculties of the soul. What is preserved for believers is God's knowledge of their faithfulness and God's promise that they will have eternal life at the second coming of Jesus.

What is the state of the dead?

The clear teaching of the Bible is that the dead know nothing and feel nothing (see Ecclesiastes 9:5, 6, 10). They have no knowledge of what is happening to their loved ones (see Job 14:21) and no knowledge of God (see Psalm 6:5). "The dead praise not the Lord, neither any that go down into silence" (Psalm 115:17). If they were in heaven, surely they would praise God.

The parable of the rich man and Lazarus (see Luke 16:19-31) is an allegory, designed to teach the danger of covetousness. It provides no support for the doctrine of the immortality of the soul. Taken literally, the parable becomes an absurdity. The beggar went to "Abraham's bosom"—obviously a symbol. The rich man in hell spoke of Lazarus's finger and his own tongue. In this parable the dead have bodies. Who imagines that it is possible for the good in heaven to converse with the wicked in hell, as they do in this parable? The rich man wanted Lazarus to go to his living brothers to warn them. That would happen if "one rose from the dead" (verse 31). That is quite different from the popular idea that dead souls can communicate with the living without a resurrection being necessary.

In his great sermon on the day of Pentecost, the apostle Peter stated that David is not ascended into the heavens (see Acts 2:34). Christ rose from the dead and ascended to heaven, but David remained in the grave, where he saw corruption. David was a righteous man; he had fully repented of his sins. But he did not go to heaven when he died. The dead sleep peacefully in their graves, waiting for the resurrection morning at the second coming of Jesus (see Job 14:14; 17:13-16; Isaiah 26:19).

The dead will live again

Jesus taught that there will be a resurrection of the righteous and a resurrection of the unrighteous (see John 5:28, 29). The resurrection of the righteous takes place at Jesus' second coming (see 1 Corinthians 15:16-22, 51-54; 1 Thessalonians 4:16-18). Those who died believing will be raised from their graves and, along with their living brothers and sisters, will be given immortality.

The dead are not raised as disembodied spirits; they will be given perfect, immortal bodies, free from all physical ills and blemishes (see Romans 8:11, 23; Philippians 3:20, 21). Believers in Christ receive their eternal reward at His second advent (see Luke 14:13, 14).

The lost are not raised at the second advent; they remain in their graves until the end of the thousand years (see Revelation 20:5). Then they are raised in the *second* resurrection to receive their reward of eternal death, ultimate separation from the Lord they have rejected (see Revelation 20:9, 10, 13-15).

What a thrilling day it will be when Jesus comes the second time to raise our dead loved ones! Mothers and fathers will be reunited with their little ones, wives with their husbands, friend with friend. It will be a great reunion day. Never again will there be suffering, separation, or death. "And God shall wipe away all tears from their eyes; and there shall be no more death, neither sorrow, nor crying, neither shall there be any more pain: for the former things are passed away" (Revelation 21:4).

Jesus is, indeed, the resurrection and the life (see John 11:25). Just as surely as Jesus raised Lazarus from the dead, so He will raise His faithful ones at the end of time. When the great silver trumpet sounds, the sleeping saints will come forth to receive their eternal reward.

Where will you be in that day? Do you plan to be among the redeemed? This can be your happy lot. Now is the time to make your calling and election sure by committing your life to the loving care of your heavenly Father. If you allow Him to raise you from spiritual death now, you can have a certain part with Him in His glorious kingdom. Death may come as a temporary sleep, but it will never separate you from the love of Christ (see Romans 8:38, 39). Will you, just now, give your heart fully to Jesus?

Chapter 26

The
New Millennium

As we enter the third one-thousand-year period since the birth of Christ, many are asking, What is about to happen? Will this new millennium turn out to be the millennium foretold in the book of Revelation? Is Christ soon to come?

The Bible teaches that Christ's second advent occurs before the millennium. The millennium is the thousand-year period that takes place after the second coming of Jesus. The term *millennium* is not found in the Bible, but is derived from two Latin words—*mille*, meaning "one thousand," and *annum*, meaning "year." In discussions of the prophecies, Bible students use the term to refer to the one thousand–year period outlined in Revelation 20. During this time, the earth will be utterly desolate, occupied only by Satan and his angels. At its close Christ with His saints and the Holy City will descend from heaven to earth. The unrighteous dead will be resurrected and with Satan and his angels will be destroyed by fire from God. The universe will be freed from sin forever.

There are three basic millennial views held by people today: *a*millennialism, *post*millennialism, and *pre*millennialism. Amillennialism takes the position that the one thousand years of Revelation 20 is a figurative expression. Postmillennialism turns from the figurative to a spiritualized interpretation of the thousand years. Those holding this position generally believe that a future golden age of blessedness will take place before Christ comes the second time. But the Bible teaches that the world will suffer conflict and trouble before Jesus comes. The third view, premillenialism, was accepted by the pioneers of the Seventh-day Adventist Church. They believed and taught this at a time when the religious world in general predicted a thousand years of peace and prosperity prior to Christ's second coming. On the authority of the Bible, Adventist pioneers preached that the world will progressively grow more wicked, that God's people will be in heaven during the millennium, and that no human beings will be alive on earth.

God raised up the Seventh-day Adventist Church for the special purpose of proclaiming the everlasting gospel to the world in the setting of the three angels' messages. At the heart of these messages is the announcement that the "hour of his judgment is come" (Revelation 14:7). The judgment began in 1844 as Christ commenced His Most Holy apartment ministry in the heavenly sanctuary. There are four phases in the work of judgment that is being carried on in heaven.

Phase 1. *The investigative judgment of the righteous.* "Judgment must begin at the house of God" (1 Peter 4:17). In 1844 "the judgment was set, and the books were opened" (Daniel 7:10; see also Daniel 8:14). The records of those whose names are recorded in the book of life are opened to the universe to show who on earth is fit for eternal companionship with sinless heavenly beings.

Phase 2. *The executive judgment of the righteous.* Jesus tells us that this will take place at His second coming. It involves bringing His people the reward He has promised (see Revelation 22:12).

Phase 3. *The investigative judgment of the unrighteous.* In order to satisfy any questions that may arise concerning the justness of His judgments, God allows the records of those from earth who were not taken to heaven to be investigated during the millennium (see Revelation 20:4).

Phase 4. *The executive judgment of the unrighteous.* When all are satisfied that God has been fair in determining the fate of the unrighteous, final judgment is pronounced and executed. Sin and sinners will be no more. In this chapter we will show how these four phases of the judgment fit into the framework of the millennium of Revelation 20.

The period between two resurrections

The millennium begins with a resurrection and ends with a resurrection. The Bible calls the resurrection that begins the thousand-year period the "first resurrection" (Revelation 20:6). The righteous dead, those who are "blessed and holy," come out of their graves when the voice of Jesus calls them at the time of His second coming.

But the rest of the dead are not resurrected until the end of the millennium (see Revelation 20:5). Whereas the righteous who are raised in the first resurrection come forth from their graves with perfect, immortal bodies, the wicked are raised in the second resurrection with the same kind of weak, mortal bodies they had when they died.

Jesus distinguished between the two resurrections by calling the first the "resurrection of life" and the second the "resurrection of condemnation" (John 5:29, NRSV).

Events at the beginning of the millennium

1. *The return of Jesus.* This is the climactic event of earth's history. There should be no break between chapters 19 and 20 of Revelation, because chapter 20, the millennium chapter, concludes the prophecy that begins in chapter 19. In Chapter 19 Jesus is pictured coming as a Conqueror. He is coming to reign as "KING OF KINGS, AND LORD OF LORDS" (Revelation 19:16). It is at the second advent that the resurrection takes place that begins the millennium.

2. *The righteous dead raised.* Revelation 20:4 describes the righteous in heaven. How did they get there? Revelation 20:6 explains that they came up in the "first resurrection." The Bible connects the resurrection of the righteous with the second coming of Christ in such scriptures as 1 Thessalonians 4:15-17.

3. *The living saints caught up.* First Thessalonians 4:16, 17 also indicates that those caught up in the clouds to be with Jesus include both the righteous who are living when Jesus comes and those who are resurrected at His coming. The righteous do not remain on the earth. Before Jesus went away, He gave the wonderful promise: "I will come again,

and receive you unto myself; that where I am, there ye may be also" (John 14:3). That place is in heaven. According to Revelation 20:4-6, the saints will live and reign there with Christ during the thousand years.

4. *The wicked slain.* The term "the rest of the dead" in Revelation 20:5 refers to the wicked who were slain at Christ's coming (see Revelation 19:21) as well as all the dead who were not raised in the first resurrection. They do not live again until the end of the millennium.

5. *Satan bound.* Revelation 20:1-3 describes Satan being bound at the beginning of the one thousand years. What does it mean for Satan to be bound? Ever since he first tempted Adam and Eve in the Garden of Eden, Satan has occupied himself with trying to deceive people and lead them into sin. But with the righteous in heaven and the wicked in their graves, he will have no one to tempt. Revelation describes him as being bound with a chain and confined to a bottomless pit (see Revelation 20:2, 3). The chain is symbolic, not literal.

6. *The earth desolated.* Jeremiah 4:23-27 describes the desolation of Judah during the captivity in terms that indicate there would be a broader, more significant application at the end of time. Thus it can be applied to the condition of this earth after Jesus has taken the saints to heaven.

Because Isaiah 24:1-6 originally was addressed to literal Israel and intended to describe the destruction of their land by their enemies, not everything in these verses can be applied to the millennium. But the destruction described is so vast and universal that it cannot be limited to the destruction of Israel. Many Bible students believe that it contains a broader description that is applicable to the destruction of the earth at Christ's second coming.

Events in heaven during the millennium

Those who have gained the victory over the beast and its image and have been taken to heaven at the second coming are pictured in Revelation 15:2 standing on the sea of glass. What are they doing there?

Before entering the City of God, the Saviour bestows upon His followers the emblems of victory and invests them with the insignia of their royal state. The glittering ranks are drawn up in the form of a hollow square about their King, whose form rises in majesty high above saint and angel, whose countenance beams upon them full of benignant love. . . . Upon the heads of the overcomers, Jesus with His own right hand places the crown of glory. . . . In every hand are placed the victor's palm and the shining harp (Ellen G. White, *The Great Controversy*, pp. 645, 646).

Think for a moment how long it will take for Christ to personally place a crown on the head of every redeemed individual who stands on the sea of glass. We don't know how many there will be, but let's say there are more than a billion redeemed. How long will that take? Who cares! We'll be in heaven for one thousand years. We'll never get tired, but will stand there rejoicing as Christ welcomes each saint. When He is finished, we will be able to play our harps, without having had any lessons, as we join in a great victory song, praising the One who made it possible for us to be there.

In addition, after we enter into the New Jerusalem, we will be asked to verify God's justice in excluding those who are not there by examining their records. This examination is known as the investigative judgment of the records of the wicked and must be accomplished before God pronounces final judgment upon them. This phase of judgment is essential in order to demonstrate to the universe that God is both just and merciful in destroying sin and sinners.

Although there will be much to do during the thousand years, we will take time to enjoy the wonderful sights of heaven that up until then we could not even begin to imagine. We will also spend many happy hours and days visiting with those from whom we have long been separated.

What takes place on earth during the millennium?

At the second coming, the saints will be taken to heaven to reign with Christ during the thousand years, while the wicked will have been destroyed by the brightness of His coming. Revelation 20:5 states that the "rest of the dead" will not live again "until the thousand years [are] finished." This leaves the earth depopulated except for Satan and his angels, who have nothing to do except brood and quarrel about their responsibility for what has happened to them.

For a thousand years, Satan will wander to and fro in the desolate earth to behold the results of his rebellion against the law of God. During this time his sufferings are intense. Since his fall his life of unceasing activity has banished reflection; but he is now deprived of his power and left to contemplate the part which he has acted since first he rebelled against the government of heaven, and to look forward with trembling and terror to the dreadful future when he must suffer for all the evil that he has done and be punished for the sins that he has caused to be committed (Ellen G. White, *The Great Controversy*, p. 660).

Events at the close of the millennium

1. *Christ, the saints, and the city descend.* Revelation 20:9 speaks of the "camp of the saints," or the "beloved city," being on earth at the end of the millennium. How does it get there? Revelation 21:2 tells us that it comes "down from God out of heaven." Not only the New Jerusalem but its inhabitants, including God Himself, come to earth to dwell (see Revelation 21:3).

2. *The wicked dead raised.* Revelation 20:5 indicates that there will be another resurrection at that time. The wicked come to life at the end of the one thousand years with the same thought patterns and rebellious attitudes they had when they went to their graves.

3. *Satan loosed.* Because the wicked dead have been raised, Satan once again has someone to deceive. That is how he is said to be "loosed" for a little season (see Revelation 20:7, 8).

4. *The last judgment.* The executive judgment of the wicked will then take place. God will be forced to do away with sin and its effects forever (see Revelation 20:9-15).

5. *Satan and sinners destroyed.* The fire God uses to destroy Satan, sin, and sinners does not burn eternally. It is the consequences that are eternal. Malachi 4:1 makes it clear that, as the result of the fires of the final judgment, the wicked will be destroyed. They "shall be stubble," the fire "shall burn them up," and "neither root nor branch" shall be left.

6. *The earth cleansed and renewed.* After Satan and those who have followed him in rebellion have marched against the Holy City and have been destroyed by fire, God will re-create this earth as the eternal home of the saved.

The great controversy is ended. Sin and sinners are no more. The entire universe is clean. One pulse of harmony and gladness beats through the vast creation. From Him who created all, flow life and light and gladness, throughout the realms of illimitable space. From the minutest atom to the greatest world, all things, animate and inanimate, in their unshadowed beauty and perfect joy, declare that God is love (Ellen G. White, *The Great Controversy*, p. 678).

The signs of Christ's coming outlined in the Bible indicate that He is soon to come and that the Bible millennium is about to begin. Contrary to much that is taught today, the Bible teaching about the millennium makes it clear that it begins with the second coming of Christ. Jesus does not touch the earth when He returns the second time but takes the resurrected and living saints, who have been caught up with Him into the clouds, to heaven with Him (see 1 Thessalonians 4:16, 17). At the end of the thousand years He returns to this earth to dwell here forever with His followers in the New Jerusalem that has come down from God out of heaven.

During the thousand years, the wicked dead who were left behind on earth are not aware of anything taking place. Because the righteous are in heaven, only Satan and his angels are alive on this desolate planet. For the righteous in heaven the thousand years will be a time of reflection as they are engaged in a work of judgment, an investigation into why the wicked were lost. This work of judgment will lead to a verification of the love and justice of God in destroying sin and sinners. The millennium also will be a time of reflection for Satan and his fallen angels, and thus a part of their final punishment. At the close of the one thousand years, there will be a final destruction of everything that has brought death, disease, and unhappiness to our world. Then Planet Earth will be restored to its Edenic beauty and become the eternal happy home of the saved. Here God Himself will dwell with those who have been redeemed, those for whom He gave everything possible in order that they might become His sons and daughters. God longs to be with us. Do we long to be with Him?

Chapter 27

Free at Last!

The poems and hymns of Fanny Crosby have had a profound influence on the spiritual lives of millions of people in many lands. The phenomenon of a blind woman being able to express in verse the deepest sentiments of the believer's heart captured the imaginations of nineteenth-century Christians. Her hymns are also sung with genuine appreciation by modern churchgoers.

Fanny's cousin, Dr. Howard Crosby, a Presbyterian minister, died of pneumonia at age sixty-five. His last message stirred Fanny to the depths of her soul. He had written that no one need fear death, and added: "If each of us is faithful to the grace which is given us by Christ, that same grace which teaches us how to live will also teach us how to die."

Taking up her pen, in just a few minutes Fanny wrote the famous poem that soon after became the well-known hymn "Saved by Grace."

Fanny was lifted beyond the struggles and vicissitudes of this sad old world to the glories of the kingdom that Jesus promised to prepare for those who love Him (see John 14:1-3). The joys that she anticipated will begin at Jesus' second advent, when He will take His faithful followers to the heavenly Jerusalem. There they will dwell with Him for one thousand years while this earth will be in a state of desolation, inhabited by Satan and his evil demons.

Then, at the end of the millennium, Christ, His people, and the New Jerusalem will descend to this earth (see Revelation 21:2).

The wicked will be raised, and the final judgment will take place (see Revelation 20:7-15). The entire desolate earth will be purged by a fierce, consuming fire that will destroy sin and sinners for eternity. At last Satan, who masterminded the terrible rebellion against God, will be eliminated.

Then the earth will be restored to that superb state of natural loveliness with which God originally endowed it (see 2 Peter 3:13, 14; Revelation 21:1). Writing hundreds of years before the time of Christ, the prophet Isaiah looked forward with earnest longing for the new world order that God will introduce at the end of the millennium:

> Behold, I [the Lord] create new heavens and a new earth: and the former shall not be remembered, nor come into mind. But be ye glad and rejoice for ever in that which I create: for, behold, I create Jerusalem a rejoicing, and her people a joy (Isaiah 65:17, 18).

> For as the new heavens and the new earth, which I will make, shall remain before me, saith the Lord, so shall your seed and your name remain (Isaiah 66:22).

It is futile to look for any lasting improvement in the condition of our world today. The Bible predicts that things will get worse, not better. Sin, sorrow, war, and destruction will become more and more prevalent, right up to the second coming of Jesus. Only then can we hope for deliverance from the frustrations and sufferings of this life. The millennium will be a time of wonderful peace and perfection in heaven. And when the earth is renewed after that, God's people will have an eternity of joy in the most ideal environment He can give them.

What will the saved be like spiritually and physically? What differences will there be between the condition of the natural kingdom then and its condition now? It is difficult for us in our present mortal state to imagine a world free from temptation to sin, from hatred, discrimination, war, sickness, disease, and death. Is there any possibility that evil will reappear after the earth has been re-created by God? Will the saved live in complete freedom from fear of their perfect paradise ever again being threatened by the incursions of evil? Will they truly be free at last?

How can we be sure that Fanny Crosby's dream will be realized? For whom will this dream come true? And how do we prepare to inhabit the earth made new?

The capital of the new earth

No human pen can describe adequately the magnificence of the New Jerusalem. We can only read the Bible description and try to imagine what it will be like.

The New Jerusalem is called "the bride, the Lamb's wife" (Revelation 21:9). The saved were "married" to Christ during the pre-advent, investigative judgment. John calls this judgment the "marriage of the Lamb" (Revelation 19:7). As described in Revelation 19:7, 8, the true believers in Christ, who have received the gift of His righteousness by the Holy Spirit, are His bride. Both Christ's people and the city are called the bride because the city is the eternal home of the people. The city is called the bride because it is inhabited by the true bride, Christ's faithful church.

The number 12 and multiples of 12 occur frequently in the description of the New Jerusalem. It seems that twelve is a symbol of the city's complete symmetry and of the spiritual perfection of the people who inhabit it. The faithful, living on the earth when Jesus comes, who have never experienced death, are called the 144,000 (see Revelation 7:1-8). Because this number occurs in a highly symbolic prophecy, it does not indicate that only 144,000 living believers will exist on the earth when Jesus comes the second time. The number is a multiple of twelve (twelve times twelve times one thousand). This number seems to represent the spiritual wholeness or symmetry that will be enjoyed by those who allow Christ to reign in their hearts perpetually.

Similarly, the New Jerusalem is depicted as a perfect square (or maybe a cube). The number 12 figures largely in its dimensions. It has twelve gates and twelve foundations. It is not known whether the measurement of 12,000 furlongs (1,378.4

246 THIS WE BELIEVE

miles, since a furlong is 606.5 feet) is the measurement of the circumference of the city or the length of one side (see Revelation 21:16). If this distance is the circumference, the city would be about 344.6 miles to a side—a very large city. But we cannot be sure that our human measurements are correct. The important point seems to be that the number 12 and its multiples figure largely in the dimensions. Revelation 21:17 says that the measure of the wall will be 144 cubits (twelve times twelve)— "according to the measure of a man, that is, of the angel." Since it is an angel's measurement, we cannot be sure that our computations are satisfactory. Nor do we know whether 144 cubits (210 feet) is intended to be the height of the wall or its thickness.

The purpose of the city's measurements and of the symbolic number of the living believers when Christ comes (144,000) seems to be that the city is a perfect home of a spiritually perfected people.

The description that follows boggles the imagination (see Revelation 21:18-21). The city of translucent gold, the wall of jasper, the foundations of precious stones, the gates of pearl, the massive, glorious structure, all suggest to the mind the most outstanding architectural wonder the human mind could possibly conceive.

There will be no temple in the New Jerusalem, "for the Lord God Almighty and the Lamb are the temple of it" (Revelation 21:22). The temple in heaven (see Revelation 7:15; 20:4) is the heavenly sanctuary (see Hebrews 8:1, 2), where the sin problem is finally disposed of during the millennium. After that, there is no need of a temple because sin has been excluded from the universe. The Lord Himself provides the light needed for the Holy City, and there is no night there (see Revelation 21:23, 25). The nations of the saved will inhabit the city (see verse 26), and God will dwell with them (see verse 3). There will be no defilement or corruption of any kind in the New Jerusalem (see verse 27). Only redeemed souls in whose lives the power of Christ is reigning will ever enter there. These are the ones who in the pre-advent judgment have had their names retained in the Lamb's book of life (see Daniel 12:1; Revelation 3:5).

The spiritual life of the saved

Jesus said, "My kingdom is not of this world" (John 18:36). His kingdom is spiritual, not temporal. Even though His kingdom will ultimately be established on this earth, the basis of His government and of the society He establishes will not be worldly power or human pride and achievement. His eternal kingdom in the earth made new will be a spiritual realm in which His holiness reigns supreme in every citizen's heart.

God Himself will dwell with His people (Revelation 21:3), and the Holy City will be the center of His government. The victorious character of each citizen is described in Revelation 21:7: "He that overcometh shall inherit all things; and I will be his God, and he shall be my son." Throughout the book of Revelation, the great emphasis is on the blessings for the overcomer (see Revelation 2:2, 7, 11, 17, 26; 3:5, 12, 21). Christ wants us to have victory over sin as He had victory (see Revelation 3:21). Not only does He offer all the necessary power to make us conquerors (see Jude 24), but He also assures us that what we give up for Him is minimal compared to the wonder of our eternal inheritance in the earth made new (see Romans 8:18).

Throughout eternity, the saved partake of the tree of life (see Revelation 22:2) and of the water of life (see Revelation 7:17; 21:6). This means that their perpetual existence both spiritually and physically will be maintained by their constant union with Christ. The promise of Jesus to the woman of Samaria will be fulfilled for the redeemed in the most complete way. Because they constantly drink deeply of the water of life, they will never die (see John 4:14).

The Sabbath will be the weekly day of worship in the new earth (see Isaiah 66:23). Worship will be a daily experience, but especially meaningful on the day that reminds us of God's creative work and His infinite redeeming grace. The Lord who mercifully and tenderly fosters the spiritual lives of His redeemed people will be the constant object of their adoration. There will be no deceiver to turn their minds away from God or to seduce them into imagining that the Lord is responsible for evil and suffering. Because the demonic source of all such deception is now no more, those who fully acknowledge their debt of gratitude to the Source of all life can enjoy life to the fullest.

Our worship here and now should be a preparation for that thrilling day when we will worship our Lord in the new earth. Daily worship is vitally important to each one of us, and Sabbath worship is intended to be a foretaste of the blessed Sabbath days that will be an unending feature of Christ's new world order.

The physical and material blessings of the saved

One of the most exciting features of the new earth is that we will be real people in a real world. We will not be ethereal spirits divorced from work, social activities, and emotional fulfillments that are meaningful to humans.

The redeemed inhabitants of the new earth will be physical beings with bodies similar to Christ's body after His resurrection from the dead (see Romans 8:23; 1 Corinthians 15:44, 49; Philippians 3:20, 21). We will not have the physical limitations of fallen beings, but neither will we be disembodied spirits. We will know our friends and loved ones, and they will know us (see 1 Corinthians 13:12). We will have the privilege of working with our hands and of enjoying the fruits of our labors (see Isaiah 65:21-23). It will not be the arduous labor of this fallen world, but the most satisfying and creative work. In Christ's new world order, every talent will find expression and every noble ambition will be realized.

Isaiah described the uninterrupted temporal security that will be experienced by the inhabitants of the new earth (see Isaiah 65:17-25). Isaiah 65:20 does not mean that sin and death will exist on the new earth: "There shall be no more thence an infant of days, nor an old man that hath not filled his days: for the child shall die an hundred years old; but the sinner being an hundred years old shall be accursed." Isaiah's message regarding the new world order had a dual application: to Israel as a nation and to the end-time situation, when earthly kingdoms will be swept away and God's kingdom established. Israel could have enjoyed great spiritual, physical, and material blessings if she had followed God's will. There would have been minimal infant mortality and physical sickness. Because Israel turned from

God's purpose, the promises to her have been inherited by the Christian church (see Galatians 3:28, 29). Now the secondary application of Isaiah's prophecy applies. Those features of the prophecy involving sin and death no longer have relevance. The predictions concerning the "new heavens" and the "new earth" still apply because they are confirmed by John's predictions in the book of Revelation.

Elsewhere Isaiah speaks of the joys awaiting the saved in the new earth. "They shall not hurt nor destroy in all my holy mountain: for the earth shall be full of the knowledge of the Lord, as the waters cover the sea" (Isaiah 11:9). Animals that are incompatible in our fallen world will dwell together in perfect harmony (see verses 6-8). There will be no deserts or barren places (see Isaiah 35:1, 2). The book of Revelation adds that there will be no huge sea as we know it today (see Revelation 21:1).

One of the most wonderful assurances is that "the former things are passed away" (Revelation 21:4), and "the former shall not be remembered, nor come into mind" (Isaiah 65:17). The Lord will not allow the memories of earth's struggles, disappointments, and heartaches to destroy the peace and contentment of His people. Moreover, the sin problem will never rise again. "Affliction shall not rise up the second time" (Nahum 1:9). Because the entire universe has seen the devastating results of evil, all are convinced that God's way is best and that He is entirely righteous and just. Never again will anyone wish to diverge from perfect obedience to His righteous will.

Are you ready for the new earth?

Jesus wants each of us to share His kingdom. Shortly before His death, He prayed: " 'Father, I desire that they also, whom thou hast given me, may be with me where I am, to behold my glory which thou hast given me in thy love for me before the foundation of the world' " (John 17:24, RSV). Because we are the creatures of His hand, and because He has given all to save us, His most earnest desire is to see us delivered from all evil, sharing the eternal benefits of His new world order.

The Bible spells out the conditions under which we can inherit the new earth: " 'As I live, says the Lord God, I have no pleasure in the death of the wicked, but that the wicked turn from his way and live; turn back, turn back from your evil ways; for why will you die'" (Ezekiel 33:11, RSV). "'He who conquers shall have this heritage, and I will be his God and he shall be my son'" (Revelation 21:7, RSV). Christ's gospel offers great power to the one who believes (see Romans 1:16, 17). Faith in Christ—living, abiding, constant faith is the means of spiritual power and purity. "This is the victory that overcomes the world, our faith" (1 John 5:4, RSV).

You can be an overcomer as you maintain your spiritual union with Christ. He will dwell within you by the Holy Spirit (see John 14:23; 17:23). He will live out His life through you (see Galatians 2:20). There are enormous material and physical advantages in being among the saved in the new earth. But the real issue confronting us today is spiritual. Christ is offering spiritual advantages; victory over all sin, purity of heart and mind, and purity of behavior (see 2 Corinthians 7:1; 1 Peter 1:15, 16). These blessings can be ours for eternity; we can be perfect souls in a perfect world. But the spiritual qualities that will characterize the saved are to be ours now—because Jesus offers Himself to us now. His righteousness is available to us now (see Romans 8:9, 10). His abiding presence in our hearts can be ours now (see John 14:18).

Will you receive Christ as your present and immediate Saviour from sin? Will you resolve to join us in seeking Him daily so that each of us can have the abiding assurance of eternal salvation?

DATE DUE

HIGHSMITH 45-220